The Legacy of Ernest Mandel

The Legacy of
Ernest Mandel

Edited by
GILBERT ACHCAR

VERSO
London • New York

First published by Verso 1999
© This edition published by Verso 1999
© Individual contributions the contributors 1999
© Introduction Gilbert Achcar 1999
All rights reserved

Verso
UK: 6 Meard Street, London W1V 3HR
US: 180 Varick Street, New York, NY 10014–4606

Verso is the imprint of New Left Books

ISBN 1–85984–703–X

British Library Cataloguing in Publication Data
A catalogue record for this book is available from the British Library

Library of Congress Cataloging-in-Publication Data
A catalog record for this book is available from the Library of Congress

Typeset in 10pt Baskerville by SetSystems Ltd, Saffron Walden, Essex
Printed by Biddles Ltd, Guildford and King's Lynn

In the last instance I am a Marxist because only Marxism makes it possible to keep believing in humanity and its future without self-deception – despite all the terrible experiences of the twentieth century, despite Auschwitz and Hiroshima, despite famine in the 'Third World' and the threat of nuclear annihilation. Marxism teaches us to take a positive attitude toward life and human beings and to love them, without a false gloss, without illusions, in full awareness of the never-ending difficulties and unavoidable setbacks in the millions of years which it has taken our species to progress from ape-like creatures to global investigators and stormers of heaven. To conquer conscious control over its social existence has today become a matter of life and death for this species. In the end it will succeed in realizing the noblest of all its aspirations: the construction of a humane, classless, non-violent world socialism.

Ernest Mandel

Contents

           Ernest Mandel**

10   The Luck of a Crazy Youth   217
     Ernest Mandel interviewed by Tariq Ali

11   Material, Social and Ideological Preconditions for the Nazi
     Genocide   225
     Ernest Mandel

12   Why I am a Marxist   232
     Ernest Mandel

     Ernest Mandel's Book-Format Works in English   261

     Notes on the Contributors   269

Preface and Acknowledgements

This book is based on papers presented at the first seminar organized by the Ernest Mandel Study Center on the premises of the Amsterdam International Institute for Research and Education (IIRE), from 4 July to 6 July, 1996. The theme of this seminar was 'The Contribution of Ernest Mandel to Marxist Theory'.

A special debt is owed to Peter Drucker who contributed greatly to the editing of this book. He also translated Michel Husson's contribution and Ernest Mandel's theses on the 'Material, Social and Ideological Preconditions for the Nazi Genocide' from French. Thanks are also due: to Penny Duggan who helped put the book into correct English; to Cesar Ayala who translated the contribution of Jesús Albarracín and Pedro Montes from Spanish; to Jurrian Bendien who translated Mandel's article 'Why I Am a Marxist' from German; to Wilfried Dubois who revised this translation; to Jurrian Bendien, Petra Lubitz and Wolfgang Lubitz whose previous research we relied on in compiling the bibliography published at the end of this volume; and to Charles Post who copy-edited the final manuscript.

We are also indebted to those who attended the seminar and helped enrich the discussion of the papers collected here. Among them were Alan Freeman, Janette Habel, Joost Kircz, Marcel van der Linden, Livio Maitan, Jakob Moneta, Jaime Pastor, Charles-André Udry and Robert Went. Thanks are of course due as well to all those who presented the papers collected here.

We also thank Kindler Verlag (Munich) and Editions du Cerf (Paris), as well as Anne Mandel Sprimont, for authorizing us to use the two articles by Ernest Mandel which are published for the first time in English in this volume.

Gilbert Achcar

NB: Except when quoted directly, references to Ernest Mandel's book-format works available in English will not be given, since they are all listed in the bibliography published at the end of this volume.

Part I

The Marxism of
Ernest Mandel

Introduction
Ernest Mandel (1923–1995):
An Intellectual Portrait

Gilbert Achcar

Ernest Mandel belonged to a species that has become increasingly endangered in this second half of the twentieth century: theoreticians of militant Marxism. He was one of those few men and women in the history of the socialist movement who were able to combine the untiring activities of revolutionary leaders with a body of intellectual work that fulfilled the scholarly criteria for scientific research and compelled respect in academic circles. He was one of those who conceive Marxist theoretical activity as both a scientific endeavour and an integral part of revolutionary activity – in the sense in which Marxist theory is a guide to action, as Friedrich Engels said, and its 'theoretical production' is an essential, inseparable dimension of class struggle, not just speculative acrobatics.

Ernest Mandel was so entirely devoted to this struggle, to which he had decided to dedicate his life, that, even when he happened to write a little book on a 'trivial' subject like crime stories, he produced a telling dissection of bourgeois society – although the 'Pharisees' whom he denounced in his preface to *Delightful Murder* would not acknowledge the value of this exercise.

One key to his personality as a tireless fighter and a fundamental optimist is to be found in that famous episode of his youth when his force of character and physical strength allowed him to escape from the Nazi camps.[1] The two fellow Trotskyist militants of his generation whose intellectual abilities he admired most, Marcel Hic and Abraham Léon (Abram Leon), could not survive this darkest hour of the century:

both died before they were thirty. Mandel thus brought to his work an ardour enhanced by the sense of owing a moral debt to these two comrades, whose loss he deeply regretted. He put the will to survive that saved him from the Holocaust in the service of a movement that, in the aftermath of the Second World War, seemed to be on the verge of dying out. Like Leon Trotsky in exile, he threw himself into 'uninterrupted work in order to ensure the succession'. And when he jubilantly witnessed the new youth radicalization of the 1960s, he redoubled his efforts, setting himself, like his mentor, the task of 'arming a new generation with the revolutionary method'.[2]

In a half-century of unbroken labour, Ernest Mandel often managed despite everything to write 'as a happy man', as he noted in the dedication of one of his books.[3] He left an extraordinarily impressive body of writing behind him, which could easily fill several dozen volumes. Mandel was a prolific writer, to be sure; he could write letters, an article or a brochure or finish off a chapter of his current book while participating attentively and actively in a meeting. But with him quantity seldom came at the expense of quality. Whether or not one agreed with all the ideas he expressed, a political or theoretical writing by Ernest Mandel was always a rich and stimulating document, even if it was merely one of the personal discussion letters of which he wrote so many.

The erudition of this uncommon man was of a kind that the constant, cumulative progression of printed knowledge is putting further and further beyond human reach. It impregnated all of his spoken statements as well. Mandel was someone whom you could listen to for hours, always with the feeling of learning more and discovering new horizons. And he was certainly not a man to hug his knowledge jealously to himself. Not that he showed off his encyclopaedic culture out of pedantry, far from it. But he felt a duty to pass on what he knew, to communicate his thirst for knowledge and his intellectual passions. These concerns marked all his works.

An exhaustive survey of Ernest Mandel's writings – even if it were restricted to published works, books, brochures and articles, leaving out his voluminous correspondence – would be an undertaking on the scale of a doctoral dissertation. We can only mention here the high points, the most striking marks left along the trail, of this immense body of work, written mainly in English, French, or German, the three languages that Mandel used best (besides Flemish, his 'mother tongue').[4]

It was in May 1960 that he completed, in French, his first major work, the one that would make him an internationally recognized

Marxist economist. The book appeared in 1962 under the somewhat misleading title of *Traité d'économie marxiste* ('Treatise on Marxist Economics', which became *Marxist Economic Theory* in English and most of the many translations). The French title was misleading because it sounded like one of those scholastic Stalinist-inspired manuals. In reality the book embodied a gigantic effort (ten years of work, a fifty page list of works consulted) to breathe new life into Karl Marx's most important contribution to scientific knowledge, which the Stalinists had petrified and twisted out of shape.

Mandel's goal, as he explained in the preface, was 'to start from the empirical data of the science of today' in order 'to reconstitute the whole economic system of Karl Marx' and 'de-Westernise' it.[5] On top of this he made a similar effort to update the Trotskyist analysis of the Soviet Union and the problematic of the transition to socialism. This first, refreshing work was presented (already then!) as 'an invitation to the younger generation of Marxists', an invitation that was widely taken up to judge by the book's great success.

The theoretical audacity of *Marxist Economic Theory* was limited by the fact that its main purpose was to defend and illustrate the Marxist heritage. Only after having written it – and probably dissatisfied with its on the whole rather traditional analysis of what he still called 'the epoch of capitalist decline', at a time when the post-war long expansive wave was reaching its climax, flouting most Marxists' predictions – did Mandel turn to the theory of 'long waves of capitalist development'. He came to believe that capitalism had entered a new, third historical phase after the Second World War (after the classic and imperialist phases). Accordingly, he drew the outlines of what he then called 'neo-capitalism' in a 1964 article that was added as an appendix to later editions of *Marxist Economic Theory*, and in the best known of his many pedagogical pamphlets, his *Introduction to Marxist Economic Theory*, which was first published in French that same year, 1964.

Not wanting to be consigned to the 'historico-empirical' school of economics by 'Western Marxists', Althusserians or other professional Marxist philosophers, Ernest Mandel wrote his most 'philosophical' book, *The Formation of the Economic Thought of Karl Marx* (first published in French, in 1967). Through that work he intervened directly in the debate, very fashionable at the time, over the relationship between the 'young Marx' and the mature Marx (the period covered by the book ends just as Marx is about to write *Capital*). He also made worthwhile contributions on other fashionable topics, such as 'the Asiatic mode of production', the theory of alienation, and its relation to 'industrial civilization' (Mandel never accepted the term 'post-industrial'). This work would be completed later with introductions to a new English edition of the three volumes of Marx's *Capital*, which appeared one after another in London in 1976, 1978 and 1981.[6]

Europe vs America was first published in Germany, in 1968 (*Die EWG und die Konkurrenz Europa–Amerika*). A milestone in Mandel's thinking about the third phase of capitalism, the work takes up the issues of inter-imperialist contradictions between the United States and the Europe of the Common Market, their monetary consequences and their implications for the prospects for European integration. The book is out of date now, but interesting nevertheless since the problems it raised are still quite relevant and its key assumptions were based on an accurate prognosis of a generalized recession.

During the years immediately after the shock wave of 1968, several important theoretical texts by Mandel, the length of a pamphlet or a long article, were published in several languages. Most noteworthy were his lectures on bureaucracy (originally in French), his two texts on fascism and on the Leninist theory of organization (originally in German), and many polemical works, often written in English, particularly those debating the theory of state capitalism in the USSR. In 1970 he published in French a voluminous anthology with a long introduction on a theme that was dear to him as a revolutionary activist and former trade-unionist: *Contrôle ouvrier, conseils ouvriers, autogestion* (Workers' Control, Workers' Councils, Self-Management).

In 1972, at last, Mandel's work on the third phase of capitalism was published in German: *Der Spätkapitalismus* (the revised and updated English edition appeared in 1975 as *Late Capitalism*). He would consider this book his *magnum opus*, and would rightly be proud of it. It was indeed an innovative work in several respects: particularly because of its updating and refinement of the theory of 'long waves' (which it linked to the falling tendency of the rate of profit); its theory of crises; and its analysis of the connections between the third technological revolution, what he called 'the tendency to permanent innovation', and the arms race, on the one hand, and the structural transformations of capitalism, on the other hand, in light of the laws of capitalist development that Marx had discovered. *Late Capitalism* is above all the first serious attempt – the only one so far – to sketch an overall Marxist picture of contemporary capitalism, integrating the various dimensions that Marx intended to cover, including issues such as social classes, the state and the world market which the author of *Capital* had no time to deal with in his masterpiece.[7]

This was a formidable endeavour, especially for one man on his own.[8] The work he produced in the end can certainly be debated. How could it be otherwise, given the extreme complexity of the contemporary world and the multitude of issues he addressed? But it is undeniably a respectable and respected work, although academic economists have mostly preferred to ignore it rather than risk a debate with its author. The book shows the intellectual scope of this man we have lost, whom it would be legitimate to consider as the most fertile and universal Marxist mind of his generation.

In articles written in French beginning in 1975 and published in 1978 as *La Crise* (in English: *The Second Slump*), Mandel tried to show that the generalized recession of 1974–75 confirmed the ebb of the long wave that he had foreseen. It was thus an expression of a long-term depressive tendency. Above all, it was the ineluctable result of capitalism's internal contradictions and their cumulative exacerbation over a long period, not a simple accident due to exogenous factors (such as the oil crisis). The subsequent evolution of the world capitalist economy has largely borne out this 'Mandelian' diagnosis, leading therefore to a growing international interest in the theory of 'long waves', which Ernest Mandel had done more than anyone to rehabilitate since 1964.

One relatively early result was the invitation to the author of *Late Capitalism* in 1978 to give a series of lectures on long waves as the Alfred Marshall Lectures for that year at the University of Cambridge. An expanded and more detailed version of these lectures was published in 1980 as *Long Waves of Capitalist Development: The Marxist Interpretation*. In this work Mandel returned to the theses he had already expounded in his *magnum opus*. He tried to make a link between long waves and 'cycles of class struggle', and for the first time took strong exception to the idea of a cyclical sequence of long waves. The man who had for years predicted the crisis and the end of the post-war expansive long wave thumbed his nose at the capitalists by refusing to predict recovery once the crisis had arrived. The turn from an expansive to a recessive long wave flows from the system's inherent contradictions, he explained, but there is nothing automatic about a turn back toward protracted expansion. For that, the role of exogenous factors is indispensable.

On a completely different subject, articles written in French were collected and completed with unpublished chapters to make up Mandel's book *Critique de l'eurocommunisme* in 1978 (*From Stalinism to Eurocommunism* in English), followed by *Réponse à Louis Althusser et Jean Elleinstein* the year after. Also in 1979 a series of interviews with Ernest Mandel was published in London under the title *Revolutionary Marxism Today*, in which he passed judgement and made predictions on many different historical, theoretical, and current political issues. Giving his thoughts free range, the Fourth International's leader, speaking as such, showed his strengths as well as his weaknesses, which were noticeable above all in excessive optimism or defensiveness. Last of all in 1979, Ernest Mandel published in English his *Trotsky: A Study in the Dynamic of His Thought*. This essentially didactic work was devoted to the formation of the thought of the great Marxist whom he venerated and constantly re-read, always marvelling anew at the perspicacity of the man Isaac Deutscher called a 'Prophet'.

The first years of the 1980s brought an ebb in struggles. They gave Ernest Mandel an opportunity to write and publish in English his book on detective novels, *Delightful Murder: A Social History of the Crime Story* (1984). It was a rough sketch of a work on the relationship between capitalism and crime that death would prevent him from completing. He finished and published in 1986, again in English, *The Meaning of the Second World War*. Not merely a Marxist interpretation of this terrible mid-century (which shaped the young Ernest Mandel), it is also a fierce denunciation of capitalism 'with a human face', and a penetrating reflection on some key issues of the materialist conception of history. *The Place of Marxism in History* (1986), a didactic presentation of Marxism's historical and intellectual genesis, was the result of his teaching at the Amsterdam-based International Institute for Research and Education (IIRE).

Also in 1986, Mandel debated Alec Nove in *New Left Review* on the relationship between plan and market in a post-capitalist economy. He vigorously criticized the idea of 'market socialism', and defended the democratic socialist project of the revolutionary Marxist tradition. This debate, a new version of the irreducible conflict between the 'realism' of reformist resignation and the 'utopia' of revolutionary intransigence, continued until 1988.[9] It reflected the spirit of the time, the heyday of Gorbachevism.

Mandel grasped very early that this was a turning point in Soviet history, at a time when many people still tended to minimize it. However he was clear-headed enough not to have any illusions about Mikhail Gorbachev's chances of success, unlike many admirers of this sorcerer's apprentice of bureaucratic reform. (Khrushchev in his time had evoked identical hopes.) He did err nevertheless, carried away by his characteristic revolutionary optimism, by underestimating the effects of decades of Stalinist dictatorship on the consciousness of the Soviet working class and overestimating the will of both Soviet workers and bureaucracy to resist the dynamic of capitalist restoration, overdetermined by the global context. Both the strengths and weaknesses of his analysis appear clearly in Mandel's *Où va l'URSS de Gorbatchev?*, published first in French in 1989 and in English as *Beyond Perestroika: The Future of Gorbachev's USSR.*

Mandel was bitterly disappointed by the reactionary turn of events in Eastern Europe after 1990. He probably felt it more intensely than others because of the intensity of the hopes he placed on the thaw, which ended in a debacle. He then calmly finished the theoretical work on bureaucracy that he had been planning for a long time, *Power and Money: A Marxist Theory of Bureaucracy*, published in London in 1992. Events impelled Mandel to give this book a function that he had certainly not originally foreseen: to explain the roots of the Soviet and East European bureaucracies' restorationist turn, as he stressed in his introduction, and to criticize his own past errors of judgement along the way. It was also an opportunity for him to re-argue the case for a socialism based on self-management, for which he had always fought.

The same year he defended the Russian revolution against its detractors, whose ranks swelled in the wake of the Soviet collapse. In his second IIRE Notebook: *October 1917: Coup d'état or Social Revolution?*, Mandel presented a balance sheet based on long familiarity with this subject. His defence of the Russian revolution did not preclude a critique of its shortcomings in the spirit of Rosa Luxemburg, whom he always profoundly admired. At the request of the German PDS's publishing house he then presented a defence of Leon Trotsky. Its title, *Trotski als Alternativ* (*Trotsky as Alternative* in English) echoed former East German left-wing dissident Rudolf Bahro's book, which had made a stir in 1977. Mandel defends Leon Trotsky and his struggle passionately before the court of history, though again in a critical spirit. He stresses his belief that Trotsky's contributions were Marxism's only coherent response to the major problems of the twentieth century (except the ecological issue).

Much weakened by declining health, and in spite of a first coronary in December 1993, Ernest Mandel found the energy to finish preparing a new, revised and expanded edition of his book, *Long Waves of Capitalist Development*. Published in London shortly before his death, it was supplemented by two chapters in which he reviewed the copious literature that had appeared on the subject since the 1980 edition. He returned at length to the debates raised by this literature, and re-affirmed his conviction that the conditions still do not exist for an end to the depressive long wave of this last quarter-century.

*

Ernest Mandel died on 20 July 1995: by a remarkable coincidence, this was just fifteen days before the first centenary of the death of a man whom he admired profoundly – Friedrich Engels, who died on the 5th of August 1895 at a similar age to Mandel's.

One could draw an interesting parallel between these two figures. Both held a quasi-epicurean conception of life, which stood light-years from any ascetic misconception of what a communist revolutionary ought to be. Both displayed a sharp sense of humour, and used to laugh loudly and frequently. Both were characterized by their fluency in writing and linguistic gifts. The two men were outstanding erudites and had a truly encyclopaedic curiosity and culture, matched by a tremendous capacity for intellectual labour, although neither of them was a 'workaholic'.

Both showed an inexhaustible commitment to revolutionary politics and a tireless dedication to building the international movement to which they belonged. Both were thoroughly internationalist in theory and practice, manifesting a deep contempt for all brands of narrow-minded nationalism, especially when these nationalisms ran counter to what they saw as the requirements of social progress. Both were obsessed by the 'prophetic' warning that, short of socialism, the fate of humanity could only be barbarism (Rosa Luxemburg borrowed her famous formula from Engels).

Both were 'scientific utopians' one could say, not without a dash of irony. They were both hard rationalists, believing in the limitless capacity of scientific knowledge – true 'positivists' actually, if we free that concept from the heavily pejorative connotation with which it is usually endowed. And yet, both men were real utopians, dreaming of a society that looked more like the one imagined by Charles Fourier than like any brand of realistic, not to say 'really existing', socialism.

Several other common features of the two men could be added to this already long list. To be sure, there were also many differences between their two lives and characters, mostly related to the huge differences between their respective centuries. They also had different social origins: Engels was the heir of a capitalist family, whereas Mandel was truly a 'natural-born Marxist', the son of a learned communist activist. Mandel was a typical representative of that remarkable category of thinkers that Isaac Deutscher labeled 'the non-Jewish Jew'.[10] Engels was of Protestant descent, although he was the alter ego of Marx, the most famous of all 'non-Jewish Jews', a fact which indicates a strong kind of 'elective affinity', although different, to be sure, from the one Michael Löwy described in his *Redemption and Utopia*.[11]

From this brief comparison emerges an indisputable fact: like Friedrich Engels, Ernest Mandel was a multifaceted personality, a multi-talented mind, a complex thinker as well as a thinker of complexity. This implied a difficult choice of topics to be discussed in this volume and at the seminar where these papers were originally presented. Material reasons forbade the discussion of all aspects of Mandel's thought. To be sure, all the topics discussed here are central elements of Mandel's contribution to Marxist theory, key aspects of Mandel's intellectual production seen from a macroscopic point of view. Positively, our choice is undoubtedly legitimate. However, the exclusion of certain topics needs some explanation.

Many of Mandel's voluminous writings were devoted to questions which are hardly discussed or even referred to in this book. Like his two bearded intellectual guides of the nineteenth century, Mandel was closely involved in actual working-class activities during his life, and deeply involved in the day-to-day life of the international Marxist organization he strove to build, the Fourth International, an organization which dealt with almost all the fields of social and political struggle during the fifty years that Ernest Mandel spent in its leadership. In this militant capacity, Mandel commented on a very long list of issues, writing extensively on topics as varied as trade-union tactics in Western Europe and guerrilla warfare in Latin America.

The fact that we did not confront most of these issues in our seminar and this book – including the key activity of Ernest Mandel to which he dedicated his whole life, the building of the Fourth International – has to be explained. To avoid any misunderstanding, we must state categorically that our choice does not stem in the least from any belittling of Mandel's intellectual production directly related to these activities. It does not proceed from any assessment in the vein of Isaac Deutscher's well-known negative judgment on Trotsky's fight for the Fourth International, a judgment that irritated Mandel very much. Whatever opinion one may have about the movement Mandel led, it is beyond doubt that his specific political commitment informed most if not all of his writings.[12]

Mandel's theoretical production did not occur *despite* his involvement in militant revolutionary politics. It occurred rather *because* of this involvement, which shines through all his publications, including such major works as *Marxist Economic Theory* and *Late Capitalism*, read far beyond the Trotskyist ranks. In that sense, whatever choice of topics we were to make, the discussion of Mandel's theoretical legacy could not avoid dealing with his political views and commitment, as these proceedings of our seminar definitely show.

It is possible, however, even necessary, to separate the appraisal of

Mandel's theoretical achievement from the assessment of the militant endeavour that motivated it; to separate the appraisal of his contribution to Marxist theory from the discussion of his innumerable writings on conjunctural issues, or his proclamatory statements which were often a display of wishful thinking, as is usually the case for that peculiar brand of literature. After all, to cite a great example, does anyone base an appraisal of Marx's *Capital* on an evaluation of the International Workingmen's Association which he founded and led?

Our goal then was to emphasize those aspects of Mandel's contribution to Marxism which can be acknowledged and appraised regardless of any judgment on the specific political and organizational choices through which he attempted to translate his Marxist convictions, being a firm believer in the inseparability of revolutionary theory from revolutionary praxis. Mandel's theoretical production cannot be separated from his commitment to revolutionary class struggle, to be sure, but it can be assessed independently of the concrete ways through which he channelled his revolutionary praxis.

This does not mean that we wished to avoid a discussion on Ernest Mandel's concrete politics, or that any of our contributors would have been embarrassed by such a discussion. The fact is only that not everyone interested in discussing Mandel's contribution to Marxist theory is interested in assessing his militant career. The former circle is far larger than the latter, and it is the larger circle that our seminar and this book wished to address. Besides, it is too soon to draw a balance-sheet of Mandel's life as a revolutionary fighter: we lack historical perspective in that respect. It is already quite possible, however, to assess critically some key tenets of his theoretical contribution, whether in relation to post-war capitalism or to Stalinism. On both levels, major shifts have already occurred that enable us to compare Mandel's views with history, which remains the highest criterion.

Finally, one can easily infer from what is said here that our goal was never to avoid discussion in general. On the contrary, although tributes are generally meant to praise a person's life and work, we definitely wanted our tribute to Ernest Mandel's theoretical legacy also to be an occasion for a critical examination of several aspects of his work.

After all, this is certainly the way he would have liked it to be. His liberal conception of democracy applied to the very ranks of the small organization he led, which can be singled out among all brands of organized Marxism for the very high tolerance for debate and divergences that it exhibited under Mandel's leadership. This is also part of Mandel's legacy: a truly open conception of revolutionary politics, reviving the party tradition that existed before Stalinism infected most brands of Marxist organizations, whether Stalinist, non-Stalinist or even anti-Stalinist.

As a matter of fact, the best tribute to the democratic example set by Ernest Mandel is that this is perhaps the first time that the key leader and theoretician of a political movement is not sanctified by his own co-thinkers – a category to which many of the participants in our seminar and several of the contributors to this book belonged – immediately after his death. As the French eighteenth-century writer Beaumarchais said eloquently in a famous sentence: '*Sans la liberté de blâmer, il n'est point d'éloge flatteur.*'[13] This is how we intended this posthumous tribute to Ernest Mandel: as critical, and therefore truly flattering!

Notes

1. 'I was almost happy at being deported to Germany. I had a crazy confidence: I was going to find myself at the centre of revolution. That was our state of mind. I wonder if I could have survived physically and morally, and if our little organization would have survived, without this confidence.' Ernest Mandel, in an unpublished interview with Rodolphe Prager, dated 12 November 1977. See also Mandel's interview by Tariq Ali, published under the title 'The Luck of a Crazy Youth', in *New Left Review* (hereafter NLR), 213, September–October 1995 and reproduced in this volume, pp. 217–24.
2. Quotes from Leon Trotsky's *Diary in Exile*, Cambridge (MA) 1958, p. 47.
3. *The Formation of the Economic Thought of Karl Marx* is dedicated 'to Gisèle [Scholtz – Ernest Mandel's first wife who died in 1982] who enabled me to write this book as a happy man'.
4. Due to space limitation, this introduction ignores deliberately the many anthologies of articles written at very different dates, published by Mandel himself or with his consent, such as *La Longue marche de la révolution* (1976), *De la Commune à Mai 1968* (1978), *Revolutionäre Strategien im 20. Jahrhundert* (1978), *Les Etudiants, les intellectuels et la lutte des classes* (1979), *Karl Marx: Die Aktualität seines Werkes* (1984), etc. The same goes for the very many collective works to which Ernest Mandel contributed or that he himself edited, alone or jointly, such as *Fifty Years of World Revolution, 1917–1967* (1968), *Ricardo, Marx, Sraffa* (1984), *New Findings in Long-Wave Research* (1992), etc. For a complete list of Mandel's book-format works in English, see the bibliography at the end of this volume.
5. *Marxist Economic Theory*, London 1968, vol. 1, pp. 17, 20.
6. The three introductions were later published together in one volume in Spanish under the title *El Capital: Cien Años de Controversias en Torno a la Obra de Karl Marx*.
7. In his *Considerations on Western Marxism* (London 1979, p. 99), Perry

Anderson describes *Late Capitalism* as 'the first theoretical analysis of the global development of the capitalist mode of production since the Second World War, conceived within the framework of classical Marxist categories'.

8. Mandel was aware of the necessary limitations of his work. He had modestly subtitled the original German edition 'Versuch einer marxistischen Erklä-rung' ('An Attempt at a Marxist Explanation').

9. Mandel, NLR 159, 1986; Nove, NLR 161, 1987; Mandel, NLR 169, 1988.

10. What has been said above about Mandel's contempt for all brands of narrow-minded nationalism makes it obvious that he never succumbed to what Hannah Arendt described in 1946 as 'that Jewish brand of chauvinism automatically produced by secularization, which somehow persuades the average de-Judaized Jew that . . . he is still a superior being simply because he happened to be born a Jew – the salt of the earth – or the motor of history.' ('The Jewish State: Fifty Years After – Where Have Herzl's Politics Led?' in *Zionism – The Dream and the Reality*, Gary Smith, ed., London 1974, p. 73). This is certainly one of the clues which make it possible to under-stand the relative discretion and restraint that Mandel showed for a long time regarding the Nazi genocide. The resurgence of anti-Semitism, among other forms of racism and barbarism coinciding with the protracted crisis of European societies, led him to abandon this reserve, which could almost be seen as an underestimation. All those who knew Ernest Mandel well know for sure that this was never the case. On this question, aside from the contribution by Norman Geras to this book, see Enzo Traverso's afterword to the second French edition of his work on *The Marxists and the Jewish Question* (*Les Marxistes et la question juive*, Paris 1997): 'De l'école de Francfort à Ernest Mandel. Interrogations et impasses du marxisme devant Auschwitz', pp. 317–41 (English translation in Traverso, *Towards a Critique of Modern Barbarism: Marxism and the Nazi Genocide*, forthcoming from Pluto Press, London).

11. Michael Löwy, *Redemption and Utopia*, London 1992.

12. The last lines of one of the most lyrical texts Ernest Mandel ever wrote (at the age of 23) – the 1946 preface, signed 'Ernest Germain', to the first edition of the 24-year-old Abraham Léon's extraordinary work on the Jewish question, written two years before Léon's death at Auschwitz – bear witness to the meaning that Ernest Mandel wanted to give his own life:

> Among those who learn the story of his life there may be some who will perhaps ask why a man of such remarkable qualities tied his destiny to a small revolutionary organisation. . . . They will ask them-selves: why did the Marcel Hics, the Martin Widelins, the A. Leons, who were among the most gifted European intellectuals, choose a movement which could promise them neither success nor glory nor honors nor even a minimum of material comfort, but which on the contrary demanded of them every sacrifice, comfort, including their lives, and which required long, ungrateful work, frequently in isola-tion from the proletariat to whom they wanted to give everything? And if they are able to recognize in these young revolutionists, along with their intellectual gifts, exceptional moral qualities, then they will

say to themselves that a movement capable of attracting such men solely by the power of its ideas and the purity of its ideal and capable of leading these rationalist dialecticians to such heights of self-denial and devotion – is a movement that cannot die because in it lives everything that is noble in man.

'A Biographical Sketch of Abram Leon' in Abram Leon, *The Jewish Question: A Marxist Interpretation*, New York 1970, p. 26.

13. 'Without the freedom to blame, there is no flattering praise.'

2

The Unexpected Dialectic of Structural Reforms

Robin Blackburn

Ernest Mandel, who died at the age of 72 on 20 July 1995, was one of the world's leading Marxist economists, author of more than twenty books and an inspiring speaker in half-a-dozen languages. He was a passionate defender of the ideas of Leon Trotsky and a leading member of the Fourth International for over four decades. He commanded respect and admiration from wide layers of the Left. Perhaps more than any other single person he was the educator of the new generation recruited to Marxism and revolutionary politics by the student revolts of the sixties, especially in Europe and the Americas. For several years the United States, France, West Germany, Switzerland and Australia denied him entry, deeming his very presence a threat to 'national security'. For over thirty years Ernest Mandel was a regular contributor to *New Left Review* (hereafter NLR), the journal I now edit; his books, many of them published by Verso in English, were translated into more than thirty languages. His *Introduction to Marxist Economics* (1968), sold over a hundred thousand copies. The present appreciation and critique will first sketch an overall assessment and then develop a more specific argument to do with socialist transition.

Ernest Mandel was born to Belgian Jewish parents in 1923. In a remarkable interview published in NLR 214 (1995) Mandel described his early contact with a Trotskyist group before the outbreak of the Second World War and his experiences in the Resistance and in a German prison camp. Following the end of the war he studied at the University of Brussels and the Ecole Pratique des Hautes Etudes in Paris. His first major work was a two volume *Treatise on Marxist Economics* (published in French in 1962 and in English in 1967) though he had already made his mark as a gifted polemicist, contributing, under the name Ernest Germain, both to Trotskyist disputes and to the debate in *Les Temps Modernes* aroused by Jean-Paul Sartre's *Les Communistes et la Paix.*

Mandel's Marxism was attractive to the new team at NLR in the early sixties because it was focused on current politics and informed by wide reading of anthropology, history and economics. Mandel was asked to write on Belgium. The resulting article, published in NLR 20 (1963), started from the revolution in the Low Countries in the sixteenth century, showed why nineteenth-century Belgium had been 'the classic European bourgeois state', analyzed the Belgian general strike of 1960–61 and concluded with a sketch of the 'structural reforms' needed to take matters forward.[1] This essay was to furnish one of the models for NLR's subsequent series of country studies. His *Treatise* was reviewed in NLR 21 by the eminent economist H.D. Dickenson.

Mandel's two most distinctive and widely noticed contributions to the NLR of the sixties were a vindication of Trotsky in debate with Nicholas Krasso and a much reprinted lecture entitled 'Where is America Going?'. Krasso was a former student of Lukács who had played a role in the establishment of the Budapest Workers' Council in 1956. His article in NLR criticized what he saw as the 'sociological' reductionism of Trotsky's concept of 'permanent revolution' and work- ers' state. Mandel's two lengthy replies ranged widely over the history of the century, defending the necessity of building a Marxist alternative to Stalinism and arguing that Stalinism was not merely a wrong and dangerous theory but also the expression of 'an autonomous social layer', namely the bureaucracy. Krasso and Mandel were both too inclined to judge Trotsky by a Leninist yardstick, Krasso criticizing Trotsky for not having displayed Lenin's political skills in his battle against Stalin and Mandel being over-cautious in differentiating Trot- sky's legacy from Leninist orthodoxy. When I taxed him with this once he referred me to his pamphlet on 'The Leninist Theory of Organiz- ation' (1976) where he had been more forthright: 'Lenin, in his first debate with the Mensheviks, very much underestimated the danger of the apparatus becoming autonomous and of the bureaucratisation of the workers' parties . . . Trotsky and Luxemburg recognized this danger more accurately and earlier than Lenin.'[2]

While many prominent writers influenced by Trotsky became histor- ians, like Trotsky himself (Isaac Deutscher, C.L.R. James, Daniel Guérin, Pierre Broué), Mandel's writings are more redolent of Rosa Luxem- burg's influence, with their sinewy analysis of capitalism and thorough- going commitment to Marxist universalism. Despite his obeisance to

Lenin's memory he was also committed to a rather unLeninist view of the creativity of the workers' movement in action. It could also be said that his own creativity often flourished in contexts where he was not preoccupied by the reaction of the less enlightened wing of the Trotskyist movement – when addressing a public rally or writing for the *Frankfurter Rundschau.*

Re-reading 'Where is America Going?' (1969) it is striking how accurately it forecast the consequences for the US of intensifying competition and declining profitability. The future would see stagnant or declining wages, growing public squalor and financial speculation divorced from productive investment.[3] Mandel was at this time engaged on writing his single most important work, *Late Capitalism*, with its sustained analysis of the dynamic and limitations of the post-war boom. At this time the leading mainstream economists and commentators all wrote as if capitalism had permanently smoothed out the trade cycle and ensured conditions of permanent full employment and constant growth. On the left the notion of state monopoly capitalism asserted that there now reigned a managed capitalist system, under US hegemony, where inter-capitalist competition was of less account. *Late Capitalism* published in 1972 in Germany and 1974 in Britain offered a very different, and as it turned out immensely prescient, analysis. In an original redeployment of Kondratiev's theory of 'long waves' of capital- ist development Mandel argued that the post-war boom had run out of steam and that the conditions had been created for a period of lower profits, the erosion of real wages in the US and the re-emergence of mass unemployment in the advanced countries. It can fairly be said that *Late Capitalism* still ranks as the commanding Marxist work on the post-war development of capitalism.

Ernest Mandel earned his living from his writing and political work. His contacts with the academic world were few. However in 1978 he was invited by the University of Cambridge to give the Alfred Marshall Lectures. The book which resulted, *Long Waves in Capitalist Development*, has just been republished with two new chapters surveying the course of global recession over the last two decades and responding to other students of world economy. While Mandel analyzes the inexorable structural tendencies underlying the capitalist trade cycle he also argues that the preconditions for an upturn are essentially political and social in character.

Mandel's political predictions were less accurate than his economic prognostications, often proving too optimistic. Like many others, he saw the general strike in France in 1968 as harbinger of a new wave of struggles by workers and students that would challenge the capitalist order throughout Western Europe and join up with renewed anti-bureaucratic revolution in the East and anti-imperialist movements in the Third World. He sought to make sense of the Prague Spring, the Tet offensive and the May events within a single framework. Mandel's French associates played a prominent role in the revolt in Paris and elsewhere; he was himself discovered by an English journalist on a barricade beside the burnt out ruins of his own car, exclaiming 'C'est beau, c'est la révolution!'. Mandel's great ability as an orator in Flemish, French, German, English, Spanish and Italian made him the emissary of the message of '68 throughout Europe and beyond. I remember a friend's report of the astonishing spectacle of a thousand phlegmatic Finns rising to their feet and cheering wildly following one of Ernest's stirring perorations.

While Mandel was to prove mistaken about the destiny of the diverse struggles of '68, he encouraged young people to commit themselves to movements whose effects were emancipatory. Whether in Czechoslovakia or Poland, Spain or Mexico those engaged and inspired by Mandel's vision played a modest but not insignificant role in pushing back the bounds of dictatorship and oppression. In later years the Mandel levy have generally merged with the new Marxist parties like Rifundazione in Italy, Izquierda Unida in Spain and the Greens or the PDS in Germany.

Mandel had a breadth of vision not normally encountered in those who make politics their profession. I first met him at a conference organised by the Labour Student organization in Folkestone in 1963. As Secretary of the Oxford Labour Club I had been obliged to entertain the likes of Harold Wilson and Richard Crossman. The leonine Mandel, with his disdain for petty calculation and ability to think historically, could not have been more different from these clever foxes. Mandel insisted that we take time out from the Conference to visit Canterbury Cathedral; my school-induced reluctance to enter an Anglican place of worship soon evaporated as Mandel discoursed on the fine points of Gothic architecture and the achievement of the artisans who had built the Cathedral – we paused for a moment at the grave of the Archbishop martyred during the Peasants' Revolt, a plaque inviting us to pray for industrial peace. Subsequently I had the pleasure and instruction of accompanying Mandel on a trip to Tenochtitlan – and to canals on the outskirts of Mexico City which had only recently, Mandel explained, recovered the levels of agricultural productivity achieved in Aztec times. However Mandel's diversions were not consistently so exalted. His deplorable addiction to crime thrillers led him to write a book on the subject – the only work of his to be translated into Russian prior to the Soviet collapse.

We were glad to publish not only Mandel's long range economic analysis but also essays and books in which he addressed other matters. These included a fine response to Solzhenitsyn's work and a marvellous reconsideration of 'the role of the individual in history'.[4] In the eighties he also published *The Meaning of the Second World War*, a book which sought to grapple with the complexity of what he saw as five wars-within-a-war.

In a special category was 'In Defence of Socialist Planning', an article especially written for NLR in response to Alex Nove's *The Economics of Feasible Socialism*. Mandel had earlier grappled with these issues in the sixties when his advice had been solicited by Che Guevara; at that time he had made a distinctive contribution in support of Guevara's argument that the world market should neither be ignored nor should it be allowed to dictate priorities. Like his mentor Trotsky, Mandel did not favour vain attempts to anticipate a complete suppression of the market, but still less did he put any credence in 'market socialism'. His powerful arguments for the essential role of far-reaching democratic planning of economic life if capitalist inequality and waste was to be overcome stimulated much discussion both in NLR and elsewhere.[5] While warning of the dangers of reliance on the market, Mandel remained implacable in his indictment of bureaucratic dictatorship. Following the collapse of the Soviet Union he remained hopeful that a new workers' movement would surface in the East and predicted that capitalism would not be swiftly or easily re-established.[6]

The last occasion I saw Mandel speak at a public event was in December 1991 in Madrid when he debated the future of socialism with Felipe Gonzalez. The Spanish Prime Minister unwisely elected to lecture Mandel on the virtues of constitutionalism and respect for human rights. Mandel drew a stark picture of the plight of Europe's thirty million unemployed and attacked social democracy for its capitulation to the deflationary dictates of the Bundesbank. He also drew attention to the contradiction between Gonzalez's oration and the fact that several thousand young pacifists were languishing in Spain's jails as he spoke. There can have been very few in the hall, or watching on TV, who did not see the frail, seventy-year-old Ernest Mandel as the vigorous and principled defender of socialism and Gonzalez as the miserable, compromised prisoner of power.

Mandel's Theory of Socialism and the Transition

I have said that Mandel was too optimistic in political prediction, and this is true, but he was also, perhaps, exposed to the danger of disillusionment by the unrealistic nature of some of his hopes. The central thesis of Ernest Mandel's political writings was the political capacity of the working class, as embodied in trade unions, workers' parties and, at the moment of rupture, institutions of dual power such as workers' councils or soviets.

By comparison with the inclination of early Marxists to stress the limitations of trade unions or with Lenin's strictures on economism Mandel was strongly committed to the developmental possibilities of the labour movement, notwithstanding bureaucratic encrustations. While registering Lenin's critique Mandel was willing to endorse at least some of Luxemburg's positions on the inherent logic of workers' struggles and workers' organizations in the direction of a challenge to the logic of capitalism.

In Mandel's view this logic would be unleashed by the crisis-logic of late capitalism. The analysis of late capitalism, as we have seen, constituted one of the most original aspects of Mandel's thought. If his prediction of a coming era of crisis had been made simply on the basis that nothing had changed in capitalism then this would not have been such an achievement. But Mandel did register the new role of the state in post-war capitalism, arguing not that it could suppress the trade cycle but that it could fundamentally affect its form. Mandel's theory of workers' struggles growing to the point of challenging capitalist power and his programmatic proposals for 'structural reforms' were congruent with this perspective.

However there was a central flaw in Mandel's vision of a rise of workers' democracy virtually neutralizing and hence by-passing representative democracy. Historically there are few cases of institutions of dual power emerging in this way. The Russian soviets emerged out of the wreckage of Tsarism; curiously they were first set up at the instigation of a Tsarist Senator in 1904–5. Clearly they did not confront a functioning bourgeois democracy. The workers' council movement in Italy and Germany stopped a little way short of bidding for power. In Germany it was the defence of bourgeois democracy which mobilized the workers' movement at the time of the Kapp putsch; and, of course, the failure to defend bourgeois democracy which paved the way for the rise of

Nazism. Subsequent experiences of workers' councils in countries such
as Spain, Hungary, Portugal and Chile, confirm, in my view, that they
did not constitute an appropriate nucleus for a new state. In May 1968
in France, or in Italy in subsequent years or in Portugal, the counter-
position of workers' democracy to the representative state made little
headway and resulted in the hegemony of often fairly undemocratic
forms of the latter. I would argue that 'centrist' proposals to reform
and improve representative institutions by making them more genuinely democratic, by introducing checks on the executive and by
stimulating forms of self-administration in civil society are more promising and necessary than the abstract 'dual power' conception.

Mandel's concept of 'structural reforms' sought to build on the logic
of reform of welfare capitalism, strengthening the element of planning
and redistribution to the point where its logic encroached on the logic
of capital. However in contrast to left social democratic thinking
Mandel's notion of structural reforms did seek to nourish workers' self-
management tendencies, through watchwords such as 'Open the
Books'.

From the perspective of the 1990s I think these proposals were
inadequate, though there is something of their method which is useful
to retain. Methodologically Mandel's programmatic ideas developed
from the analysis of 'late capitalism', taking to a higher level the
objective tendency towards 'socialisation of the forces of production'.
However, Mandel's political economy did not sufficiently register the
important role played in some advanced capitalist economies by financial institutions connected to pension and insurance funds. In a
number of countries these institutions now play a major role in the
accumulation process; pension and insurance funds currently supply a
half of new capital formation in Britain every year. However, the
employees who are the nominal beneficiaries of these schemes have
absolutely no control over them. This is a rather stark species of the
workers' economic 'alienation' about which Mandel wrote, since workers find their own pension funds used in speculative attacks against
their own industries and living conditions. Yet there is something about
these schemes which seem to invite workers' participation.

Throughout Europe the form of pension provision has become a
crucial stake in political struggle. This first became clear in the controversies over the Meidner Plan in Sweden in the 1980s. The defeat of
the Meidner proposals left the Swedish multi-nationals free to withdraw
huge sums from Sweden, thus undermining and eventually destroying

the Swedish welfare model. Most recently social struggles in France, Italy and Germany have highlighted the importance of the form and scale of pension provision. What is at stake in such clashes is the shape of the future, so they are not only of concern to employees approaching retirement age. Pension funds under the control of the latter, and backed by appropriate state encouragement, could begin to foster social priorities, to ensure proper housing and social facilities and to guarantee industrial regeneration within the framework of a sustainable economy.

The old ideas of 'workers' control' or of 'open the books' wrongly supposed that the path of capitalist economy was determined at the level of the factory or workplace. The coordination of capitalist economy in fact takes place at the financial level where the key investment decisions are made. Structural reforms or transitional demands have to apply to this level if they wish to play a hegemonic role. The riposte to today's 'grey capitalism' should be a species of pension socialism. This was not a conclusion Mandel ever reached but it is, I believe, consistent with his method and his fundamental goal.

Notes

1. Ernest Mandel, 'The Dialectic of Class and Region in Belgium', *New Left Review* (hereafter NLR), Summer 1963, pp. 5–31.
2. Ernest Mandel, 'The Leninist Theory of Organization ', in Robin Blackburn, ed., *Revolution and Class Struggle: A Reader in Marxist Politics*, London 1977, pp. 78–135, p. 100.
3. Ernest Mandel, 'Where is America Going?', NLR, March/April 1969, pp. 3–17.
4. Ernest Mandel, 'Solzhenitsyn, Stalinism and the October Revolution', NLR, 86, July/August 1974, pp. 51–61; 'The Role of the Individual in History: the case of World War Two', NLR 157, May/June 1986, pp. 61–77.
5. Ernest Mandel, 'In Defence of Socialist Planning ', NLR 159, September/ October 1986, pp. 5–37. Nove replied to Mandel in NLR 161 and Mandel came back with 'The Myth of Market Socialism' in NLR 169 (May/June 1988), pp. 108–20. Other responses to Mandel included Auerbach, Desai and Shamsavari in NLR 170 and Diane Elson in NLR 179.
6. Ernest Mandel, *Power and Money*.

3

Ernest Mandel's Revolutionary Humanism

Michael Löwy

Ernest Mandel is known not only as the main theoretician of the Fourth International, but also as one of the great Marxist economists of the second half of the twentieth century. However, the audience for his work goes well beyond the ranks of the movement founded by Leon Trotsky or the circle of economics students.

There are many reasons for this wide appeal, interest and sympathy, from Paris to São Paulo, from Berlin to New York, and from Moscow to Mexico City. One of them is certainly the revolutionary humanist dimension of his writings.

This dimension is one of the unifying principles of his thought, a red thread running throughout his work, whether he was dealing with the economic debate in Cuba, poverty in the Third World, Marxist political economy or revolutionary strategy today. He related each economic or political issue, each event, conflict or crisis, to a global viewpoint, to the struggle for a universal and revolutionary human emancipation. His work was not the prisoner of a narrow standpoint, a narrow technical or tactical approach, an economistic or 'politistic' method, but always embedded in a wider, world-historical, revolutionary humanist perspective.

This is why his economic writings are never concerned only with abstract forces or 'economic laws', but with concrete human beings, their alienation, their exploitation, their suffering – as well as the history of their struggles, their refusal to submit to the rule of capital.

Of course, Mandel's humanism had nothing in common with the vague 'humanitarianism' that is so fashionable nowadays. For him, as a

Marxist, the future of humanity depended directly on the class struggle of the oppressed and exploited.

Marxist humanism is not the object of any specific writing by Mandel: it is found throughout his work. In the following brief notes I shall attempt to bring together and, to some extent, systematize and criticize – without any pretension to being exhaustive – his ideas in this area. Needless to say, this is an *interpretation* – largely inspired by such 'heterodox' Marxists as Lucien Goldmann and Walter Benjamin – of his thought. I am going to focus particularly on three central topics, intimately linked and dialectically articulated: the inhumanity of capitalism, socialism as the realization of human potentialities, and the argument for anthropological optimism.[1]

There are some surprising lacunae in his work: one can find very little on the debate around Althusser's 'theoretical anti-humanism' or on the discussion about the Marxian concept of human nature. But this can be explained by his reluctance to engage in strictly philosophical controversies. More disturbing is the limited attention paid to the crimes against humanity: the Stalinist Gulag, Hiroshima, and even (until 1990) Auschwitz.[2] It is not that these historical events are absent from his writings: they are often mentioned (particularly during the last ten years) but they are somewhat marginal and not always given their full world-historical significance, as disasters of modernity.

Mandel was too much of a (proud) heir to the *Aufklärung*, a follower of the French Enlightenment and its optimistic philosophy of historical progress, to perceive these events as civilizational breaks, as central landmarks of the twentieth century, and as arguments for a general critique – in the spirit of the Frankfurt School – of the whole modern, industrial civilization. He did not understand them as a challenge to the idea of progress inherent in a certain 'classical' interpretation of Marxism nor as a major turning point in human history, requiring a different interpretation of our century.[3]

The critique of capitalism as an *inhuman* system is for Mandel – as for Marx himself – one of the main arguments for the need to struggle against this mode of production and for its revolutionary abolition. Of course, Mandel, like Marx, refers to the civilizing role of capitalism and its contribution to human progress through the exponential development of the productive forces. But he emphasizes that since its origin, 'industrial capitalism has developed a combination of progress and regression, of productive forces and destructive tendencies'.[4] The regressive and 'inhuman' nature of capitalism shows itself in the mutilation of human life, of human nature, and of the human potential for freedom, joy and solidarity.

Capitalism is a system that produces and reproduces exploitation, oppression, social injustice, inequality, poverty, hunger, violence and alienation. The concept of alienation, i.e. the enslavement of human beings by the products of their own labour, by the 'laws' of commodity production, and by the social organization of life transformed into a hostile and independent force, is an essential component of Mandel's critique of capitalism. Because of alienation, human beings, after escaping – to some extent – from the tyranny of natural fatality, have become victims of a social fatality, which seems to doom humanity to crisis, wars, dictatorships and perhaps, tomorrow, nuclear disaster.

Alienated labour is an alienation of human nature, a negation of the human being as a social and political being, because it subordinates human relationships to an irrational accumulation of goods. Through such forms as the division of labour it mutilates the human person in a way that is contradictory to human nature itself, as well as to the harmonious development of the individual.[5] (It is worthy of note that it is here that one does find some of the few passages where Ernest Mandel employs the concept of human nature, though without attempting to define it in one way or another.)

In his book on *The Formation of the Economic Thought of Karl Marx*, Mandel polemicizes against those Marxists – usually linked to the Communist Parties, like Wolfgang Jahn, Manfred Buhr, Auguste Cornu, Emile Bottigelli and of course Louis Althusser – who reject the term 'alienation' as 'non-scientific', 'pre-Marxist', and belonging to the humanist/Feuerbachian intellectual universe of the 'young Marx'. In opposition to this view, Mandel argues that *Entfremdung* (alienation, in German) does not at all disappear from Marx's late economic writings: a study of his intellectual evolution shows the passage from an anthropological conception of alienation, characteristic of the *Manuscripts of 1844*, towards a historical one, which can be found in *The German Ideology*, the *Grundrisse* and even *Capital*.[6]

Capitalist alienation also produces and reproduces the universal venality and commodification of social life: everything is to be sold or bought in the market. The frenetic privatization of consumption and of life destroys the living texture of human relationships, increasingly diminishing oral communication and common action, depriving human beings of the links of affection and sympathy that flow from collective groups, and producing more and more solitude and cynicism.

Egotistic individualism, competition and greed dominate social relations, leading to the *war of all against all* which uproots and destroys the feelings, values and motivations for action which are the most characteristic of humanity: protection of the weak; solidarity; the desire for cooperation and mutual help; love of one's neighbour.[7] (The Marxist atheist Ernest Mandel did not hesitate to use this 'Christian' commandment in his writings.)

Homo homini lupus and *bella omnium contra omnes* are the quintessential expression, not of human nature – as Hobbes and so many bourgeois ideologists pretend – but of the spirit of capitalism. The logic of the system leads to massive forms of social violence, such as the brutal destruction of pre-capitalist societies throughout the process of primitive accumulation and colonization described by Marx and Engels: they were 'too passionate humanists not . . . to revolt against these abominable crimes'.[8] With the advent of imperialism, the colonial forms of violence are transferred, at even more destructive levels, to the advanced metropolis, in the form of wars and fascism. There has not been one single year without war since 1935. The First World War, which cost the lives of ten million people, was a turning point in human history because of its level of brutality and violence. But it was by far surpassed by the Second World War, with its eighty million dead and new levels, hitherto unknown, of barbarism: Auschwitz, Hiroshima. 'What will the price of the Third World War be?'[9]

Capitalism does not have a monopoly on barbarism: its rival and alter ego, the Stalinist bureaucratic system, is also responsible for monstrous crimes. The trials and 'purges' of the 1930s constitute, for Mandel, 'a whole chain of tragedies and crimes on a gigantic scale', with the murder of millions of victims, including the bulk of the communist cadre of the Soviet Union. A list of Stalinist crimes begins with the forced collectivization in the USSR and ends with the horrors of the Pol Pot regime in Cambodia.[10]

Preventing new wars and preventing new outbursts of modern barbarism are among the most urgent reasons to struggle against the capitalist system – as well as against its bureaucratic counterpart. 'Socialism or Barbarism': Rosa Luxemburg's formulation often appears in Mandel's writings, dramatically highlighting the idea that the advent of a socialist world is not at all inevitable, but only one of several possibilities in future historical development. Not by accident the title chosen by Mandel for the 1992 Manifesto of the Fourth International was *Socialism or Barbarism on the Eve of the Twenty-First Century*.

This way of posing the alternatives shows that Mandel wrote less as an 'oracle' – i.e. someone who pretends to predict the inevitable future

– than as a 'prophet', i.e. in Biblical terms, a figure who announces what will happen if a people forgets its best traditions. The prophet voices only a conditional anticipation: he speaks of the imminent disaster, if action is not taken against the danger. Understood in these terms, prophecy is an essential component of all strategic revolutionary discourse – as in Lenin's well-known pamphlet from 1917, *The Impending Catastrophe and How to Combat It.*[11]

After 1985, 'socialism or barbarism' is increasingly replaced, in Mandel's discourse, by a new choice: 'socialism or death'. Capitalism leads to suicidal catastrophes that threaten not only civilization but the physical survival of the human species – *if* there is no worldwide revolutionary action against the system.[12]

Is this a too 'apocalyptic' conception of the future? Mandel was not afraid of using 'apocalyptic' images to illustrate his warnings. In his 1990 essay on the future of socialism, he sees the four horsemen of the apocalypse already running amok: the threat of nuclear war, the danger of ecological disaster, the impoverishment of the Third World, and the threats to democracy in the metropolis. Mandel was particularly indignant at the death, because of hunger and curable diseases, of *sixteen million children* every year in Third World countries (according to UNICEF sources): 'Every five years, this silent massacre claims as many victims as World War II – including the Holocaust and Hiroshima. This is the equivalent of several world wars against children since 1945: that is the price paid for capitalism's survival during this time.'[13]

In spite of Mandel's 'anthropological optimism' (about which more will be said later) there is no easy and complacent belief in irreversible 'progress', no blind faith in the future in his discourse. If Marxism has to combine, as Gramsci once suggested (quoting an expression from Romain Rolland), 'pessimism of the intellect' and 'optimism of the will', there is no lack of rational pessimism in Mandel's 'prophetic' warnings. For instance, in one of his last published books, *Power and Money* (1992), he argued: '*If* irrationality continues to prevail' in relation to nuclear weapons and the threat of environmental disaster, 'humankind is doomed to extinction.' The survival of the human species depends on its capacity to stop 'the trend towards self-destruction'.[14] In other words: if things continue 'as usual', if no revolutionary action takes place, the 'natural' course of history, the spontaneous trend of capitalist pseudo-rationality will lead to catastrophe. This *pessimism of the intellect* is one of the reasons for the feeling of moral and political urgency conveyed by Ernest Mandel's writings, and for the superiority of his diagnosis over so many weak and bland forecasts of 'social progress'. Mandel did not believe in linear progress and insisted on the need to explain and give an account, in Marxist terms, of the 'succession of periods of barbarism and civilization throughout human history'.[15]

Only the proletarian revolution and the establishment of a new mode of production, a new way of life, a new civilization based on cooperation and solidarity – i.e. *socialism* – can prevent the disaster. For Mandel, the destiny of humanity is intimately linked to the victory of the international working class. The emancipation of humanity as a whole depends on the emancipation of the proletariat, but the two are not identical: 'Proletarian emancipation is an absolute precondition for general, human (*gesamtmenschliche*) emancipation, but it is only a precondition, not a substitute.'[16] Universal emancipation requires not only the liberation of the working class but the abolition of *all* the forms of human oppression and exploitation: of women, dominated races or nations, and colonized peoples.[17]

In fact, for Mandel, the proletarian revolutionary struggle – defined in classical Marxist terms[18] – is the legitimate heir and the executor of thousands of years of emancipatory efforts by toiling humanity, from Spartacus to Thomas Münzer and Babeuf. There exists a historical continuity in the fight against social injustice, a powerful tradition of human struggles against inhuman conditions which nourishes proletarian emancipatory action.[19]

The modern revolutionary cause is based on the objective material interests of a social class – the wage earners, in the broadest sense – but it is also inspired, according to Mandel, by ethical values, by a *categorical imperative* (in the Kantian meaning of the term, but with an entirely different content) formulated by Marx himself: to struggle against all social conditions in which human beings are exploited, debased, oppressed, alienated.[20]

To fight on the side of the victims against injustice, against inhumanity (*Unmenschlichkeit*), against inhuman social conditions that transform the world into hell is an elementary duty, based on an axiomatic principle: the only supreme value for human beings is human beings themselves. Far from contradicting this moral obligation, historical materialism and the defence of the proletariat in the class struggle only provide it with additional reasons.[21]

This duty to struggle against exploitation, injustice, oppression, and inhuman circumstances is not motivated by any assurance that it will end with the triumph of socialism. Even if science proved that in the foreseeable future such a struggle has no chance to succeed, the categorical imperative remains valid:

Is one not a better human being, if one tries to pull the whip from the hands of the slaveholder who is flogging his slave, or if one tries to organize an uprising against mass murder (as in the Warshaw Ghetto)? Resistance against inhuman conditions is a human right and a human obligation – independently of any scientific knowledge or prediction.[22]

If revolutionary socialism represents the hope of interrupting the catastrophic course of humanity towards self-destruction, and the opening of a new era, it is not, for Marxism – as so many superficial critics argue – 'the end of history', the 'paradise on earth', perfect happiness and stable harmony: it is only the end of human 'pre-history', the end of dramas that are unworthy of human beings, and the beginning of real human history, the real human drama. Class conflicts will disappear, and will be replaced by new types of conflicts, not animal and debased, but worthy of the human species.[23]

Socialism is also the first step towards the *realm of freedom*. Conscious control by associated individuals over production – democratic planning – is the beginning of the accomplishment of freedom through the community, suppressing the alienated external constraints created by the economic laws of commodity production, the so-called 'iron laws of economics'.[24]

In one of the most powerful passages of his *Marxist Economic Theory*, Mandel categorically rejects the positivist variant of Marxism, for whom the laws of economics are 'objective' and 'necessary', and freedom consists only in the 'consciousness of necessity': taking sides with the 'true humanist tradition of Marx and Engels' – for whom 'the realm of freedom begins *beyond* the realm of necessity' – he argues that freedom does not consist in a 'freely accepted' constraint, but in the free self-development of human beings, in a permanent process of change and enrichment. In socialism, there are no more 'iron laws', and there is no more room for 'political economy' in the strict sense, since production is based on free and democratic choices by associated individuals, according to the social needs of their communities.[25]

For the revolutionary humanist Ernest Mandel, socialism is not a 'productivist' goal. He emphasizes, in his economic writings, that the development of the productive forces ceases to be, in socialism, an end in itself, and becomes only a means for human ends: the growth of socially rich individuality. Goods are increasingly distributed through means other than monetary circulation, according to need. Instead of the accumulation of things, the production of more and more commodities, the aim is the many-sided development of human beings, the realization of all their human potentialities. The criteria for wealth will become *free time*, the time for creative expression and social interchange, allowing each individual his or her self-development as a complete and harmonious personality.[26]

The modern *homo faber* has neither the time nor the possibility for free creativity, for play, for the spontaneous and unselfish exercise of his capacities – the specific character of human *praxis*. The socialist human being will become again, as in the pre-capitalist past, at the same time *faber* and *ludens* – in fact more and more *ludens*, without ceasing to be *faber*:

> Material disinterestedness is crowned by the creative spontaneity which brings together in the same eternal youth the playfulness of children, the enthusiasm of the artist and the 'eureka' of the scientist.[27]

In other words: socialism is not a 'state', a 'system', but a *process*, a historical process of progressive humanization of social relationships, leading to the rise of a new set of human relationships between individuals – instead of reified relationships between things – and finally to a new human being: 'the socialist humanism which puts human solidarity and love of one's neighbour first among the motives of human action' is a notable contribution to the birth of the new human being.[28]

Is this just another *utopia*? In spite of his admiration for Ernst Bloch, Mandel does not usually describe his views on a possible socialist alternative as 'utopian' – an adjective which has too often been used to eliminate radical proposals for social change as 'impossible', 'unrealistic', 'impracticable' or 'unfeasible'. But in *Power and Money*, he refers to Lenin's famous rehabilitation of the dream, in order to challenge the conventional and restrictive definition of the term 'utopia':

> Lenin of all people . . . actually drew attention to the 'right to dream', nay the 'need to dream', provided that the dream is about what does not yet exist but could come about under a certain set of circumstances . . . Utopia in the broadest sense of the word, has been one of the great motors of the eventual achievement of historical progress. In the case of slavery, for example, its abolition would not have happened when and as it did if revolutionary or 'utopian' abolitionists had limited themselves to a struggle to better the conditions of slaves within the 'peculiar institution'.[29]

In Mandel's view, the revolutionary dream, the imaginary horizon of the future, the hope of radical change are essential components of human life: following Ernst Bloch – one of his favourite contemporary Marxist authors – he insists that the human being is a *homo sperans*, moved by the 'Principle of Hope'.[30] Of course, for Mandel, this utopian dimension is not opposed to the scientific one: both are necessary components of the socialist movement for revolutionary emancipation.

Science can demonstrate the existence of class struggle, but not its outcome: 'socialism or death'. In a commitment to the proletarian socialist cause there is, necessarily, an element of *faith*, i.e. (to use Lucien Goldmann's definition) a belief in transindividual values, whose realization cannot be the object of a factual or scientific proof.[31] In one of his first long essays, the article on 'Trotsky, the Man and his Work' (1947), the young Ernest Mandel already wrote:

> In the heart of every true Marxist is a belief in man, without which all revolutionary activity is devoid of meaning. Throughout the last 20 years of his life, years of battling in retreat, of struggle against infamy, calumny, and the growing degradation of humanity, he [Trotsky] maintained that unshaken faith, without being ensnared by illusions . . . But his faith in man has nothing of the mystic or irrational in it. It is only the highest form of consciousness.[32]

This faith in 'man' – in human beings – is intimately linked, in revolutionary Marxism, with the belief in the emancipatory potential of the exploited class. In an article under the astonishing title 'Leon Trotsky's Victory' – published in 1952, at the worst moment of the Cold War! – Mandel argued:

> Trotskyism is above all the belief, the *unshakable faith* in the capacity of the proletarians of all countries to take their destiny into their own hands. Nothing distinguishes Trotskyism more from the other currents of the labour movement than this belief . . . Trotsky's conviction was not an irrational or mystical faith; it was based on a deep understanding of the structure of our industrial society.[33]

Lucien Goldmann discovered a common matrix to Pascal's *wager* on the existence of God and the socialist wager on the historical accomplishment of a true human community: both require faith, and both include risk, the danger of failure and the hope for success.[34] In an obvious reference to Goldmann's thesis (which he knew well) Ernest Mandel argued in his essay on the reasons for founding the Fourth International (1988) that since the socialist revolution was the only chance to ensure the survival of the human race, it was reasonable to wager on it by fighting for its victory:

> Never was the equivalent of the 'Pascalian wager' in relation to revolutionary commitment as valid as it is today. By not committing oneself everything is lost in advance. How can one not make that choice even if the chance of success is only one percent? In fact the odds are much better than that.[35]

At the heart of Mandel's revolutionary faith lies a sort of *anthropological optimism*, i.e. an optimism based on the belief that 'in the last instance, the striving for emancipation (*Emanzipationsstreben*) has an anthropological foundation.' Rebellion is inherently human: as long as humankind continues to exist, the oppressed and enslaved will rise against their chains and the revolutionary species will never disappear.[36]

This does not mean that Marxists hold a naive and one-sided view of the intrinsic 'goodness' of human nature: they agree with modern psychology (Freud) that humans are contradictory and ambivalent beings. Their character combines individualism and socialization, selfishness and solidarity, destructiveness and creativity, Thanatos and Eros, irrationality and rationality. However, as contemporary anthropology has shown, humans are social beings; this means that there exists the possibility of a society organized in such a way as to favour the human potential for creativity and solidarity.[37]

There are also *historical* reasons for optimism: the study of primitive societies shows that greed is not a component of 'human nature' but a product of social circumstances. Far from being an 'innate part' of the human character, the tendency towards private accumulation of wealth did not exist for thousands of years: cooperation and solidarity held sway in primitive, tribal or village communities. There is no a priori reason for them not to become universal human qualities once more, in a future, socialist world community. It is no accident that for many centuries, socialism was a dream of return to the lost 'golden age'.[38]

Incidentally, this argument is one of the rare 'romantic' moments in Mandel's revolutionary humanism, i.e. a positive reference to social and human qualities of archaic or pre-capitalist societies, destroyed by capitalist civilization and re-established in a new, utopian and modern form by socialism.[39]

Grounded in this revolutionary/humanist 'anthropological optimism', Mandel categorically rejects any form of 'anthropological pessimism': the dogma of the basically 'evil' nature of humankind is a pure superstition. It received a pseudo-scientific veneer with the Konrad Lorenz school of the alleged universal aggressiveness of human beings – a reactionary mystification denied by Freud's much deeper psychoanalytical theory, which points to *both* Eros and Thanatos as essential components of the human psyche.[40] Summarizing the issue in *Power and Money*, Mandel argues, at the book's conclusion:

> Socialists believe that Doomsday can still be averted if we increase the degree of rationality of our collective behaviour, if we strive to take the

future into our own hands. That is the freedom and self-determination
we are fighting for. To believe that humankind is incapable of it is not
'being realistic'. It is to assume that men and women are congenitally
unfitted for self-preservation. But that is utter superstition, a new version
of the myth of Original Sin.[41]

This anthropologically-grounded *optimism of the will* is a key element
of Ernest Mandel's character as a Marxist thinker and fighter: it
illuminates his whole life, his political actions and writings. Without it
one can hardly understand such incredible episodes in his life as his
two escapes from German prison camps during the Second World
War.[42] It was certainly an important component of his personal strength
and steadfastness, of his persuasive charm as a public speaker, of the
enthusiasm and hope which he was so often able to communicate to
his audiences and readers.

But, when it ceased to be 'optimism of the will' in the Gramscian
meaning (i.e. coupled with 'pessimism of the intellect') to become a
sort of ungrounded 'optimism of the intellect', or rather just plain and
simple over-optimism, it was a source of great weakness. It inspired
some of his notoriously optimistic oracular predictions, so often
repeated and so often falsified, about the 'impetuous rise of the
masses', and the imminent revolutionary upsurge, in the USSR, in
Spain, in Germany, in France, in Europe and in the whole world. This
pattern that frequently reproduced itself, started very early as shown by
the following example: in an article from 1946 'E. Germain' (Mandel)
insisted that the uprisings of the years 1944–45 were only 'the first
stage of the European revolution', soon to be followed by a second.
There will be no 'relative stabilization', he said: the present situation is
only 'the calm before the storm', 'a transition towards a general
revolutionary upsurge'. Cutting short any counter-argument, 'Germain'
concluded: 'this is not optimism, it is revolutionary realism'.[43] No
comment is needed.

Mandel's over-optimistic predictions were short-lived. But his
humanist/revolutionary message is as relevant as ever:

> Marxists do not fight against exploitation, oppression, massive violence
> against human beings, and massive injustice, only insofar as this struggle
> promotes the development of productive forces or narrowly defined
> historical progress ... Even less do they fight against these phenomena
> only insofar as it is scientifically demonstrated that the struggle will end
> with the victory of socialism. They fight exploitation, oppression, injustice
> and alienation as inhuman, unworthy conditions. This is a sufficient
> ground and motivation.[44]

Ernest Mandel's unswerving moral and political commitment to the emancipation of humanity, his powerful dream of universal human solidarity will remain with us for many years to come, and will inspire the struggle of future generations.

Notes

1. If I follow a thematic rather than a chronological order, it is because there is an impressive continuity in his Marxist/humanist reflection. However, on many important issues – socialist democracy, self-emancipation and self-organization, the new social movements, Marxian dialectics – there was a significant enrichment of his views from the 1940s to the 1970s and 1980s.

2. In the 208 pages of Mandel's otherwise interesting book on *The Meaning of the Second World War*, there are only four pages on the Holocaust and one on Hiroshima. It should be said that the first limitation is corrected by his brief but remarkable essay 'Material, Social and Ideological Preconditions for the Nazi Genocide' (1990), published in English for the first time in this volume.

3. Mandel's Marxist culture was impressive, but apparently he was not familiar with the writings of Benjamin, Adorno, Horkheimer or Marcuse.

4. 'The Future of Communism', *International Viewpoint* 179, February 26, 1990, p. 15.

5. *Marxist Economic Theory*, London 1968, vol. 2, p. 681; *Socialism or Barbarism on the Eve of the Twenty-First Century: The Programmatic Manifesto of the Fourth International*, International Viewpoint, 1993, p. 15 (this document was written by Ernest Mandel).

6. *The Formation of the Economic Thought of Karl Marx: 1843 to Capital*, London 1971, pp. 157–88.

7. *Marxist Economic Theory*, vol. 1, p. 173; *Socialism or Barbarism*, pp. 18–19.

8. *The Place of Marxism in History*, IIRE *Notebooks for Study and Research* no. 1, Amsterdam 1986, p. 28.

9. 'The Current Situation and the Future of Socialism', in *Socialism of the Future*, vol. 1, no. 1, London 1992, p. 56. This article is one of Mandel's most powerful political essays.

10. *Zur Geschichte der KPdSU*, Frankfurt 1976, p. 170; 'The Current Situation', p. 51. It can be argued, however, that Mandel did not pay sufficient attention to the importance and significance, as crimes against humanity, of the Soviet concentration system (the *Gulag*) and of the Cambodian genocide. They are mentioned as examples of Stalinist crimes (among others), but there is no clear hierarchy drawing attention to their world-historical scope and meaning. This failure is perhaps linked to his conviction that the USSR and the other so-called 'workers' states' were, in spite of everything, more 'advanced' social formations, in the scale of human progress, than the capitalist societies.

11. I refer to Daniel Bensaïd's most insightful distinction between the 'oracle' and the 'prophet' in his recent book *Marx l'intempestif*, Paris 1995, pp. 71–2.

12. This new formulation appeared for the first time in 1985, in a paper on 'The Actuality of Socialism' that Mandel wrote for the collection of essays from the Cavtat Conference in Yugoslavia, *Socialism on the Threshold of the Twenty-First Century*, Milos Nicolic, ed., London 1985: '. . . current trends may lead to the destruction of human life on earth . . . the alternative is no longer "socialism or barbarism". It is "socialism or death"' (p. 147).

13. *Socialism or Barbarism*, p. 8 (see also 'The Current Situation', p. 56). Moreover:

> The resources to feed, care for, house and educate these children certainly exist on a world scale – provided that they are not squandered on arms spending, that they are distributed to benefit the most destitute and that control over them is taken out of the hands of those whose sole consideration is their own thirst for private riches.
>
> (Ibid., p. 8)

14. *Power and Money: A Marxist Theory of Bureaucracy*, London 1992, pp. 243–6.

15. 'Solzhenitsyn, Stalinism and the October Revolution', *New Left Review* 86, July/August 1974, p. 56.

16. *Karl Marx: Die Aktualität seines Werkes*, ISP Verlag, Frankfurt 1984, p. 77. This quotation, like most of what follows from this collection, is taken from the essay 'Emanzipation, Wissenschaft und Politik bei Karl Marx', first published in 1983.

17. Ibid., p. 105.

18. Sometimes with an 'economistic' twist, as when Mandel deduces the revolutionary potential of the proletariat from its 'capacity to bring the capitalist economy as a whole to a halt' (see for instance 'The Current Situation', p. 23).

19. *Karl Marx: Die Aktualität*, p. 78 and *The Place of Marxism*, pp. 18–19. This is what Walter Benjamin called 'the tradition of the oppressed', as against history as written by the winners.

20. This reference appears often in Mandel's writings, with slight variations. The exact formulation of Marx is: '*alle Verhältnisse umzuwerfen, in denen der Mensch ein erniedrigtes, ein geknechtes, ein verlassenes, ein verächtliches Wesen ist*' (*Zur Kritik der Hegelschen Rechtsphilosophie, Einleitung*, in *Marx-Engels Werke*, vol. 1, p. 385) – 'to overthrow all relations in which man is a debased, enslaved, forsaken, despicable being' (Karl Marx and Friedrich Engels, *Collected Works*, vol. 3, New York 1975, p. 182). See Mandel, *Karl Marx: Die Aktualität*, p. 75.

21. Ibid., p. 76.

22. 'Die zukünftige Funktion des Marxismus', in H. Spatzenegger, ed., *Das verspielte 'Kapital'? Die marxistische Ideologie nach dem Scheitern des Realen Sozialismus*, Salzburg 1991, p. 173.

23. *Marxist Economic Theory*, vol. 2, p. 686; 'The Current Situation', p. 50.

24. The opposition between economic alienation and socialist freedom (democratic planning) is extensively dealt with in Mandel's 1967 speech in Korčula (the Yugoslav town where famous international socialist meetings

took place during the 1960s). See *Aliénation et planification*, La Brèche, Document 1, Lausanne 1969, pp. 5–6.

25. *Marxist Economic Theory*, vol. 2, pp. 686, 730. The argument on the supersession of political economy in socialism first appears in Rosa Luxemburg's *Introduction to Political Economy*, as Mandel emphasized in his preface to the French edition of the book (Paris 1970).

26. *Marxist Economic Theory*, vol. 2, p. 679; *Karl Marx: Die Aktualität*, pp. 171–3.

27. *Marxist Economic Theory*, vol. 2, p. 685. Mandel does not hesitate to celebrate the well known Dutch (non-Marxist) Romantic historian Huizinga, who in his book *Homo Ludens* claims that the playing human being is the true creator of culture. See *Marxist Economic Theory*, vol. 2, p. 684.

28. Ibid., vol. 2, p. 683 and *Aliénation et planification*, p. 19.

29. *Power and Money*, p. 233.

30. See his homage to Bloch, 'Antizipation und Hoffnung as Kategorien des historischen Materialismus', in Karola Bloch, Adelbert Reif, eds., *Denken heißt überschreiten: In memoriam Ernst Bloch 1885–1977*, Köln 1978, p. 224. There are often references to Bloch in Mandel's writings.

31. Lucien Goldmann, *Le Dieu caché*, Paris 1955, pp. 99–100. An English translation of this book has been published under the title *The Hidden God* (London 1964).

32. 'Trotsky, the Man and his Work', *Fourth International*, vol. 8, no. 7, July–August 1947, p. 205.

33. 'E. Germain' (Ernest Mandel), '20 août 1940 – 20 août 1952: La victoire de Léon Trotsky', *Quatrième Internationale*, vol. 10, no. 5–10, October 1952, pp. 18–9 (my emphasis, ML).

34. Goldmann, pp. 334–6.

35. 'Reasons for Founding the Fourth International and Why They Remain Valid Today', *International Marxist Review*, vol. 3, no. 2, Autumn 1988, p. 20.

36. *Karl Marx: Die Aktualität*, pp. 80, 12.

37. 'Die zukünftige Funktion', p. 174.

38. 'The Actuality of Socialism', p. 153 and *The Place of Marxism*, p. 5.

39. Another romantic moment in his thought – Mandel, a faithful heir to the spirit of classical *Aufklärung*, would not have agreed with this label! – is his above-mentioned reference to the unity between *homo faber* and *homo ludens* in pre-capitalist societies. On the relationship between romanticism and Marxism, see Michael Löwy and Robert Sayre, *Révolte et mélancolie: le romantisme à contre-courant de l'histoire*, Paris 1992.

40. Mandel, 'The Marxist Case for Revolution Today', *Socialist Register 1989*, London, p. 204.

41. *Power and Money*, p. 246.

42. See his interview with Tariq Ali, 'The Luck of a Crazy Youth' in *New Left Review* 213, September/October 1995, reproduced in this volume, pp. 217–24.

43. 'Problèmes de la révolution européenne' (May 1946), in Mandel, *La longue marche de la révolution*, Paris 1976, pp. 59–66. Needless to add that Mandel was not the only revolutionary Marxist that committed this sort of mistake. Who has not (including the author of this note)?

44. 'Die zukünftige Funktion', p. 173.

4

Late Capitalism: Mandel's Interpretation of Contemporary Capitalism

Jesús Albarracín and Pedro Montes

> *[The method of inquiry] has to appropriate the material in detail, to analyse its different forms of development and to track down their inner connection. Only after this work has been done can the real movement be appropriately presented.*
>
> Karl Marx, Postface to the Second Edition of *Capital*[1]

During the decades that followed the Second World War, capitalism's contours became significantly different not only from what it had been in Marx's time, but from what it had been before the war. The changes which the system experienced required a global analysis of the concrete forms assumed by the capitalist mode of production. The paralysis of theory produced by Stalinism and the mistakes of Western Marxism impeded the realization of that task. Ernest Mandel changed that situation. Returning to the methodology and the fundamental categories used by Marx and incorporating the theoretical advances and practical experience produced up to that point, he produced an interpretation of post-Second World War capitalism, or 'late capitalism', which represented without a doubt a considerable advance for Marxism.

The following essay analyzes the fundamental characteristics of Ernest Mandel's Marxist political economy and the most important aspects of his theory of late capitalism.

1. The recovery of Marx's method

The changes in capitalism after the Second World War should not have been an insurmountable obstacle for Marxism, since it possessed a method and a theoretical arsenal capable of analyzing them. However, in practice, Marxism was well prepared to accomplish the task. On the one hand, since the 1930s it had been dominated by so-called 'Soviet Marxism', an apologetic and dogmatic variant built by Stalinism. On the other hand, also since the 1930s, the fundamental axis of Marxist analysis had shifted from political economy to philosophy. Finally, Marxist political economy had been separating itself from Marx's method even before the rise of Stalinism. As a result Marxism and particularly Marxist political economy became sclerotic, incapable of understanding the forms acquired by capitalism in the second half of the twentieth century.

Ernest Mandel erected a bridge to connect the origins of Marxism with its subsequent evolution, placing economics at the centre of the analysis and recovering the fundamental categories of Marx's political economy to explain the evolution and present state of capitalism. This allowed him to lay the foundations for an analysis of the concrete forms acquired by the system after the Second World War.

1.1 Open Marxism

Marxism is not a dogmatic and unchanging system, but learns from practice, is influenced by it and is in continuous development. It is the product of a multiple synthesis that must be repeated again and again as time passes.

In the first place, Marxism is a synthesis of the principal social sciences. Marx and Engels conceived it as a synthesis of German philosophy, English political economy and French politics. But like all non-dogmatic, developing disciplines, Marxism must continually incorporate the advances of all the social sciences which contribute to understanding and transforming the world, in order to release humanity from exploitation and oppression.

Second, Marxism is a synthesis of the principal existing projects of liberation. Marx and Engels owe much to the utopian socialism of their epoch, but they surpassed it with scientific socialism. In each historical era one must do the same, because Marxism does not have a monopoly on emancipation or critical thinking. Sexual domination, the ecological crisis and national liberation, for example, are topics insufficiently treated by Marxism which should have a place within it.

Marxism must integrate all existing emancipatory contributions, in a constant dialogue which must include mutual influence. In fact, Marxism is a point of encounter, not a complete system.

Finally, Marxism is a synthesis of the emancipatory movements actually existing at each point in time. Marx and Engels adopted as a point of departure the actually existing workers' movement of their epoch, fought for its self-organization and independence from the bourgeoisie, worked to endow it with a revolutionary programme, and learned from its experiences. In the more complex world of capitalism in the second half of the twentieth century, it is not possible to avoid this task. Marxism must learn from the experiences and preoccupations of the different social movements, not only of the workers' movement, and it must submit its strategy to the verdict of practice.

With this triple synthesis, Marx and Engels built a system which had to evolve in step with the evolution of the social system it tried to analyze and fight against, while preserving its fundamental characteristics. Marxism would always have to bear in mind the historical character of capitalist society and the concrete manifestations of its laws of motion. In fact, the search for magic formulas which explain everything is foreign to Marxism, which is not exempt from the need to analyze reality at each historical moment.

However, this conception of Marxism as an open system was disfigured in the 1930s as a result of the hegemony of so-called Soviet Marxism. For almost six decades, this apologetic and dogmatic variant rooted in Stalinism has been the official doctrine of the countries of so-called 'actually existing socialism', and it has been almost completely dominant in the Communist parties of the West. The result has been a paralysis of theory and its increasing separation from practice.

Marxism bypassed its economic centrepiece and flowed instead through the philosophical channels opened by the well-known paragraph of the foreword to the *Critique of Political Economy*:

> In the social production which men carry on they enter into definite relations that are indispensable and independent of their will; these relations of production correspond to a definite state of development of their material powers of production. The sum total of these relations of production constitutes the economic structure of society – the real foundation, on which rise legal and political superstructures and to which correspond definite forms of social consciousness . . . At a certain stage of their development, the material forces of production in society come in conflict with the existing relations of production, or – what is but the

legal expression for the same thing – with the property relations within which they had been at work before. From forms of development of the forces of production these relations turn into their fetters. Then comes the period of social revolution.[2]

In this manner, economic structure, superstructure, mode of production, and so forth, and the relationships among all these concepts became fundamental. Even when dissenting voices were raised, as in the case of Althusser (though he was not the only one), they were located on the same philosophical terrain. This approach was not fit for analyzing the concrete capitalist reality facing us, but served instead to develop a culture of Marxist thought ever more removed from the needs of class struggle. At best it gave a sense of moral satisfaction to the left, through the prospects offered by Marxism, and served to comfort it with the idea that socialism was inevitable. In the imperialist countries, the development of the welfare state diminished the urgency of anti-capitalist struggle, the more so because the end of the system was theoretically and historically guaranteed.

Marxist economics always played a secondary role in this conception of Marxism. The theory of value and exploitation became a universal dogma, but its general formulation provided nothing that helped to understand the growing complexity of the capitalist economy (growing state intervention in the economy, consumer society, expansion of the service sector, technological changes and changes in the organization of work, neocolonialism and unequal exchange, and so forth) or the concrete manifestations of its laws of motion (tendency of the rate of profit to fall, rising organic composition of capital, and so forth). The fundamental concepts of Marxism became progressively decrepit, and served only to demonstrate the unavoidable end of capitalism, once again to the satisfaction of the left, while also serving to estrange its thought from the tasks of class struggle. The huge advances in the social sciences, particularly in economic theory, were considered bourgeois and were despised as such. Only those authors who had come out of mainstream economics escaped this trend (Sweezy, Baran, the New Left, those originating from the Cambridge school, and others), but the Communist parties always regarded them with a certain suspicion. The advances in sociology, in political science, or in the rest of the social sciences met the same fate. This was 'waterproof' Marxism, impermeable to social realities other than the vision of the Western Communist parties, which had in turn adopted the decrepit version of Stalinism.

It was very difficult to understand the characteristics acquired by

capitalism in the second half of the twentieth century with these
resources, much less to combat it. Ernest Mandel turned this situation
on its head. In 1962, the date of publication of the first French edition
of *Marxist Economic Theory*, Mandel recovered the tradition of classical
Marxist political economy, which had disappeared from the literature
for decades, enriched it with subsequent contributions from the field
of Marxism and from without, applied it to the capitalism that he had
before him, and drew political conclusions in the process. *Marxist
Economic Theory* alone would require us to consider Mandel as a classical
theoretician of Marxism, directly connected to the founders of the
tradition, Marx and Engels. The importance of this work was not only
theoretical. *Marxist Economic Theory* was published in many different
languages and became an essential reference point for many Marxist
fighters in all corners of the planet. With the appearance of *Late
Capitalism*, first published in German in 1972, and of the multiple
articles and books which followed, Mandel fully developed and mod-
ernized Marxist political economy and used it to accomplish a profound analysis of post-Second World War capitalism.

His open Marxism allowed him to incorporate not only all the
theoretical arsenal of Marxist economics within his reach, but also
the useful parts of the new developments in mainstream economics.
In the pages of *Marxist Economic Theory*, *Late Capitalism* and many of his
articles and books, one can find a thorough exposition of a good part
of the debates within academic economics during the last decades,
Mandel's positions in these discussions, and the positive aspects which
Marxism could incorporate from those advances. Many teachers of
economic theory in Western universities are surprised, when they look
at his work, by the vigour, wealth and depth with which he approaches
many of the problems that occupy them, and the same happens when
the topic of discussion is the validity of Marxist economic theory. The
introductions to the Penguin edition of *Capital* shows that there was no
discussion on Marxist economics, within or outside the family (Ricardians, Sraffians, Keynesians, and others) that was foreign to him. In
particular, his positions on the theory of value in the discussion with
the Ricardians are revealing.[3] One is surprised by the way in which he
integrated the greatest advances in mainstream economics into Marxist
economics to demonstrate the validity of the latter, and at the same
time used these advances to develop it. And theory was always linked to
practice, to the class struggle from which, as a leader of the Fourth
International, he was never absent. His theory of late capitalism was
not so much an academic exercise as an attempt to understand and lay
bare the system, in order to combat it better. His internationalism took

him beyond the horizon of one country and one culture, as he became involved in the political struggle of many countries, paying a high personal price. But the benefits to Marxism were immense: he linked analysis and theory to the vicissitudes of class struggle, recovered the role of political economy within historical materialism, and contributed decisively to the analysis of capitalism in the second half of the twentieth century.

Without a doubt, there are shortcomings in Mandel's work from our current perspective. His synthesis failed to integrate certain social phenomena, and he did not carry certain ideas to their logical conclusion. This is particularly true with respect to the detailed analysis of the subjective factors that can affect the force, organization and fighting disposition of the working class, a topic on which he always had an excessively optimistic position, or feminism, with which he dealt very insufficiently, or environmentalism, where he did not surpass the most general contradictions between capitalism and the ecosystem. But this cannot be a critique, but rather a recognition of the enormous theoretical work he undertook, of the complexity acquired by the current social system and of the tasks which remain for Marxism to accomplish. What is important is that his method, open Marxism, permits, as no other method does, an analysis and comprehension of present-day capitalism, a task to which all those who lay claim to the heritage of the thought and political work of Ernest Mandel must pay sufficient attention.

1.2 Political economy – central axis of analysis

Understanding capitalism required a radical break with the approaches and objectives of the kind of Marxism that was dominant in Mandel's epoch. Recasting Marxism successfully and in depth is, without a doubt, one of Mandel's main contributions.

Political economy occupies a central place within Marxism. At the beginning, Marx approached the analysis of capitalism using all the elements of intellectual training within his reach. German philosophy and French politics occupied a central and dominant place. But this arsenal was not sufficient to understand an economic system in which the market, price formation, the division of the product between the working class, bourgeoisie and landed classes, the economic evolution of society, and so forth are central. That is, these problems are hardly approachable using philosophy or politics exclusively. After the *Manuscripts of 1844*, Marx understood the huge potential of English political economy to analyze all these phenomena.[4]

The first products of the incorporation of political economy into the analysis of capitalism were the manuscripts written in 1857–58, published in 1939 by the Marx-Engels-Lenin Institute of Moscow under the name *Grundrisse der Kritik der politischen Ökonomie*. The *Grundrisse*,[5] which can be considered a first draft of *Capital*, were followed by a series of manuscripts in which Marx analyzed economic developments and developed his explanation of capitalism: those of 1861–63, from which Kautsky extracted the *Theories of Surplus Value*,[6] those of 1864–65, which contain topics which appear in volume 3 of *Capital*, and those of 1865–70, from which Engels extracted the materials for volume 2 of *Capital*. Finally, in 1866–67, volume 1 of *Capital* was published.

Thus, beginning in the 1850s, Marx concentrated his work on political economy. In his hands it acquired a dimension totally different from that of the classical economists and, henceforth, it became the fundamental element of his analysis of capitalism. The integration of German philosophy and French politics took place around the central axis of the economic dynamics of capitalism. It can be said that the *Grundrisse* and, above all, *Capital* represent a sort of break with Marx's previous work, which produced an integration only of philosophy and politics. What makes *Capital* the most important revolutionary text of all time is not its philosophical speeches or political proclamations, but the way in which it unveils the functioning of the capitalist economy, how the exploitation of the workers takes place, what its internal contradictions are and why it is impossible to do away with social injustice within the system.

However, in the recent history of Marxism, political economy has not always played the prominent role it should. Perry Anderson argues that changes in class struggle explain the displacement of Marxism from political economy to philosophy.[7] As a result of the defeat of the workers' movement after the Russian revolution (suppression of the uprisings in central Europe between 1918 and 1922, rout in Spain and France in the 1930s, the inability of the anti-fascist resistance to win lasting political hegemony after the Second World War), the development of Marxism was displaced from the unions and political parties to the universities. After the Second World War, there have been hardly any Marxist theoreticians who have not held a post in academia, while very few have been directly involved in political struggles. This separation of Marxism from class struggle was reflected in a changing approach. While in Marx, political economy was the backbone sustaining philosophy, sociology and politics, after the 1930s philosophy held the pre-eminent position.

The paralysis of Marxism provoked by Stalinist degeneration also explains the loss of the central role of political economy. In a context in which Soviet Marxism was hegemonic, many authors wanted to distance themselves from the official doctrine of the Communist parties and sought a more subtle version of Marxism in the writings of the young Marx, which led them to focus on problems of method. The theory of value and its development, the laws of motion of capitalism, and the fundamental concepts of Marxist economics were turned into dogmas which were taken for granted, as Marx had formulated them. There was no possibility of incorporating new theoretical advances, or they were dismissed as useless. The starting point of the analysis of capitalism was henceforth based not on material production, which conditions distribution and demand, but problems such as the subject, the economic structure, its relationship to the superstructure, the formation of class consciousness, and so on. Thus Marx's political economy remained frozen and its place was occupied by philosophical developments which, however much they enriched the leafy tree of Marxism and represented a considerable advance in some of its fundamental aspects, did not tackle the quintessential aspects of the system against which they struggled. Examples of this are the existentialist Marxism of Sartre and the structuralist Marxism of Althusser, and the same could be said of the projects of Adorno, Marcuse, Habermas, and Bloch, for instance. As a rule, Marxist thought produced books which, in keeping with the authors' positions in academia, answered more to the needs of a small number of individuals bound to intellectual environments than to the requirements of class struggle.

This situation began to change with Mandel's *Marxist Economic Theory*, published in 1962. But the definitive restoration of the role of the political economy in Marxism did not occur until the *Grundrisse* were recovered, well into the 1960s. The *Grundrisse* were published for the first time in 1939, but the Western world did not know them until they were reprinted in 1953 in Berlin. This means that one of the fundamental works which deepens the political economy developed by Marx in *Capital* was not available until almost a century after it was originally written. However, in a period in which Soviet Marxism was hegemonic and in which philosophy had become the central axis of Marxism, as happened after the Second World War, it took some years before they began to have an influence on Marxism.

This did not happen until 1968, with the first appearance in German of Roman Rosdolsky's (1898–1967) posthumous book.[8] Rosdolsky, who was not an economist but a historian, undertook the reconstruction of the mature economic thought of Marx, through an extensive analysis of the *Grundrisse* and their relationship to *Capital*, in order to lay the foundations for a subsequent development of Marxist economics capable of a deep analysis of postwar capitalism. As aforementioned, four years later, in 1972, the first German edition of Mandel's *Late Capitalism* appeared, integrating the theoretical corpus developed by Rosdolsky and the advances in Marxist and mainstream economics, producing the most profound analysis of contemporary capitalism to date. The English edition, published in 1975, contains a prophetic analysis of the economic crisis as part of a theory of the long waves of late capitalism that remains, in essence, valid today. The analysis is all the more insightful given that *Late Capitalism* was written before the 1975 recession!

Late Capitalism played a fundamental role in the recovery of Marxist political economy. But there is no doubt that even today, a quarter-century after the beginning of the economic crisis, philosophy continues to occupy a pre-eminent position within Marxism. With the exception of the publications of Mandel and his followers, or the authors grouped under the generic term 'Regulation School', the volume of literature which approaches the development of Marxism from a philosophical angle remains overwhelming.

1.3 Concrete analysis of concrete situations

Marx used political economy not to build a theoretical edifice, but to understand the system facing him and to seek the means to combat it. For him, capitalism was not an abstract system, but a concrete social formation, with differences from one country to the next, whose laws of evolution it was necessary to uncover as it unfolded in time. The objective of the system, generalized commodity production, would be the same no matter how much the system evolved. The law of value and the laws of motion of capitalism would remain in place so long as the system endured, but the form they would acquire at each moment in time would differ as the capitalist mode of production evolved. Understanding the system and fighting against it required avoiding the separation between theoretical analysis and empirical data – it required the integration of theory and history. When one reads *Capital* today one has the sensation that its analysis fits late-twentieth-century capitalism better than it does the period in which it was written[9] – the fact that Marxism is not simply a nineteenth-century theory. This demonstrates the analytical power and prognostic character of *Capital*. What is important is that Marx saw capitalism as an evolving system and, consequently, theory could not stand still, but had to adapt at each moment of time to the concrete forms acquired by the system. This meant that for Marx theory and history were inseparable.

However, this integration of theoretical analysis and empirical data has not been reproduced after Marx except on a few occasions. This failure has prevented a correct understanding of the successive stages traversed by the capitalist mode of production. In part, this is due to the temporary paralysis of theory provoked by Soviet Marxism and by the displacement from economics to philosophy. But Marxist political economy also bears its share of responsibility, since it has developed according to an internal logic that has prevented it from formulating theories adequate to explain concrete phenomena. In the first chapter of *Late Capitalism* and the introductions to the Penguin editions of the three volumes of *Capital*, Mandel indicates which aspects of the internal logic of Marxist political economy have been fundamental, in his opinion, in preventing Marxist economics from integrating theory correctly with history. The most meaningful have been:

- The abusive utilization of the reproduction schemes to explain the laws of motion of capital. The function of the reproduction schemes is to prove that the capitalist mode of production can exist. They show how a system based on the anarchy of the market can operate normally, how periodic equilibrium is produced, and so forth. However, the crisis cannot be explained simply by the disproportionality of value among the different branches of production, by the laws of motion of capitalism presented in the reproduction schemes. This mistake has dominated a large part of Marxist literature from the beginning – a mistake which in one way or another, Rudolf Hilferding,[10] Rosa Luxemburg[11] and Nikolai Bukharin[12] all made. It was also a characteristic mistake of Soviet Marxism. The reproduction schemes have been used widely in Western Marxism to analyze the dynamics of capital, especially by those authors who came from a Keynesian background. In short, for a long time, volume 2 of *Capital* thoroughly overshadowed volumes 1 and 3.
- The monocausal analysis of the development of the capitalist mode of production. On too many occasions, the dynamics of capitalism have been deduced from only one variable, so that all the other laws formulated by Marx would be a function of that single variable. The single cause that underlay all the laws of capitalist development has been different according to the authors: overaccumulation is the fundamental motor of the capitalist dynamic in Henryk Grossmann's *The Law of Accumulation and Breakdown of the Capitalist System,* the difficulty of realizing surplus-value in Rosa Luxemburg or Paul

Sweezy,[13] competition in Rudolf Hilferding, and so forth. There is
no doubt that, contrary to Marx's own approach, Marxist economics
has been guilty of excessive reductionism, perhaps a product of the
influence of the Cartesian method of mainstream economics. Even
today, Mandel's analysis of late capitalism is commonly reduced to
long waves, determined by one variable, the rate of profit. Mandel
repeated incessantly that late capitalism was a complex phenomenon
that could not be reduced to long waves; that these were concrete
historical phenomena and, as such, also complex; and that the rate
of profit was not more than an indicator that summarized many
other phenomena. We will return below to this point.

Marxist economics has been unable to formulate more complex
theories adapted to reality because it misunderstood the laws of motion
of capital and devoted all its efforts to a useless search for a universal
mechanism that explained the entire course of history. Breaking with
this untenable situation required a radical shift, and this is what Mandel
accomplished. The system which is the object of his analysis is not
abstract capitalism, but the concrete form capitalism acquired after
the Second World War. The nature of this capitalism was the same
as the one described by Marx, but profound transformations had taken
place: the correlation of forces between classes had been altered as
result of the Second World War and fascism; a new technological
revolution, the third in the history of capitalism, was unfolding; corporate productive processes and products had changed, and with them,
the organization of work also changed; the minimal, liberal state had
given way to a state that was intervening increasingly in the economy.
The world economy was restructured (falling prices of raw materials,
structural change of monopoly capital, changes in the process of
unequal exchange, deepening differences in the rates of profit between
centre and periphery, and so forth) and the international monetary
system was based on fixed exchange rates under the hegemony of a
single capitalist power, the United States, which made it possible. The
dominant ideology changed so that liberalism and the ideas of the
neoclassical school yielded to Keynesianism. Full employment, wage
growth, the volume of commodities put at the disposal of the workers,
and the welfare state gave the system a certain legitimacy which it had
not enjoyed before.

In Mandel's analysis of late capitalism, political economy returns to
centre stage and politics and philosophy become the ancillary disciplines. The reproduction schemes perform their proper role, that is, to
show how the capitalist system operates, how periodic equilibrium is

reached, while military spending acquires a growing importance. The development of the capitalist mode of production is not the result of the evolution of a single variable, but of the interaction of many: the evolution of the organic composition of capital and its sectoral distribution, the evolution of the distribution of constant capital among circulating and fixed capital, the development of the rates of exploitation and accumulation, the turnover cycle of capital, and the relationships of exchange between Departments I (production of the means of production) and II (production of the means of consumption), among others. Class struggle plays a key role through its effects on the rate of exploitation and the rate of profit. There is no effective equalization of the rates of profit, which is decisive not only for some theoretical discussions (transformation of values into production prices) but for understanding some fundamental features of the system (changes in the structure of monopoly capital, the growing gap between centre and periphery).

1.4 The dynamics of capitalism: moving beyond Marx

In traditional Marxist literature, the dynamics of capitalism were defined by two different kinds of cycles: on the one hand, its life cycle as a social regime, determined by the laws of motion of the mode of production (growth of the organic composition of capital, formation of the industrial reserve army, falling rate of profit, technological advances); on the other, short-term movements determined by periodic industrial crises. For Marx, these movements were not independent of one another, and above all could not be conceived as mechanical phenomena.

In the long-term the fall of the rate of profit was unavoidable, but a series of factors (increases in the rate of exploitation, imperialism, decreases in the turnover time of capital, and so forth) could offset this decrease for some time. As a result, the laws of motion of capital could not be used as a philosopher's stone to understand capitalism at each historical moment. Again, the concrete analysis of concrete reality became unavoidable.

In this context, economic cycles, that is, recurrent industrial crises, were an expression both of the form acquired by the laws of motion of capital at each moment of time and of many other factors. Some of these factors may not be determinant in the analysis of capitalist trends, but could have a very marked impact in specific historical periods. It was not possible, then, to formulate a general theory of industrial crises which could explain capitalism in the first half of the nineteenth century, for example, as well as post-Second World War capitalism.

However, throughout the history of Marxism, the rigid utilization of Marx's concepts and analysis has led to important mistakes in studying the dynamics of capitalist development.

The law of the falling rate of profit has been used and abused to justify the theory of the collapse of capitalism, that is, to demonstrate that the socialist mode of production will inevitably succeed capitalism. But what is truly important to understand in order to fight against the system is not this general, ahistorical deduction, but rather, the fact that the rate of profit can recover over long periods of time as a result of the counteracting tendencies to the law, described by Marx in volume 3 of *Capital*. To assume that capitalism will collapse sooner or later, regardless of the concrete characteristics of the system in each historical period, is totally contrary to Marx's method.

A similar analysis of short-term cycles is also common. At least three different versions of the periodic crises have been formulated, according to the cause that determines them: disproportionality between Departments I and II (Tugan Baranovski, Rudolf Hilferding), under-consumption by the masses (Rosa Luxemburg, Paul Sweezy) and over-accumulation. Only on rare occasions has the analysis of such crises been framed in terms of specific historical periods. Periodic crises are in fact determined not only by the form acquired by the laws of motion of the capitalist mode of production, but also by many other factors: dominant ideology, hegemonic power, degree of technological development, degree of class organization and consciousness, structure of the capitalist world market, the monetary system, and so forth. Between the trends and periodic crises one must interpolate a third movement: long waves of capitalist development. Marx could not formulate a theory of long waves, because when he published *Capital* only one long wave, that of the first half of the nineteenth century, had completed its course. However, there is no reason not to move beyond his analysis, based on the method he established.

Long waves had already been an object of some interest in the past century, among Marxists as much as neoclassical authors. Jevons (1884), Wicksell (1894), Casel (1918) and van Gelderen (1913), among others, accepted the existence of these long cycles. But it was Kondratieff in the 1920s who made the first statistical study with data from France, England and the US. The data, which spanned the period from the end of the eighteenth century to the 1920s, suggested the existence of 'long waves' with an average length of fifty years. Kondratieff considered long waves as an expression of the internal forces of capitalism. They flowed from causes inherent to the essence of the capitalist economy. Their functioning was 'endogenous' and not 'exogenous'. The cyclical behaviour of the capitalist economy was determined by internal forces and not by the influence of any external factor. For Kondratieff, therefore, technological innovation does not create long waves. They are rather generated by deeper forces which shape the development of the capitalist economy. In addition, Kondratieff observed a broad spectrum of economic and social phenomena which were formed endogenously: wars and discoveries of gold deposits, geographical expansion of markets, and so forth. Technological innovations exercise a great influence on capitalist development but do not cause it; they are themselves a response to endogenous factors. As is evident, the concepts of 'endogeny' and 'exogeny' should not be defined in reference to capitalist society as a whole, since in this case, everything would be endogenous, but in relation to its basic economic mechanisms. In this sense, the explanation of Kondratieff is not correct, as Trotsky pointed out in a short but substantial article which he wrote in 1923 at the time Kondratieff formulated his theory of long waves.[14]

The exogenous character of long waves has been defended from two very different vantage points. The first, whose outstanding representative is Schumpeter,[15] starts from the idea that the long cycles are caused by processes of innovation. The second takes as a point of departure the idea that long waves are determined by external factors, not by technological innovations but by non-systemic and non-periodic phenomena which are different in different phases of capitalism. Within this second position one must locate authors such as Rostow. However, during the 1950s and 1960s the hegemony of Keynesianism in mainstream economics and of Soviet Marxism in Marxist economics led to the disappearance of the study of long waves from the economic literature.

In this context, Ernest Mandel recovered the theory of long waves and developed it, turning it into the missing link between the law of the falling rate of profit and periodic industrial crises.[16] The rate of profit falls, but does so in an oscillating pattern over long periods of time. Each one of these oscillations determines a long wave, with its corresponding falling and rising phases. Multiple external factors intervene in each long wave's beginning and development, determining the operation of the laws of capitalist development in each historical period. The evolution of the rate of profit summarizes all these external and internal phenomena, but each long wave must be considered as a distinct period, with its own characteristics. Furthermore, long waves are not movements that can be explained mechanically, in the fashion of mainstream economics' explanation of the business cycle, nor by an endogenous mechanism of the capitalist system itself, as Kondratieff argued and the regulationists argue today. External factors, most importantly class struggle, intervene at the beginning of a long expansive phase. Therefore the explanation of long waves does not attempt to build an abstract theoretical model, but to facilitate the analysis of the evolution of the laws of capitalist development. In this sense, each long wave has been different because the laws of motion of capital have been fulfilled in a different way each time.

2. The long wave of late capitalism

Ernest Mandel's theory of long waves of capitalist development has been considered, not without reason, as his main contribution to contemporary Marxism. It makes possible a conceptual framework that allows us to interrelate multiple economic, political, technological and social variables and factors in the context of the internal dynamics of capitalism in each historical period, thus linking up with the preoccupations and objectives of classical Marxism. However, the importance of Mandel's theory of long waves does not reside so much in its capacity for explaining the past evolution of capitalism, although it is an invaluable instrument for this task, as much as the way in which this theory clarifies the dynamics of post-Second World War capitalism.

In late capitalism, the laws of development of the capitalist mode of production take a concrete form that is distinct from the system's normal life cycle. The factors that determine this separation are numerous, and played a very different role in the decades of expansion following the Second World War than in those which followed the economic crisis unleashed in the early 1970s. During the decades of expansion, all these factors resulted in an increase in the rate of profit which was sustained for a long time, but this increase was no more than the reflection of what was happening in an entire historical era. In the same way, the downward phase began with a declining rate of profit, but this decrease and the events that have occurred since, are the result of the interplay of multiple factors.

Thus, analyzing the long wave of late capitalism requires analyzing late capitalism piece by piece. Ernest Mandel broke down each one of these pieces, criticized the previous mechanistic mistakes of Marxist analysis, applied Marx's method to each concrete aspect of the more complex capitalism which evolved after the Second World War, incorporated the theoretical advances produced in the mainstream social sciences and, in addition to all this, composed a framework that described each concrete aspect of late capitalism. He then articulated all these dimensions into the conceptual framework of the long wave, and from this combination emerged the theory of late capitalism, Mandel's Marxist interpretation of contemporary capitalism. Briefly, the explanation is the following:

In the aftermath of the Second World War, two processes converged which laid the foundation for an historically unprecedented phase of capitalist expansion. On the one hand, the weakness and, in part, atomization of the working class, provoked by the successive routs suffered after the rise of fascism and the end of the Second World War, permitted a formidable increase in the rate of exploitation in most of the industrial countries, which was expressed in a reduction of real wages in comparison with prewar levels. There was also an extension of the working day, above all in the initial years. This provoked an extraordinary increase in the rate of profit, which, when combined with the need to rebuild the productive capacity destroyed in the war, considerably favoured the process of capital accumulation. On the other hand, the technological advances initially developed in military industries (electronics, atomic energy, synthetic raw materials, plastics, and so forth) were extended to all branches of industry, generating what has been called the Third Technological Revolution. As a result, there was a massive spread of new productive processes which manufactured new products that quickly replaced previously existing ones, changed the organization of work, notably increased the productivity of labour, and reduced the cost of machinery and materials in relation to the value of production. In short, the recovery of the rate of profit induced further capital accumulation, which incorporated new technological advances, which in turn reinforced the growth of profits.

From then on, a virtuous circle emerged which favoured generalized economic expansion. The Third Technological Revolution required the appearance of new markets. This was accomplished not geographically, but through the replacement of some products: glass and wood with plastic, natural fibres by artificial ones, and so forth. Rising production and productivity made possible a certain growth of real wages without affecting the rate of profit, which meant the creation of demand for those new products. Wages were growing, driving demand and with it, production. In this context, large industrial sectors were articulated around mass consumption. Expansion generated higher incomes, higher incomes led to higher tax receipts, and this greater possibility of financing government spending played an important role

in satisfying collective needs. Thus health facilities and public instruction were established, pension systems became generalized and unemployment insurance expanded to cover all the unemployed. What is
now known as the welfare state emerged. This greater state intervention
in the economy was used to put in practice a policy of maintenance of
demand which favoured economic growth considerably by absorbing
the shocks of the periodic crises. And in the wake of all this, full
employment, which was emerging as a fundamental objective in the
programmes of all the political parties, whether of the left or the right,
became in practice the 'normal' state of affairs in all the developed
capitalist economies.

In this expansive context, Keynesianism became the ideology that
inspired government social and economic policy in all the industrial
countries, displacing from the official bureaux and international organizations the ideas of the neoclassical school that had been the theoretical basis of hegemonic liberalism before the Great Depression. It was
the ideology that corresponded to the needs of capitalist expansion
and to the fact that, for the first time in the history of capitalism, a very
powerful material and ideological competitor, so-called actually existing
socialism, had emerged. Since the crises that periodically struck capitalism were due to insufficient demand, economic policy had to be
directed at avoiding them, which meant creating full employment. Real
wages were to grow as productivity increased, which would guarantee
the growth of consumption without affecting the rate of profit. Additionally, the state had to intervene in the economy creating demand,
and what better way of doing it than by broadening the welfare state?
This served at the same time to counter the power of attraction which
'real socialism' exercised on workers in the West. Employment did not
depend on the characteristics of the labour market, but on the operation of the economy as a whole, and it was therefore useless if not
detrimental to allow the laws of the market to determine the state of
labour relations.

This policy became the basis of what came to be known as the
Keynesian consensus. The state guaranteed full employment and growing social spending to meet collective needs (health, education, pensions, and so forth): the so-called welfare state. Collective bargaining
took care of keeping real wages growing in step with productivity,
improving workers' standard of living and maintaining demand without
affecting profits. Labour relations were based on the regulation of
labour rights instead of the mechanisms of the market. In exchange
for all this, the only thing that workers' organizations had to do,
whether trade-union or political organizations, was guarantee social

peace and, above all, not question the operation of the system. This Keynesian consensus was the base sustaining social democracy during the decades following the Second World War.

The result was a considerable improvement in the standard of living of most of the population of the industrial countries. Full employment, higher wages, the huge bulk of consumption goods that were put at workers' disposal and the extension of the welfare state in most of the developed countries gave capitalism a certain legitimacy, in spite of the fact that exploitation, poverty, inequality and social exclusion continued to exist. But all this was procured at a very high ecological cost. Dirty and energy-intensive technologies, the waste introduced by the Third Technological Revolution, and the generalization of consumption standards based more on the absorption of capitalist production than on the satisfaction of human needs implied a qualitative leap in attacks on the environment and are the main cause of the planetary ecological crisis facing humanity.

The downward phase of the long wave began towards the end of the 1960s. A series of factors that had been developing during the preceding expansive phase became mature at that point, and provoked a marked fall in the rate of profit. Full employment and the growing organization of the workers' movement in the main industrial countries blocked increases in the rate of exploitation. The Third Technological Revolution had become generalized, stopped being a source of profits and became instead a source of overproduction and increased competition. The deliberate application of Keynesian anti-crisis techniques accentuated inflation and finally provoked a crisis of the international monetary system, with negative repercussions on trade and the circulation of capital. Finally, the era of cheap raw materials and energy came to a close, provoking serious problems in the operation of the capitalist system. Following mainstream terminology, this was not a crisis of demand, because the change in production trends and accumulation was not a product of capital's difficulties in selling its commodities. It was rather a supply crisis determined by the fact that production was not profitable for capital because costs were too high.

At first, most governments responded with Keynesian-style demand policies, similar to those which had been practised during the decades of expansion in the aftermath of the Second World War. But such policies did not address the fundamental cause of the crisis.[17] Higher consumption or government spending, for example, did not translate into capitalists increasing their production, because the problem was not insufficient demand, but a reduced rate of profit. Under such conditions, greater demand would only provoke price increases. For the same reasons, investment would not grow in response to increased demand, because there were serious difficulties finding profitable projects. If investment did not increase, neither would employment and, on the contrary, capitalists were forced to cut their payrolls to restore profitability, which was squeezed by high costs.

As a result, economic policies based on increasing demand did not help overcome the crisis, because they did not lead to recovery of the rate of profit and thus did not have any positive effect on production and investment. On the contrary, they were inflationary and aggravated rather than prevented rising unemployment. Thus the economic crisis became the crisis of Keynesianism. The dominant class looked to the past to seek a solution to its problems. Capital found in neoliberalism the ideology to formalize social and economic policies favourable to its interests. As time went by, neoliberalism became hegemonic among all the industrial countries' governments. Whatever their political labels, they all apply neoliberal economic policies. Overcoming the downward phase of the long wave will not come about mechanically, nor by endogenous causes. The organization and degree of consciousness of the classes in conflict and their future evolution, that is, class struggle, will be decisive.

3. Late capitalism and the current downward phase

The first edition of *Late Capitalism* was published when the stage was already set for the beginning of the downward phase, but the crisis had not yet appeared in full force. Since then, a quarter-century of the downward phase has elapsed. Capitalism and the working class have undergone considerable transformations. Consequently, the mechanical transposition of the theory of late capitalism to the world of today would imply falling into one of the mistakes in the Marxist tradition that Ernest Mandel criticized: the dissociation between theoretical analysis and empirical data. This does not mean that we must begin again from scratch, but only that we must adapt the theory to the changes that have been produced. The theory of late capitalism itself provides the necessary instruments to understand these changes and the situation which capitalism is traversing under the hegemony of the neoliberal doctrine.

3.1 Production, accumulation and the organization of work

During the years of expansion, industry was the fundamental motor of the economy, propelling the activity of the rest of the economic sectors, but at the beginning of the 1970s the situation was drastically modified. On the one hand, the generalization of the Third Technological Revolution and capital accumulation provoked an exorbitant growth of productive capacity relative to demand. Additionally, higher wages and rising raw materials and energy prices increased costs considerably. As a result, production surpluses and eventually losses appeared in most industrial sectors. Henceforth the industrial crisis would be transmitted to the rest of the economy.[18]

Capitalists put in place measures to restore the profitability of their companies and the ultimate objective of social and economic policy was the same. This meant breaking the virtuous circles that had maintained expansion. While previously rising wages had maintained demand, now they had to be reduced to restore profitability. Previously accumulation had expanded employment, but now the productive apparatus had to be restructured and payrolls slashed. Previously rising government spending had served to maintain demand, but now it had to be cut to facilitate tax cuts. A recessive policy was implemented which reduced the demand for industrial products, and was meant to be pursued until its final objective of restoring the rate of profit was achieved. In this way, the industrial crisis was exported to the economy as a whole.

Not all industrial sectors were affected in the same way. In the first place, the share of wages in total costs was very different, depending on greater or lesser labour intensity in production and on the wage levels that workers in different sectors had obtained. Therefore the fall in the rate of profit had very different effects in different sectors. While in some the reduction in profits was not very significant, in others (steel, naval construction, textiles) the losses quickly became considerable, causing an untenable situation. Second, the share of raw materials and energy costs was also very different. Industrial expansion had been built on the assumption of cheap energy. The huge rise in energy costs in the wake of oil price increases caused the sectors that were using it intensely to quickly lose their economic significance. Third, the economic crisis slowed capital accumulation, affecting the sectors producing traditional capital goods. Finally, slower growth of consumption affected the consumer goods sectors as they faced smaller demand due to increased unemployment, slower wage growth and the changes in relative prices produced by rising energy costs, which altered the structure of consumption.

During the phase of industrial expansion, the rapid growth of production, together with technological advances and the generalization of 'Fordist' organization of labour processes – assembly lines, semi-automation of productive processes – produced rapid growth in industrial productivity. This permitted the maintenance of a high rate of profit and, at the same time, rising wages which drove demand. With the arrival of the crisis, the growth of production decelerated and, as a result, productivity growth also slowed down. The recovery of the rate of profit required a return to growing productivity, but, in the context of stagnant markets, this could only be obtained through rationalization of the productive apparatus and the introduction of changes in the organization of work.

Since then, as happens in all long-term downward phases, most of the investments have not been directed to the increasing productive capacity, but to rationalization of existing production processes. During a first stage, the restructuring of the productive apparatus took place at the expense of employment. In sectors such as the steel industry, textiles, naval construction, and automobile production, reconversion was accomplished through reduction of surplus productive capacity and a simultaneous intensification of the utilization of labour power with the objective of increasing productivity. But afterwards, throughout the entire downward phase, investments aimed at rationalization have dominated the industrial scene. Automation, data processing and microelectronics have been introduced increasingly in continuous industrial processes (chemical production, certain branches of food production); in those based on the assembly line (automobile production being the exemplary case); and in other discrete industrial processes such as the production of large transformers or naval construction, in which their introduction is much more difficult. The result has been that, as a rule, the increases in production registered have been accompanied by parallel reductions of employment. Most industrial sectors have been affected by the same process, although unevenly.[19]

With respect to the model of labour organization, the 'Fordist' model was very useful in maintaining sufficient output to supply growing markets, but once the crisis set in, the problem became how to increase productivity with stagnant markets. Robotization, data processing and data-transmission networks were valuable instruments for achieving these goals. In the first place, they made possible decentralization of production between countries, between regions of the same country, and between different plants of the same company. Capital could flee from the traditional industrial concentrations, which were as a rule more conflictive, and install itself in rural areas or in other countries where wages were lower and the possibilities of exploiting labour were better. Capital was also able to farm out part of production to subcontractors and promote exponential growth of domestic or putting-out industry. Second, in the face of stagnant markets, the new technologies allowed firms to compete through product diversification. Thus, the statement that Ford could satisfy its clients' desires just as long as the car they wanted was black was replaced by new capacities to combine chassis, motors, colours, and so on, offering the market a wide range of products. Finally, data processing and microelectronics made possible improved management of stocks, which meant better utilization of raw materials and a greater supply of potential markets, whatever the place of production of the commodity in question. All this required more flexible employment, geographical and functional mobility, and changes in labour conditions. The change in labour organization was imposed in practice during the first stage, but afterwards it was reflected in occupational norms, which without a doubt was one of the most important sources of productivity increases.

The objective effects on the working class of the industrial countries have been considerable: employment is stagnant, unemployment continues to grow, the employed population has been redistributed away from industry towards the service sector, poverty has spread, and so on. If we also consider the changes made in the organization of work, we must conclude that the division and segmentation of the working class have increased.[20]

3.2 The state, ideology and the political economy of late capitalism

During the post-Second World War expansion, capitalist ideology and political economy played crucial roles in determining the rate of exploitation and in the very operation of the system, to the point that Ernest Mandel underscored them as one of the most characteristic elements of late capitalism. This is one of the areas in which the changes produced throughout the downward phase have been most significant.

From the beginning of the crisis, Keynesian ideology, which inspired economic policy during the period of expansion, began losing ground to neoliberalism, because the latter appeared in the eyes of the ruling class as the best means of overcoming the downward phase. To impose such policies, some fundamental ideas which had been solidly grounded in the workers' movement had to be stamped out.[21]

The idea of socialism, as a form of social organization alternative to the market, had to lose ground in workers' consciousness, because their acceptance of measures detrimental to their interests could only be achieved if they accepted that the market economy is the only possible system and that the crisis is a problem that demands sacrifices from everyone. It was necessary to portray the market economy as the only efficient system of social organization. For neoliberalism, the market is an almost perfect mechanism that permits the allocation of scarce productive resources so that production is maximized and society's needs are fulfilled. If the market operates freely, any distur- bance will tend to be corrected. If an entrepreneur makes the wrong production decisions, offering a product for which there is insufficient demand in the market, either there will be losses, the mistakes will be corrected, or the firm will disappear. If unemployment exists, it is due to workers' excessive wage demands, which exceed the levels required to achieve full employment. The market economy is therefore (suppos- edly) an almost perfect mechanism which combines maximum effi- ciency in the satisfaction of needs with maximum freedom for the individual.[22]

Additionally, the Keynesian ideas that had inspired economic policy during the period of expansion following the Second World War had to be laid aside, because the recovery of the rate of profit required a drastic shrinkage of the welfare state. For neoliberalism, the hegemony of Keynesianism during the post Second World War years of expansion led to the state's acquiring too great a weight in the economy – in most of the industrial countries government spending is between 40 and 50 per cent of GDP – and to excessive social protection, which functions as a disincentive for workers and requires high taxation. Overcoming the economic crisis required eliminating this situation and rendering unto the market that which is the market's. Economic policy must cease being interventionist and must limit itself to guaranteeing the conditions for efficient operation of the market (maintenance of basic equilibriums, elimination of obstacles to efficient operation of the labour market, and so forth). It is necessary to give the market back its proper function, reducing the weight of the state sector in the economy through privatization of public services and profitable public com- panies. Finally, the welfare state must be reduced to a minimum, although not so much as to cause social explosions.[23]

Neoliberalism and neoclassical economics were not the only alterna- tive, and in fact they were not dominant during the first years of the long downward wave. They were imposed with Reagan's election in 1980 and Thatcher's coming to power in Britain. Today it has become the social and economic policy of all governments, whatever their political label. The crisis of so-called actually existing socialism came later, and reinforced the neoliberal project. The result has been that the dominant ideology, the political economy of capitalism and the role assigned to the state after twenty-five years of a downward phase are very different from those which characterized the expansive phase after the Second World War. The consequences in all areas are huge, at both the national and international levels.

3.3 Globalization

During the phase of expansion after the Second World War II, the search for economic spaces beyond each country's domestic market was never-ending.[24] Successive GATT negotiating rounds, the birth and subsequent evolution of the European Common Market and the creation of the European Free Trade Association are proof of this. The intensive expansion of the postwar period quickly revealed the limits that national states impose on capitalist development. The narrowness of each country's domestic market impeded large-scale production, while at the same time the necessary investments to confront competition and serve enlarged markets required capital disbursements and implied risks beyond the possibilities of isolated countries. This was agreeable to multinationals, the hegemonic organizational form of big capital in the current stage of capitalism. Multinational corporations, whose theatre of operations is much larger than the internal market of specific countries, are interested in organizing their activity in the real market in which they operate. This requires demolishing the economic frontiers which hinder international circulation of commodities and capital. This process came up against the limits imposed by Keynesian hegemony on all governments. No government was interested in mortgaging the performance of internal economic policy, and this made necessary the maintenance of tariffs and restrictions on international capital mobility. With the economic crisis and the hegemony of neoliberalism, things have changed drastically.

Neoliberalism conceives the market as the best way of organizing the economic activity of society, and this has repercussions in the international arena. For neoliberalism, free trade among all countries is the basis of economic prosperity, since it permits each of them to specialize in what it produces best and to obtain what each lacks at the lowest cost. All countries can benefit, but only if there are no obstacles to international trade, which means that all duties and all quantitative restrictions that hinder the free operation of the world market should be eliminated. Along the same lines, capital movements must be freed, so that productive resources can be assigned efficiently and without any impediment.

Neoliberalism, therefore, conceives the world as one big market in which commodities and capital can move without restriction. The World Trade Organization and the multiple agreements among countries and economic areas – the Common Market and the Maastricht Treaty in Europe, the North American Free Trade Agreement between Canada, the United States and Mexico, among others – devote themselves to the realization of this idea.

Combining tariff elimination with free capital movement has decisive consequences for the economic policies of every country. Since there are no barriers shielding domestic markets, competition becomes the system's supreme regulator, and a universal struggle is unleashed to improve competitiveness and offer better conditions of profitability for capital. This reduces all governments' manoeuvring room with respect to conditions in each country and compels them to adopt economic policies based on the reducing workers' living standards, which tend to depress demand.

In fact, competitiveness depends on many factors – capitalization of the economy, level of technological development, workers' skill levels, infrastructure and social services, multinational companies, breakthroughs into foreign markets – but none of them can be transformed in the short term. Governments therefore, drenched in ideas of the global village and in neoliberal ideology, can only cut wages – direct and deferred wages, because social pensions also form part of costs through social security premiums and taxes – and increase productivity through flexible labour markets. Neoliberal policies are thus further strengthened, at the same time that competition serves as blackmail for workers to accept these new conditions and as a weapon to make workers in the entire world compete among themselves. But such policies tend to depress demand and, since this process is repeated country by country, a dismal spiral is generated which tends to aggravate the crisis (this aspect will be examined in more detail in section 3.6).

Liberalization also has consequences for other aspects of economic policy. Less competitive countries see the emergence of balance-of-payments deficits on current account, which push them into recessive monetary and fiscal policies that reduce inflation and economic activity, put a brake on imports and increase exports. While these policies produce the desired effects, deficits need to be financed and, in a world of almost absolutely free capital movements, capital will arrive only if the interest rates are higher than in other countries, exchange rates are stable and fiscal policies are sound: if governments maintain a regressive economic policy and a fiscal system. Again this process is repeated country by country, so that competitive depressions tend to reduce demand in all of them. Nobody can escape the norm, because a different economic policy favouring growth would generate untenable problems. It would increase inflation and the foreign deficit, capital would flee, and employment would shrink. For weak countries and workers, globalization becomes a trap with no escape.

3.4 Money and permanent inflation

Permanent inflation is a characteristic of late capitalism which helps account for the intensity and duration of the rising phase of the long wave as well as certain features of the downward phase. Mandel concurs with Marx that the law of value is neither annulled nor interrupted by fluctuations in the circulation of money. Relative prices among commodities (including gold, the commodity that is used as money) are determined by the labour time socially necessary for their production. However, the expansion of paper money not convertible into gold and the growth of credit money, or banking money, cause an increase in the monetary expression of the prices of commodities and services, giving way to the phenomenon of permanent inflation. Although the tendency towards continuous price increases due to monetary factors preceded the emergence of late capitalism in the postwar period, the phenomenon came into its own during this period. Inflation now occurred even in periods of recession, in contrast to previous stages of capitalism, when crises were accompanied by falls in commodities' money prices. Mandel locates the origin of this phenomenon in the Great Depression, when the state began to exercise an active role in the economy to dampen the crisis, incurring deficits that had to be monetized. This increased the quantity of money in circulation and meant that governments stopped heeding the dictates of monetary orthodoxy concerning the issue of paper money.

The advocates of monetary orthodoxy, more concerned with the fracture of their theoretical models than with the dangers threatening capitalism, rejected as irresponsible the creation of money not based on the gold standard (under which the quantity of money in circulation depends on the volume of gold reserves of the issuing bank). They argued that the alteration of the immanent laws of the system prevented adjustments imposed by the free forces of the market. 'Artificially modifying' the real process of production through credit and monetary expansion, they maintained, would have serious repercussions on the system's equilibrium and the healthy recovery of activity and employment. The system's recovery would be prevented, since the cleansing of capital that takes place when the pure mechanisms of the market are allowed to function would be impeded (Mandel recognized that this argument contains a kernel of truth). The struggle between neoclassical economics and Keynesianism began, then, under very adverse conditions for capitalism. This explains the displacement of a theory which could neither anticipate, nor avoid, nor resolve capitalism's greatest historic crisis.

During the Second World War, the breach with orthodox prescriptions became deeper due to strong state economic intervention, which impelled the growth of the quantity of money with the monetization of public deficits to cover military spending. Once the war was over, the new social and economic role performed by the state – with the goals of full employment, countercyclical spending, development of the welfare state, takeover of productive activities of low profitability, long periods of maturation or of strategic interest, and so forth – created continuous pressure towards money creation. This new money creation took place under conditions where all discipline on the part of the monetary authorities, other than the commitments imposed by the Bretton Woods agreements of keeping fixed exchange rates with the dollar, disappeared. Until its bankruptcy in 1971, when the convertibility of the dollar into gold ceased, this system meant on an international scale what the credit systems meant on a national scale: the possibility of increasing liquidity without subordination to the rules of the gold standard and therefore the possibility of expansion of the economy and international trade.[25]

The new situation and the new direction of economic policy, adjusted to the dominant Keynesian doctrine, were felt profoundly in the rising phase of the long wave, stimulating growth, dampening the recessions, maintaining the rate of profit and therefore deferring its eventual fall and the change in the trend. State-propelled demand and the growth of credit to the private sector facilitated the strong rhythm and long duration of the expansion and the realization of surplus-value. But at the same time, as the advocates in favour of orthodoxy claimed, the expansion of demand and credit disturbed the cleansing function of crises, permitting the survival of capital which under different circumstances would have been devalued. The impact of permanent inflation led to an acute and traumatic crisis of overproduction, which began the change of trend of the long wave. Subsequent crises have been aggravated by previous inflationary tendencies, to the degree that a 'cleansing' of capital as deep as that required by orthodox policies did not take place during the expansive phase of the long wave.

However, one cannot say that monetary orthodoxy of the type proposed by gurus like Hayek or Friedman was restored once the crisis was unleashed, even after the neoclassical school took its revenge on Keynes by becoming the theoretical underpinning of neoliberalism. In the first place, the questioning of the role of the state is only an attempt to reduce its levels of regulation and intervention, while maintaining levels that have no parallel with those existing at the beginning of the long wave. The difference is that today there are large budget deficits, which make it very difficult to apply a strict monetarist orthodoxy. Second, the deregulation of international and domestic financial systems promoted by neoliberalism facilitates an extraordinary growth of credit and money in the financing of both public and private sectors. This again clashes with the discipline needed to reinforce the cleansing of capital and increase productivity. There is not even an international monetary system of fixed exchange rates to which national monetary evolution must submit and adjust, without prejudice either to the highly valued goal of currency stability or to the multiple attempts to restore exchange-rate stability. The Maastricht project of establishing a single European currency for the European Union is the most ambitious of these projects. Finally, we must emphasize that the zeal to re-establish orthodoxy or the convenience of maintaining restrictive monetary policies has not made the bourgeoisie lose sight of its broader interests. As in the 1930s, rather than satisfying doctrinal interests, the bourgeoisie responds to social and political problems. It is not appropriate now to follow orthodoxy to its logical conclusion given the existing level of unemployment and the social tensions generated by the crisis. In the face of serious incidents, as for example the stock market crash in the fall of 1987, monetary policy was modified. The bourgeoisie was rightly convinced that a few more points of inflation were preferable to an uncontrollable financial crisis.

The persistence for different reasons of a financial system capable of multiplying credit and money regardless of objective criteria is what has led to persistent inflation in all countries during the current downward phase, causing social tensions, dampening the consequences of the crisis, and preventing the crude and senseless form the crisis would assume if the policies of the patriarchs of orthodoxy were followed. The counterpart, as before the expansive long wave but in other circumstances, is the prolongation of strong economic imbalances and great financial instability.

3.5 Wages and class struggle

In *Late Capitalism*, Ernest Mandel criticized the mechanistic character of the dominant Marxist theory of wages. According to this theory, the growth of the industrial reserve army leads to reductions in real wages and an increase in the rate of exploitation; the reduction of the industrial reserve army leads to higher wages and a fall in the rate of exploitation. This cannot be deduced from Marx's writings, and corresponds to reality even less.

The evolution of wages takes place between two limits: on the one hand, the physiological limit below which wages cannot fall without severe social reactions; on the other, the social-historical limit above which they cannot rise because that would cause the disappearance of surplus-value and capitalism. It is true that wages fluctuate between these two limits according to the phase of the cycle and the long wave, so that economic expansion and the reduction of the industrial reserve army push them upwards, while recessions drive them downwards. But this is not decisive. Rather, the degree of organization and the level of consciousness of the two classes involved in the conflict and the characteristics of the division of labour are decisive. Therefore, wages may increase, even though unemployment increases; or they may fall, despite a reduction in the industrial reserve army. It all depends on class struggle, a factor external to capital's own laws of motion.

Mandel joined the debate on the Phillips curve which dominated conventional economics during the last decade of the expansive phase of the long wave. Conventional economic theory, anchored in the ideas of the neoclassical school, was unable to explain how wages increased even when unemployment rose. The existence of unemployment above the frictional level meant that the demand for labour power was smaller than the supply, and according to the neoclassical model, this excess in supply had to translate into a reduction of wages. The British economist A. W. H. Phillips (1914–75) tried to save the theory by arguing that there was no relation between wages and the level of unemployment. There was rather a trade-off between rising wages and the rate of unemployment: when the unemployment rate declined the growth of wages accelerated, and when unemployment increased wage growth decelerated. Wages were nonetheless always on the increase. For Mandel, the proponents of the Phillips curve were making a mistake analogous to that of mechanical Marxism. Rising wages depended not only on the rate of unemployment, but also on the degree of organization of the two contending classes. The Phillips curve explained nothing, because it moved constantly according to the fluctuations of class struggle.

This theory of wages in *Late Capitalism* fulfils a central role in explaining the long wave. The phase of expansion began due to the increase in the rate of exploitation which resulted from the defeats of the proletariat before, during and after the Second World War. Throughout the expansion, full employment, but also the high degree of organization of the workers, first blocked and eventually caused a fall in the rate of exploitation. During the recessive phase the opposite has occurred. The rate of exploitation has increased because unemployment has increased, but objective causes cannot by themselves explain this phenomenon. The ideological offensive unleashed by neoliberalism and the regression in workers' level of consciousness and organization have been as important as unemployment and the segmentation of the working class.

Class struggle, as a factor external to the fundamental economic mechanism of capitalism, will be decisive to the outcome of the recessive phase. It has intervened throughout the entire long wave. One must take into account that it was a significant factor in the transition from expansion to contraction, which leads to the conclusion that contraction did not take place exclusively due to endogenous reasons. There is a subjective component in the outcome of the present crisis to which Mandel possibly did not give all the weight it deserved. The subject was however implicit in his theory of late capitalism, with its recognition of the importance of class struggle. The social conflicts that exploded in the last years of the 1960s were of such scope and depth that one cannot ignore the bourgeoisie's reaction to the social situation unleashed during the expansion as one of the sources of the economic crisis.

3.6 The structural weakness of demand

Neoliberal policies have introduced a demand component to the current crisis. This is not new in the history of capitalism. Until the crisis of the 1930s, neoclassical economics, which was the ultimate foundation of economic liberalism, had been hegemonic among the bourgeoisie. The market was the perfect institution par excellence, because it guaranteed that any increase in production would translate into an equivalent increase in demand. As von Mises and Hayek argued in 1929, in a situation of perfect competition depressions could not happen.

The neoclassical structure was founded on the premise that the economy worked at full employment, that all deviations from full employment were conjunctural, and that the economy itself would generate the means to return to normality. Periodic crises would take place, but they fulfilled the objective function of adjusting productive capacity to demand. They caused the disappearance of the least productive or antiquated enterprises, provoked in the process a rise in productivity, and therefore created the conditions for a new recovery. It was only a matter of allowing the forces of the market to work in order to produce economic cleansing in the long term.

But this had nothing to do with the economic reality of the 1930s. Unemployment reached unprecedented levels, idle industrial capacity became the norm, and there was no indication that this situation was going to correct itself if left alone. The dangers of the situation were greater than the dangers of preventing economic cleansing or rocking monetary stability. The main capitalist groups and governments chose a change of economic policy as a way of dampening the effects of the crisis. The so-called 'Keynesian revolution' and the change in the role of the state that it implied were nothing but the conscious ideological expression of the ruling class's changed priorities. From that time on, the state played an important role in the functioning of the capitalist economy, Keynesian ideology was dominant, and governments utilized its recipes for the dual purpose of maintaining effective demand and avoiding crises and extending government social spending in order to integrate the demands of the working class.

At present, capitalism is in a situation similar to that of the 1930s in terms of the weakness of demand.[26] The economic crisis demanded wage reductions in the interest of restoring the rate of profit, the more so because there was also a fall in productivity. Growing unemployment, the deterioration of labour conditions and the segmentation of the working class have reduced the working class's ability to resist. Neo-liberal policies and continuous campaigns to blame wages have done the rest. As a result, workers' purchasing power lagged behind output in the main industrial countries in the 1980s, causing a relative weakness of wage consumption which has become structural. The insistence of liberalism on wage reduction has ignored wages' role as motors of demand, and has caused a structural weakness of consumption which is now making the recovery more difficult.

The weakness of private consumption would not be as important if public spending, exports, investment or several of these components of demand grew sufficiently to become motors of effective demand. But the obstacles facing the growth of these components are formidable.

In the case of public spending, the impact of the crisis on public revenues and spending and neoliberals' reduction of the tax rates on capital, together with rising interest on the public debt, have caused a sharp growth of budget deficits in all industrial countries. Orthodox financing of these deficits has caused a growth of public indebtedness of such magnitude that, from the point of view of the functioning of capitalism, it has finally become one of the most serious problems. In the OECD countries, public debt surpassed 20.2 per cent of GDP in 1980 and 42.4 per cent of GDP in 1994. Reducing the public deficit is a priority of all governments, which in turn impels them to implement recessive fiscal policies.

The obstacles facing investment are no less important. The decline of the rate of profit and the reduction of the rate of growth of aggregate demand, which are phenomena typical of the recessive phase, have been joined now by a rise of long-term interest rates. Such rates, which became very high during the 1980s, have declined in the last few years. But in 1994 they were still around 4.5 per cent in the European Union, and in the US they were noticeably higher than those registered before the economic crisis. High real interest rates are the logical result of the monetary policies applied in most countries (with the goal of reducing inflation and stabilizing exchange rates) and of the enormous financial hypertrophy which has developed (see the next section). An enormous volume of financial capital, which moves from country to country searching for speculative profits, combines with the general financial problem produced by high rates of indebtedness to produce high interest rates. This situation cannot change in the near future, because real interest rates will continue to be high. If we add to this the weakness of consumption and the insufficient recovery of the rate of profit, we cannot expect investment to become the motor of demand capable of upholding a sustained recovery.

For neoliberalism, the growth of effective demand must be propelled fundamentally by exports. The liberalization of world trade, the constant search for increased competitiveness, the attacks on wages and working conditions, the rigorous internal monetary policies, and so forth, have no other objective than facilitating exports. If exports grow, investment, consumption and profits will supposedly follow. On the surface, the policy has unquestionably been successful, since the exports of goods and services have increased faster than GDP in all industrial countries, and as a result their share of total demand has increased. But the problem is that with the internationalization of the different economies, imports have also grown considerably, demonstrating the incoherence of attempting to solve the crisis in each country at the expense of the others by invading their markets. The growth model of neoliberalism has failed. The policies which depress internal demand have not propelled external demand. The so-called 'global village' has not produced more growth or more profits in the imperialist countries, for the simple reason that each one of them has attempted to win the competitive war and, as a result, none has achieved a decisive advantage.

The structural weakness of private consumption caused by the crisis and neoliberalism has not been replaced by any other component of demand. The 'supply crisis' unleashed during the early years of the 1970s has now been compounded by a 'demand crisis'. The rate of profit has recovered to a certain extent, but a new problem has emerged which also hampers the solution to the crisis: insufficient effective demand. Overcoming this contradiction requires the appearance of a net external demand that is sustained over time. This in turn requires opening new markets, whose appearance is not imminent.

3.7 Financial hypertrophy

Neoliberalism is responsible for capitalism's development of a financial sphere based on paper, which has only a minimal relation to the real economy. This is not a specific trait of the present recessive phase, but has been shared by different phases of prolonged stagnation in the history of capitalism. The difficulties of realizing profits in the productive sphere lead to the search for speculative activities, which imply additional exploitation of workers. At present, financial hypertrophy has acquired unprecedented dimensions.

In the last years, high public deficits and orthodox deficit financing have created a level of public indebtedness without precedent in the history of capitalism. In 1993, the public debt of the twelve countries of the European Union represented 66 per cent of the combined GDP, that is, more than four trillion dollars. The net debt of the US government amounted to 39.6 per cent of GDP, which means another 2.7 trillion dollars. If we add the debt of the remaining OECD countries, which also constitute very high percentages of GDP, it is safe to say that the capital markets have been enlarged by a public debt approaching ten trillion dollars. In this way, states have absorbed a high volume of the capital which has been freed from the productive sphere, providing a rate of return which it could not easily find due to excess capacity and the fall in the rate of profit. Think of the fact that in the European Union the interest on the public debt reached 5.6 per cent of combined GDP, or approximately 350 billion dollars.

Add to the public debt the private debt of enterprises and families.

On these foundations, an enormous financial edifice of credit multiplic-
ation has been erected. The states create debt, the enterprises or
investment funds buy this debt, financing it with their own indebtedness,
and so on, in an endless chain which feeds a continuous process of
'financial innovation'. The result is an enormous mountain of paper
debt, what Marx called 'fictitious capital', which depends on the existence of directly productive capital and demands a share of the surplus-
value it generates, introducing great instability into the functioning of
capitalism.

Financial hypertrophy has favoured a rise in practically all stock
markets. Since the 1987 stock-market crash the stock-market indexes
have risen in all industrial countries with the exception of Japan: more
than 25 per cent in Italy and Canada, more than 50 per cent in the US,
Germany and the UK, and more than 100 per cent in France. High
prices on the stock market translate into low profitability. However,
finance capital does not expect to reap profits through the dividends
enterprises pay, but rather through capital gains generated by speculation. To summarize, the high indexes have little to do with firms' real
situation. What propels investment is not so much actual expectations
of profitability as the profits of accurate speculation. The result is that
capital markets, subjected to frantic activity, are overvalued. The adjustment of the indexes to the current situation of capitalism is pending,
waiting only to be triggered by some event.

In a context of absolute freedom for international capital mobility,
financial hypertrophy has also been reflected in foreign accounts.
Between 1981 and 1993, the external liabilities of the seven greatest
industrial nations multiplied fourfold, from 2.3 to 9.2 trillion dollars.
While foreign assets have behaved similarly, the fact is that an enormous volume of capital is moving internationally in search of profits,
in the capital markets or in the speculative exchange markets. The
result is an evident instability in the exchange markets, whose evolution
does not necessarily correspond to the evolution of the balance of
payments. Often governments cannot control them, given the volume
of activity of the speculative funds.

To all of this one must add the problem of the Third World debt,
which, far from being solved, is ever more acute, with disastrous results
for the countries involved. In 1994, servicing the foreign debt required
203 billion dollars, 4.3 per cent of these countries' GDP. In 1986 the
debt reached one trillion dollars, in 1995 1.5 trillion dollars; i.e. it had
grown almost 50 per cent, to which one must add 215 billion dollars
for the countries of the Eastern bloc. More than half of the debt is
owed by countries which have difficulties meeting payments, so that

the 'debt problem' continues to be a time bomb under the international financial system. Mexico, one of the most affected countries though not the only one, has given clear warnings.

The magnitude of the financial problem surpasses that of any preceding historical period, including the years preceding the crash of 1929. Considering present conditions – capital's internationalism, decomposition of the international monetary system, deregulation of markets – the house of cards erected through financial and credit expansion is highly unstable and runs a risk of collapse which is not easy to dismiss. Before the initiation of another expansive cycle similar to that of the 1980s and above all before the initiation of a lasting phase of recovery, a cleansing of the system which destroys part of this financial capital seems necessary. No firm recovery can take place with the burden of the current financial hypertrophy and degeneration.

Mandel always insisted that profound social and economic changes were necessary for capitalism to overcome the recessive long wave. The fact that after a quarter-century capitalism does not seem to be recovering from the depressive long wave gives credit to his contributions and to Marxist analysis. Despite the hegemony of neoliberalism, an examination of the different aspects of the 'new world order' hardly warrants confidence in the system's stability. Decisive economic events and profound class conflicts loom over the horizon.

Notes

1. Karl Marx, *Capital: A Critique of Political Economy*, trans. David Fernbach, Vol. 1, Harmondsworth 1976, p. 102.
2. Marx, 'Author's Preface' to *A Contribution to the Critique of Political Economy*, Chicago 1904, pp. 11–12.
3. See Ernest Mandel and Alan Freeman eds., *Ricardo, Marx, Sraffa*.
4. Marx, *The Economic and Philosophical Manuscripts of 1844*, New York 1964.
5. Marx, *The Grundrisse*, New York 1971.
6. Marx, *Theories of Surplus Value*, New York 1952.
7. Perry Anderson, *Considerations on Western Marxism*, London 1976.
8. Roman Rosdolsky, *Zur Entstehungsgeschichte des Marxschen 'Kapital'*, Frankfurt 1968; *The Making of Marx's Capital*, London 1977.
9. It has become fashionable to argue that Marxism is a nineteenth-century ideology, but in a sense Marx analyzed not so much nineteenth-century as present-day capitalism. In the second half of the nineteenth century, the capitalist economy was limited to Europe west of the Danube, North America and some cities or states of South Africa and Oceania. The majority of the known world was not capitalist and in the industrial countries the overwhelming majority of the population was still agricultural, so that the

MANDEL'S INTERPRETATION OF CONTEMPORARY CAPITALISM 73

working class was a small minority. The differences in wealth between capitalist and non capitalist countries were not great (in today's parameters, from 1 to 1.8) and no intelligent observer would have considered China as a civilization inferior to the European. The system analyzed in *Capital* resembles more today's capitalism than that of the nineteenth century. See E.J. Hobsbawm, *The Age of Empire (1875–1914)*, London 1987.

10. Rudolf Hilferding, *Finance Capital : A Study of the Latest Phase of Capitalist Development* , London 1981.

11. Rosa Luxemburg, *The Accumulation of Capital*, London 1951.

12. Nikolai Bukharin, *Imperialism and World Economy*, London 1972.

13. Paul Baran and Paul Sweezy, *Monopoly Capital*, New York 1966; Paul Sweezy, *The Theory of Capitalist Development*, New York 1956.

14. Leon Trotsky, 'The Curve of Capitalist Development', in *Problems of Everyday Life*, New York 1973, pp. 273–80.

15. Joseph A. Schumpeter, *Business Cycles: A Theoretical, Historical and Statistical Analysis of the Capitalist Process*, Philadelphia 1982; *Capitalism, Socialism and Democracy*, London 1976.

16. Ernest Mandel, *Late Capitalism*, and *Long Waves of Capitalist Development: The Marxist Interpretation*.

17. The crisis was not due to a problem of insufficient demand, but rather to a reduction in the rate of profit and the fact that production was not profitable. But this did not become evident until OPEC raised oil prices in 1973. This pushed the capitalist economy into a recession greater than any since the Second World War and so, in 1975, industrial production declined 6.7 per cent in the European Economic Community, 10 per cent in the United States, and 11 per cent in Japan. In most industrial sectors surpluses and losses began to emerge, and the climate of optimism which had predominated for decades turned into pessimism.

18. For an analysis of the first years of the downward long wave, see Ernest Mandel, *The Second Slump: A Marxist Analysis of Recession in the Seventies*.

19. For the characteristiscs of investment and organization of labour in the downward phase, see Jesús Albarracin, *La onda larga del capitalismo español*, Madrid 1987; and OECD, *Technical Change and Economic Policy*, Paris 1980.

20. In these pages we avoid entering into a debate that cuts across the left, but we have to point out that often there is an exaggeration of the changes in production which, without objective supporting facts, are used to justify the loss of centrality of the working class. Take for example the figures for the European Union. Between 1956 and 1991, total employment grew from 123 to 135 million people, which means that it has grown less than the population, but it has grown. Industrial employment, which represented 40 per cent of the total in 1956, has been reduced to 31 per cent, but it continues to represent a large proportion. The internal structure of industrial employment has experienced practically no changes. Textiles, garments, and shoes continue to be the industrial sectors which generate the most employment, followed by electrical machinery, food, non-electrical machinery, the chemicals industry, and so on. This means that despite appearances, the sectoral structure of the working class continues to be

similar. See Commission of the European Communities, *Panorama of EC Industry*, Luxembourg 1992.

21. For the appearance, contents and consequences of neoliberalism, see Pedro Montes, *El desorden neoliberal*, Madrid 1996.

22. Jesús Albarracín, *La economía de mercado,*, Madrid 1994.

23. See Jesús Albarracín, 'Ideologia, errores, malas intenciones', in *La larga noche neoliberal*, Madrid 1993; R. Miliband, L. Panitch, and J. Saville, *El neoconservadurismo en Gran Bretaña y Estados Unidos: retórica y realidad* (Valencia 1992).

24. See Pedro Montes, *La integración en Europa: Del plan de estabilización a Maastricht*, Madrid 1993.

25. Mandel foresaw the crisis of the international monetary system before it took place. The system was experiencing the basic contradiction flowing from the dual role of the dollar: as the currency of one country, with a tendency towards depreciation due to permanent inflation and the circumstances of the US economy; and as reserve currency and pivot of the system through its linkage to gold, which required that it be a solid and stable currency.

26. The analogies with the situation of the 1930s and the explanation of the reasons why the crisis is not as 'dramatic' now are systematically highlighted in an interview with J.K. Galbraith published in *El País* (14 January 1993). In that interview, Galbraith argues that

> at present, the U.S. economy finds itself in what I call *unemployment equilibrium*, similar to that experienced during the Great Depression of the 1930s. The difference is that we have introduced into the system an entire series of security nets, such as Social Security and similar measures, but also, above all, government support for the economy, without which we would find ourselves now in a situation of absolute banking disaster. So today, as in the 1930s, we have a similar low-yielding equilibrium, but at a high level thanks to the government's post-Depression safeguards. Should neoliberal policies deepen, these 'safeguards' could disappear.

After the Golden Age:
On *Late Capitalism*
Michel Husson

The new edition of Ernest Mandel's *Late Capitalism* as part of the Verso Classics series provides an occasion for an overview of contemporary debates. Nonetheless, this commentary does not aim to be a systematic discussion. It is rather the fruit of a self-interested undertaking, which has consisted in plunging into Mandel's *magnum opus*, not for purposes of posthumous defence and illustration, but as an invitation to critical evaluations and advances. This is, to be sure, the best way to carry on the tradition and method of open Marxism to which Mandel was so committed.

The central thesis of *Late Capitalism* is summed up in this way at the very beginning of its last chapter:

> Late capitalism is the epoch in history of the development of the capitalist mode of production in which the contradiction between the growth of the forces of production and the survival of the capitalist relations of production assumes an explosive form. This contradiction leads to a spreading crisis of these relations of production.[1]

Mandel's work was written between 1970 and 1972, and this thesis must therefore be situated in the context of that time. The social explosion of 1968 had already occurred, but the first generalized recession of 1974–75 was still to come. Mandel's proposition was thus not a simple observation but in large part an anticipation. True, there was talk of a crisis of capitalism, but more often in the form of a general crisis of civilization. The United States had entered a crisis of domination, with a very marked cyclical turning point in 1967, the end of the dollar's convertibility announced by Nixon in 1971, and of course the war of imperialist intervention in Vietnam. But the end of the years of expansion and the transition to a long period of weak growth and rise of mass unemployment were not part of the economic forecast. The critique of capital was directly social and political, and for the rest it sufficed to proclaim, 'The bosses can pay.' The actuality of socialism was once more on the agenda, but in a certain sense it was capitalism's economic successes that made the transition to another way of organizing society seem plausible. So the fact that anti-capitalist attitudes later declined along with growth rates is not completely paradoxical.

Prophecies

The prophetic dimension of Mandel's work supplies a first guiding thread for this rereading. His adversaries liked to joke that if you were always predicting a crisis, then you would obviously be proved right in the end. However, the inverse of this good-humoured jibe is not true: well-meaning souls have been promising the end of the crisis for a quarter of a century now, but time continues to pass and reality has failed to bear out their charming optimism. However, our goal here is to recreate the intellectual and political climate of a previous generation. It is thus not besides the point to recall how self-evident the affirmation of capitalism's superiority, its ability to master its contradictions, was supposed to be thirty years ago. In his book *The Second Slump* Mandel delights in citing various authorities of the time, like Samuelson, who said 'by means of appropriately reinforcing monetary and fiscal policies, our mixed-enterprise system can avoid the excesses of boom and slump and look forward to healthy progressive growth'. In 1969, Harrod wrote in his manual *Money* that fairly 'full employment should now be regarded as an institutional feature of the British economy'.[2] In 1970, in *L'Équilibre et la croissance économique* (Equilibrium and Economic Growth), Stoleru went further: 'It has often been said that a crisis such as the Great Depression could no longer take place today, given the progress made in techniques of state countercyclical intervention. These claims, presumptuous as they may seem, are not without foundation.'[3]

We cannot separate predictions from either their methods or their basic assumptions. Mandel's predictions, unfashionable as they were, were not made by accident, nor did they result from a systematic catastrophism. This is why it is useful to go back a bit further in time, as Mandel himself invites us to do when he explains, in his preface to the German edition, that the project of writing *Late Capitalism* resulted from his dissatisfaction with chapter 14 of his *Marxist Economic Theory*.

This chapter, composed in 1961, is called 'The Epoch of Capitalist Decline', and merits some discussion. It puts forward an analysis of postwar monopoly capitalism, with a particular emphasis on the state, inflation and their role in financing accumulation. (Mandel even speaks of 'overcapitalization'.) State intervention makes it possible to reduce 'the size of cyclical fluctuations', but this result is contradictory since it leads to inflation. As for the 'welfare state', its development is limited by its effect on the rate of profit, inasmuch as a policy of income redistribution in favour of wage-earners 'would tend to increase considerably the minimum subsistence wage, the "elements historically regarded as necessary" in this wage, and this not as a result of an increase in the productivity of labour but through a real redistribution of social income, that is, through a *considerable reduction in the rate of profit*'.[4]

Neo-capitalism

As early as 1962 Mandel took account of the achievements of postwar capitalism, which he called 'neo-capitalism'. The clearest exposition of his views is found in the lectures he gave in 1963 for a school of the French Parti Socialiste Unifié (PSU), which were published later as *An Introduction to Marxist Economic Theory*. There Mandel refers to Kondratieff, then adds: 'The long-term cycle which began with the second world war, and in which we still remain – let us call it the 1940–1965 or 1940–1970 cycle – has, on the contrary, been characterized by expansion.' It made possible 'a rising trend in the standard of living of the workers'. This relatively unprecedented functioning of capitalism derives from a specific configuration, which takes the form notably of increasing government intervention into economic life. It has been made necessary, to a large extent, by the Cold War and, more generally, by the challenge to capitalism launched by 'the totality of anticapitalist forces'.[5]

This continuous expansion also has a material basis, which is found in the effects of a 'permanent technological revolution', which is no longer governed by the cyclical rhythm of development described by Schumpeter in his *Business Cycles* (New York 1939) because of the disproportionate role of military research and development. The arms race constitutes from this point of view 'a real stimulus for permanent research, uninterrupted and practically without any economic consideration'. This technological revolution has the effect of reducing 'the renewal period of fixed capital' and shortening the length as well as severity of cycles. Mandel also mentions, among the available countercyclical policy instruments, the increased share of social spending in national income. This deferred wage 'plays the role of a shock-absorbing cushion by preventing too sudden and too violent a drop in the national income in the event of a crisis'.[6]

The tendency to permanent inflation is the consequence of these new arrangements, mainly of military spending. It also results from the behaviour of monopolies, which creates rigidity in prices. Economic concertation and incomes policy also contribute to reducing cyclical fluctuations and avoiding wage demands during '*the only phase of the cycle in which the relationship of class forces favors the working class*', so that the end result is a cycle 'in which the relative portion of wages in the national income will have a permanent tendency to fall'.[7] The framework was thus set. It was developed in a more systematic way in an article on 'The Economics of Neo-Capitalism' published in 1964 in *The Socialist Register.*

This perspective allowed Mandel to analyze the foundations of the 'long wave' and at the same time to forecast its imminent end. The notion of neo-capitalism is, in Mandel's framework, the opposite of a theorization of the end of capitalist contradictions. The text that synthesizes the logic of this prognosis best is the theses on the 'new rise of the world revolution' written by Mandel and adopted in April 1969 by the ninth congress of the Fourth International:

> [R]evolutionary Marxists ... have provided an overall analysis of the causes of the long period of imperialist expansion consistent with general Marxist theory ...

> This Marxist analysis reached three conclusions: first, that the essential motor forces of this long-term expansion would progressively exhaust themselves, in this way setting off a more and more marked intensification of interimperialist competition; secondly, that the deliberate application of Keynesian antirecessionary techniques would step up the worldwide inflation and constant erosion of the buying power of currencies, finally producing a very grave crisis in the international monetary system; thirdly, that these two factors in conjunction would give rise to increasing limited recessions, inclining the course of economic development toward a general recession of the imperialist economy. This general recession would certainly differ from the great depression of 1929–32 both in extent and duration. Nonetheless, it would strike all the imperialist countries and considerably exceed the recessions of the last twenty years. Two of these predictions have come true. The third promises to do so in the seventies.[8]

This text commands admiration, since it preceded the 1974–75 recession. We can see that it was one of a long series of works devoted to studying concrete capitalism, so that it cannot be accused of permanent catastrophism. On the contrary, Mandel's thinking about neo-capitalism could seem unorthodox to advocates of a dogmatic version of Marxism, which prevented them from taking account of transformations in capitalism and, consequently, from simply citing Mandel.

Wages

The analysis of the postwar long wave leads us to the issue of the rise in real wages. How can this be incorporated into a Marxist analysis? In Mandel's work, the starting point is a critique of the 'theory' of absolute impoverishment developed in particular by Stalinist economists during the 1950s. The question becomes whether capitalism can raise workers' real wages in a lasting way or, more accurately, to what extent it can give wage earners back all or part of the gains from increased productivity. This question is obviously absolutely central. Postwar experience shows that the answer must be yes, as illustrated in Table 1 (compiled from French data, which are in no way exceptional). The period from 1946–76 saw an average annual increase of 4.5 per cent in the real wage, which thus went up 280 per cent in thirty years, while there were only average annual real wage increases of 1.7 per cent in the rest of the century.

Table 1 Wages and productivity[9]

Period	Growth of real wages	Productivity growth
1896–1938 (42 years)	30 % (0.6 %/year)	100 % (1.6 %/year)
1946–1976 (30 years)	280 % (4.5 %/year)	400 % (5.5 %/year)
1976–1996 (20 years)	40 % (1.5 %/year)	60 % (2.5 %/year)
1896–1996 (100 years)	530 % (1.9 %/year)	1250 % (2.6 %/year)

This is why Mandel rightly emphasized the existence of a 'tendency of workers' living standards to rise'. Is this as a flagrant falsification of Marxist theory by postwar capitalism? If we go back to Marx, the question proves not to be inapposite. We find for example in *Capital* the following categorical statement: 'But the increasing productivity of labour is accompanied by a cheapening of the worker, as we have seen, and it is therefore accompanied by a higher rate of surplus-value, even when real wages are rising. The latter never rises in proportion to the productivity of labour.'[10] This sentence was written in a different way, however, in the French edition which Marx had checked personally and where it is reduced to a banal statement: 'By making cheaper the means of subsistence, the development of labour productivity lowers also the price of the workers.'[11] Maximilien Rubel, in a footnote to the French edition in the prestigious 'La Pléiade' series, considers this difference to be a clarification of the idea that the rate of surplus-value rises despite the increase in workers' purchasing power.

This is not pure Marxology. Marx's hesitation raises the essential question of whether the French Regulation School's concept of 'Fordism' is antithetical to the Marxist conception on this point or not. There are many reasons to think that this was the schema that Marx had in mind. In other words, Marx usually theorized from a model of capitalism incompatible with a rise of real wages parallel to the increase in labour productivity. If this is so, he was mistaken, though this error would not put in question the overall coherence of his theory. In fact, Marx's most profound discussion is to be found in the text described as an unpublished chapter of *Capital*. Here we find a comparable proposition:

> It is perfectly true, however, as our examination of the capitalist process of production has shown, that – quite apart from the prolongation of the working day – there is a definite tendency for labour-power itself to become cheaper. This stems from the fall in the prices of the goods that determine the value of labour-power and enter into the necessary consumption of the labourer. Hence also there is at the same time a trend towards curtailing the *paid* part of his work and extending the *unpaid* part . . .[12]

This argument is half macro-economic and rather static. It does show that gains in productivity make the value of labour-power fall, but what is the dynamic set in motion? Inasmuch as Marx rejects the 'iron law of wages', there is always a possibility that the composition of the value of labour-power can increase through the inclusion of additional use-values. The question of realization also arises immediately. If the rate of surplus-value increases uniformly with the growth of productivity, then the share of wages and the share of the market based on wages must fall steadily. Marx raises this very issue in the same passage, when he polemicizes against Proudhon: 'How then is it possible for the working class to use its weekly income, which consists just of "*salaire*" [wages], to buy a quantity of goods that consists of "*salaire*" + surplus-value?'[13] His classic answer is that workers only buy part of the social product. Nonetheless he has raised a different question in this context:

who buys the share of the social product that corresponds to the increase in surplus-value?

There are many postwar Marxist writings that can be read essentially as attempts to answer this question while ruling out, at least in theory, the possibility of a rise in real wages. Mandel clearly criticizes the theory of absolute impoverishment, and adopts in *Late Capitalism* a position of principled indecision:

> If, in the long term, the industrial reserve army remains stable or diminishes, then a rise in the productivity of labour will have a two-fold and contradictory effect on the level of wages. On the one hand the value of commodity of labour-power will be reduced, because the commodities traditionally needed for the reproduction of labour-power now lose some of their value. On the other, the value of the commodity of labour-power will be raised through the incorporation of new commodities into the necessary minimum of life (for example, the so-called durable consumer goods, the purchasing price of which has gradually found its way into the average wage).[14]

Chapter 5 on the rate of surplus-value then slips off in another direction, leaving aside the question of the relative rates of productivity growth and real wages growth. None of the data cited examines the development of productivity growth. The discussion bears directly on the indicators, which are often open to question, of the rate of surplus-value.

Mandel rightly emphasizes that this fundamental relationship depends on the rate of unemployment, taken as an indication of the social relationship of forces and only secondarily of the rate of accumulation. In addition, he attributes a key role to what one might call 'the primitive growth of surplus-value' in the immediate aftermath of the Second World War, which made it possible to stock up on reserves of profitability. None of this is really subject to debate. But once more the question of real wages in relation to productivity has disappeared. This is a blind spot in Mandel's analysis, which leads him to neglect the absolutely exceptional postwar productivity growth as a possible basis for rising real wages (again, see Table 1).

With hindsight this is probably the French Regulation School's major contribution, a contribution that Mandel's in some ways orthodox approach prevented him from fully appreciating. We can in fact identify two essential characteristics of his 'model'. The first is an approach to the reproduction schemes that is disconnected from the concrete mode of satisfaction of social needs. The second is – even if it leads to the introduction of notions foreign to Marxist theory – a conception of technical progress strongly biased towards more and more capital-intensive uses of capital. These two aspects are obviously linked.

The reproduction schemes

The reproduction schemes have often been used inappropriately in the Marxist tradition. According to Mandel in the introduction to *Late Capitalism*: 'In our opinion, the reproduction schemes that Marx developed . . . cannot be used in the investigation of the laws of motion of capital or the history of capitalism.'[15] This methodological position is important to remember, particularly because Mandel violates it on more than one occasion. It reminds us that there are too many parameters, so that the trends in fundamental variables are relatively indeterminate. It is thus very tempting to try to reduce the number of 'degrees of indeterminacy' by imposing supplementary conditions in order to generate a determinist model of capitalist development, for example by imposing a rule of proportionality between the two sectors of the economy.

Such constraints have no real justification, and this type of theorization of the dynamic of capital and of its crises (even of its final collapse) is based on ad hoc formulations of little interest. One cannot avail oneself of arithmetical simulations in order to prove that harmonious growth is compatible with the laws of capitalist accumulation. These counterposed versions, catastrophist or harmonicist, suffer from the same flaw: the difficulty of understanding the alternation of expansive and recessive long waves. In one case the crises seem incomprehensible. In the other case, it is the system's failure to collapse that becomes inexplicable.

A second level of criticism of the usual uses of the reproduction schemes requires a detour. We need to dispose of a simplistic vision, which counterposes a Marxism interested only in exchange-value to a neoclassical theory that attributes a central role to utility. In fact use-values come first, even within Marxism, and the concrete linkages of the reproduction schemes presuppose a certain correspondence between what is produced and what is consumed. Marx wrote for example, 'If a commodity is to be sold at its market value, i.e. in proportion to the socially necessary labour contained in it, the total quantity of social labour which is applied to produce the overall amount of this kind of commodity must correspond to the quantity of social need for it, i.e. to the social need with money to back it.'[16] This necessary correspondence of production with the concrete goods that give material form to social needs is even more compelling if we reason dynamically. It is then necessary that the structure of (effective) aggregate demand correspond over time to supply, and not only from the standpoint of the mass of value, but also from the standpoint of the use-values that are the 'bearers' of this total exchange-value. In other words, the structure of consumption must be compatible with the orientation of accumulation. Consequently, overall reproduction involves a dialectic between production and consumption that Marx stressed on occasion:

> Hunger is hunger, but the hunger gratified by cooked meat eaten with a knife and fork is a different hunger from that which bolts down raw meat with the aid of hand, nail and tooth. Production thus produces not only the object but also the manner of consumption, not only objectively but subjectively ... Thus production produces consumption (1) by creating the material for it; (2) by determining the manner of consumption; and (3) by creating the products, initially posited by it as objects, in the form of a need felt by the consumer.[17]

This is something other than a very global condition of proportionality between major departments or between accumulation and consumption. This structural correspondence must be reproduced within each of these dimensions. From this point of view, we can discern in Mandel's work a certain reluctance to tackle the question, to take into account what could have been new in the mass consumption of manufactured goods. His neglect of this central idea introduced by the French Regulation School, which constitutes in my view a deepening of Marx's analysis, leads Mandel to a first underestimation of the exceptional characteristics of the postwar period.

The organic composition of capital

On the side of production, there is a guiding thread that has an important place in Mandel's analysis. It is the idea that a permanent technological revolution leads necessarily to a rising organic composition of capital. This approach involves a rather orthodox reading of the falling tendency of the rate of profit. In a very interesting text first published in 1985, Mandel synthesizes his main theses and puts forward the following summary:

> The rise in the 'organic composition of capital' leads to a tendency for the average rate of profit to decline. This can be partially compensated

by various counter-forces, the most important of which is the tendency
for the rate of surplus-value (the rate of exploitation of the working class)
to increase, independently from the level of real wages (which can rise
under the same circumstances, given a sufficient rate of increase in
productivity of labour). However, in the long run, the rate of surplus-
value cannot rise proportionally to the rate of increase in the organic
composition of capital, and most of the 'countervailing forces' tend to be
superseded in their turn, at least periodically (and also in the very long
run).[18]

This formulation, incidentally a classical one, is not really satisfactory,
for several reasons. Once more the formulation concerning the rate of
surplus-value is not clear. The rate of surplus-value is determined by
the development of real wages and of the productivity of labour in
relation to each other. A rising productivity of labour lowers the value
of labour-power at a given real wage, but it can also compensate for an
improvement in workers' living standards without leading to a lower
rate of exploitation. There is no general law according to which the
rate of exploitation should go up or not: that depends on the rhythm
of the productivity of labour and the relationship of forces between
capital and labour. Thus we must distinguish between the two different
components of the rate of surplus-value (real wages and productivity of
labour), barring the very specific case of a middle-term stability of real
wages. But from the moment that this distinction is made, the same
holds true for the organic composition of capital.

The value ratio of constant to variable capital does not necessarily
increase according to some general law as a result of a growing mass of
dead capital relative to living capital. There are three reasons for this.
First, dead capital transmits its value little by little to commodities that
are produced. Constant capital increases with accumulation, but
declines with this transfer of value that we can call depreciation, in
such a way that the organic composition tends to stabilize. In order to
illustrate this statement, we can imagine an economy where the
expenditure of labour, and thus the total value created each year, is
constant, the rate of surplus-value is constant, and all surplus-value is
accumulated. If the rate of depreciation is constant, then the organic
composition of capital tends to remain constant.[19]

This result is rather easy to grasp. In value terms, the increase in
depreciation is proportional to capital, while accumulated new value is
a constant. The first amount increases until it progressively equals the
(constant) surplus of accumulated capital. At this point constant capital
is no longer increasing in value, because the quantity of value being
added (accumulation) is equal to the quantity being taken away (depre-

ciation). True, it is possible to construct examples in which the organic composition increases without limit. However, this tendency is obtained as a by-product of other tendencies that we cannot consider representative of the normal functioning of capitalism, for example an increase in the proportion of the social product that is accumulated, or a continual prolongation of the life span of capital, and so forth.

This outcome seems nonetheless to clash with our intuition, which says that accumulation increases the weight of capital relative to labour. This weighing down of productive combinations is an established fact, but it concerns the technical composition of capital, whose growth does not necessarily imply a higher composition in value terms. The simplest indicator is the capital per head which compares the stock of capital – say the number of machines – to the total labour force (or to the total number of hours worked). But, someone may object, such a concept of 'capital', defined as a stock of means of production, is foreign to Marxist theory and only makes sense in the context of neoclassical theory. This objection is not valid, however, because it confuses problems of measurement with the critique of a concept.

The concept of capital in marginalist theory is indeed open to criticism, because it is supposed to exist prior to relative prices. In other words, it is supposed to be theoretically possible to determine the quantity of this specific substance, of this 'factor of production' – capital in general – independently of prices and thus of income distribution. This requirement follows logically from the fact that neoclassical economists construct a theory of income distribution purporting to show that profits are determined by the marginal productivity of capital, while wages in a parallel way reflect the marginal productivity of labour. The so-called 'Cambridge' critique of this theory of capital consists in saying that it is a circular theory, and that no measurement of physical capital can exist prior to a system of pricing.[20]

All this is perfectly true, but it has nothing to do with the possibility of constructing an aggregate called 'fixed capital'. Nobody denies the validity of the notion of productivity of labour, which depends on measuring a 'physical' product as an aggregate, a 'basket' of use-values which cannot be added up without the help of a system of pricing. As for a stock of capital, it too sums up several generations of investments and is entitled to similar conventions, to which is added a reasonable law of depreciation.

Capital per head thus goes up: this is an empirical fact that no one questions. Then why can we not deduce from this a rising tendency of the organic composition of capital? This impossibility results essentially from the effects of the productivity of labour, which a minimal formalization enables us to see.[21] The passage from technical composition of capital to organic composition of capital depends on the development of productivity and of real wages. Given a constant rate of surplus-value, the organic composition of capital increases only if the technical composition of capital grows more quickly than the productivity of labour. In other words, an identity between a rising technical composition of capital and a rising composition of capital in value terms cannot be posited as a general rule.

The rate of profit

These considerations give rise to a hypothetical case in which everything – real wages, the productivity of labour, and capital per head – grows at the same rate. This is what Joan Robinson called a 'golden age' and defined as follows:

> When technical progress is neutral, and proceeding steadily, without any change in the time pattern of production, the competitive mechanism working freely, population growing (if at all) at a steady rate and accumulation going on fast enough to supply productive capacity for all available labour, the rate of profit tends to be constant and the level of real wages to rise with output per man. There are then no internal contradictions in the system ... We may describe these conditions as a *golden age* (thus indicating that it represents a mythical state of affairs not likely to obtain in any actual economy).[22]

In this case, the organic composition of capital, the rate of surplus-value and the rate of profit are constant. Demonstrating a tendency of the rate of profit to fall requires demonstrating why this configuration is impossible (the strong version) or untenable in the long term (the weak version). The strong version must be rejected in both its variants. The first variant depends on a technical hypothesis, according to which capital per head always increases more quickly than the productivity of labour. We have already seen that such a hypothesis is untenable. The second variant stipulates that wages can never rise as quickly as productivity, so that there exists a universal law that the share of wages must fall, which in its turn would contribute to a rising organic composition of capital. But the development of real wages is a product of the class struggle and, here again, nothing allows us to assume that they rise more slowly than productivity.

What we see here is in the last analysis an underestimation of the achievements of Fordism, which were historically short-lived. Mandel addresses this point indirectly when he analyzes the four main elements that enable capitalism in general to surmount the problem of outlets for its products. First, there is the self-development of the department of means of production, which has obvious limits since in the last analysis the demand for machines is a result of the demand for consumer goods. The second element is demand coming from other social classes besides wage-earners. These two factors played a relatively secondary role during the postwar expansion. Mandel adds the fact that the capitalist class 'can sell an increasing portion of consumer goods on credit rather than in exchange for income'.[23] This formulation is not correct, since the realization of value is always carried out by exchange 'for income' and the function of credit is to reallocate current income; it cannot constitute an autonomous market.

Finally, the last factor has to do with 'mass consumption', notably by wage-earners. But Mandel adds immediately that its growth 'is proportionately less than that of total commodity values, so that the production of relative surplus-value increases'.[24] So we come back to a 'classical' expression of the tendency of the rate of profit to fall:

> An increase in the social average rate of surplus-value has two contradictory consequences, which must ultimately generate a reduction of the social rate of profit – in other words, of the relation between the total social capital and the total quantity of social surplus-value. It leads, on the one hand, to a growth in the accumulation of capital; on the other, to a fall in the share of living labour in the total social expenditure of labour. Since only living labour produces surplus-value, however, it is only a matter of time before the increase of the organic composition of capital caused by accelerated accumulation surpasses the increase in the rate of surplus-value. At that point, the rate of profit – including that of monopolies – begins to fall once more.[25]

The weak version of the tendency of the rate of profit to fall focuses on two essential characteristics of the dynamic of capitalism: competition among capitalists and class struggle. The former pushes capitalists to look incessantly for productivity gains by means of increasing capital per head: the goal is to gain ground over the competition, but also over wage-earners, by cutting back the workforce. Class struggle, at various different levels, is aimed for its part at keeping wage increases below the growth of productivity. The lack of social control over this process leads to the idea that the exceptionally complex, fragile conditions that make possible the system's harmonious progress can only be established relatively briefly in historical terms. After a certain period of time, the contradictions triumph over the best regulations. Resistance to wage increases and over-investment end up undermining profitability.

Stagnation, monopolies, inflation

Despite what has just been said about his orthodoxy, Mandel's work clearly cannot be classed among the dogmatic versions of Marxism. Two essential aspects of his method preserve him completely from this: first his historical perspective; second, his analysis of the capitalist system as a whole, which thus appears 'as a hierarchical structure of different levels of productivity, and as the outcome of the uneven and combined development of states, regions, branches of industry and firms, unleashed by the quest for surplus-profit'.[26] The three main sources of this surplus profit are transfers of value originating in agrarian regions, colonies or semi-colonies, or less technically developed industries.

Mandel proposes a periodization marked by a progressive displacement of the dynamic of capitalism. The centre of gravity of laissez-faire capitalism 'lay in the regional juxtaposition of development and underdevelopment'. In classical imperialism, the main dynamic factor was to be found in the 'international juxtaposition of development in the imperialist states and underdevelopment in the colonial and semi-colonial countries'. As for late capitalism, its dynamism is more internal and takes the form of an 'overall industrial juxtaposition of development in growth sectors and underdevelopment in others, primarily in the imperialist countries but also in the semi-colonies in a secondary way'.[27]

This historicized approach goes together with a consistent project aiming to show how capitalism's fundamental contradictions – what one could call its classical contradictions – reproduce themselves through new forms that only displace them. At the time three themes dominated heterodox debates: monopolies, inflation and military spending. On each of these points Mandel takes a theoretical middle position between 'modernists' and 'conservatives', in other words between two ways of looking at transformations of capitalism. Modernists stressed the functional side of these transformations, which supposedly enabled the system to overcome its contradictions and proceed with a radically new rhythm. The notion of 'organized capitalism' was dominant at the time. The task of Marxist critique was to challenge this harmonicist vision, without falling into a catastrophist dogmatism that would bear little relation to reality. The 'conservatives' sought on the contrary to show that nothing had changed and that the same contradictions were at work as always.

On the subject of monopolies, Mandel never subscribed to stagnationist theses either of Keynesian inspiration (like Steindl's) or of Marxist inspiration (like Baran and Sweezy's).[28] Concentration of capital did not mean for him the end of competition. Mandel adopted as his own a thought of Marx's – 'if capital formation were to fall exclusively in the hands of a few existing big capitals, for whom the mass of profit outweighs the rate, the animating fire of production would be totally extinguished'[29] – and presented as self-evident the fact that 'capitalism without competition is capitalism without growth'.[30] But taking up an idea already put forward in his *Marxist Economic Theory*, he tries to theorize its mode of functioning under monopoly capitalism: 'A tendency equivalent to the *equalization of surplus-profits* thus arises i.e., *two* average rates of profit come into existence side by side, one in the monopolized and the other in the non-monopolized sector of the imperialist countries.'[31]

This transfer of value allows him to reconcile the price-fixing ability attributed to monopolies and the phenomenon of permanent inflation with the law of value. Much of the debate among Marxist economists concerned in fact this issue of prices and profits. Many simplistic arguments emphasized the point that inflation was a means of guaranteeing the rate of profit, even if this meant admitting that there was a certain disconnection between the price and value of commodities. One of the founding works of the French Regulation School focused in fact on the analysis of inflation, supposedly made possible by the transition to 'monopolist regulation'.[32] This discussion was also linked to a more theoretical debate over the transformation of values into prices, opened up by the Neo-Ricardian critique of Marxist theory, starting in particular from Sraffa's work. The double equalization of profit rates and the analysis of permanent inflation put forward by Mandel provided elements of a generally correct response to this challenge to the law of value. His central idea was that no arrangement, even one as permissive as credit expansion, can lead to the creation of value going beyond the surplus-value engendered by the exploitation of wage labour, or compensate lastingly for the fundamental mechanisms that hold down profitability.

Mandel's treatment of the arms economy fits within the same logic. For a whole stagnationist Marxist current, military spending plays an absolutely central role in postwar capitalism. Baran and Sweezy wrote, for example:

> Here at last monopoly capitalism seemingly found the answer to the 'on what' question: On what could the government spend enough to keep the system from sinking into the mire of stagnation? On arms, more arms, and ever more arms.[33]

For Mandel, military spending does not constitute a lasting response to the falling tendency of the rate of profit, because it draws on social surplus-value and contributes, in the same way as other industries, to a rise in the organic composition of capital.

The watershed

What accounts for the end of the long expansion? We have here a major theoretical problem. Concrete history has to be made compatible with theoretical schemas integrating both the possibility of phases of expansion and the ineluctability of crises. This articulation is extremely complex, since the theories must not 'explain too well'. There are 'catastrophist' readings for instance that explain the crisis so well that it becomes difficult to understand why the crisis is not permanent. On the other hand, 'harmonicist' approaches lead us to ask how such a well-oiled machine could have ever derailed. Nor can we demand that theoretical formulations provide a universal, timeless interpretative matrix, applicable to all crisis situations; this would mean denying their historic dimension.

Another way of expressing the same difficulty is to emphasize the contradiction that exists between the structural causes of the crisis and the forms in which it suddenly appears. We can easily show that the moment where the crisis erupts always points towards an 'unjustly accused' factor, a superficial cause. In 1973–74 economists spoke about the oil crisis, merrily confounding a factor that directly triggered the recession with its underlying causes. The stock exchanges are the favourite place for crises to emerge, not because the financial dimension is primary, but because they are the natural location for the necessary, violent devalorization of capital to be revealed. This interpretative problem also exists within the most traditional Marxism: how, and under what conditions, can a tendency such as the tendency of the rate of profit in fact engender periodic crashes? A comparable difficulty is revealed by the various different meanings of the term 'crisis', which is applied both to the sudden shock of a crash and to the slide into a longer-term crisis. Three theoretical tropes enable us to move forward in these areas: accumulating contradictions; the reversal of virtuous circles; and the distinction between long-term and short-term variables.

The first useful metaphor in interpreting the crisis is that of accumulated tensions. We can use the image of a dam giving way: the catastrophe itself takes place very quickly, but it is the result of a slow wearing away. The first breach may be minuscule, but it unleashes a process of qualitative transformation and creates a disequilibrium that becomes a break. It does not matter where the first fissure opens up: spotting it gives no indication of any kind of causality. To stretch out the metaphor, Mandel's standpoint consists in observing the dam before it has given way and showing why it has held up until this moment and why it cannot resist the accumulating pressures. Forgetting either side of the prediction leads to a one-sided discourse that is easy to criticize. This explains incidentally why Mandel was caught between mutually contradictory critiques. Defenders of dogma attributed to him the thesis that capitalism had overcome its contradictions. But others, from the opposite side, reproached him with always predicting the system's collapse.

A second conceptual tool leads us to observe how stabilizing arrangements can gradually be transformed into their opposite, thus becoming in a sense accelerators of contradiction. Inflation for example has many advantages for financing capital, but it only draws out contradictions in time, to the point where it is transformed into its opposite, that is an obstacle to capitalist crisis management. We have seen that inflation plays a central role in analyses of postwar capitalism, and Mandel was undoubtedly the best in showing its dual role. But the neoliberal turn also took place around the rallying cry of the fight against inflation, the real objective obviously being to impose wage restraints as a new norm. To this end it was necessary to put a brake on inflation, an earlier regulatory tool that was becoming an obstacle to deploying policies to get out of the crisis. The same reasoning can be applied to social spending or, more recently, to military spending. Everyone agreed that they had an anti-recessionary effect, but Mandel was one of the few economists to grasp their contradictory dimension, that is, the growing drain that they constituted on profits.

Finally, one last distinction needs to be made, between long-term and short-term variables. The transition from an expansive long wave to a recessive long wave can only be understood as a modification of the overall capitalist configuration, which Mandel proposes to analyze starting from what he calls 'partially independent variables'. The main such variables are: (1) the organic composition of capital in general and in the two departments; (2) the division of constant capital between fixed and variable capital; (3) the development of the rate of surplus-value; (4) the development of the rate of accumulation (the relationship between productively and unproductively consumed surplus-value); (5) the duration of the capital renewal cycle; and (6) the terms of exchange between the two departments. The thesis that Mandel upholds is that

> ... the history of capitalism, and at the same time the history of its inner regularities and unfolding contradictions, can only be explained and understood as a function of the interplay of these six variables. Fluctuations in the rate of profit are the seismograph of this history, since they express most clearly the result of this interplay.[34]

Nevertheless these variables, on their own, are not enough to make conjunctural turnarounds intelligible. The generalized recession of 1974–75, which closed the period of expansion, cannot be explained directly by tendential variations in productivity rates, and still less by the slow development of aggregate demand. It is nonetheless these slow, underground tectonic shifts that lead to crises (and then to the failure to get out of crises), even if crises take the form concretely of eruptions, earthquakes or tidal waves. Accounting for crises and giving an historical analysis of long waves thus requires a mastery of the various 'times out of joint'.[35]

Why the crisis?

Despite the critical reservations that we have just expressed, the explanation of the crisis that flows from Mandel's analysis seems much more coherent than the French Regulation School's account, even if it rests on incomplete premises. What in fact do the Regulationists say? In their eyes the crisis is linked to the exhaustion of productivity increases, which is essentially right. But what is the cause of this slowdown? Here the Regulationists swing back and forth among several different accounts, which can be classified under three headings. The first kind of explanation is technological: everything that could be gotten out of a 'Taylorist paradigm' had been gotten out of it, the assembly lines were running at top speed, and Taylorism had begun to deliver diminishing returns. The second explanation is more 'workerist', highlighting resistance to intensification of work rhythms. The third explanation, finally, is classically Keynesian, stressing the exhaustion of mass markets through their progressive saturation.

Each of these explanations has a certain measure of validity, but all of them contradict the original Regulationist theoretical contribution. With this theory, paradoxically, it is difficult to understand why a well-regulated capitalism could not carry out the necessary shifts towards new forms of organization of labour, a transitional adjustment of wages, and the satisfaction of new social needs. In keeping with their own logic, the Regulationists have also sought since the early 1980s to sketch the outlines of a 'post-Fordist' system of regulation, but have not managed to construct a scenario that would be an alternative to the neoliberal steamroller.

Mandel got the better of the argument with the Regulation School, because his analysis and predictions take account of the contradictory nature of the capitalist mode of production and the fact that it is not oriented towards optimal satisfaction of human needs. The Fordist system of regulation was to a large extent imposed on capitalism. Its inner logic came into contradiction with the direction in which the expansive long wave was headed, a direction leading in effect to a progressive socialization and reorientation of aggregate demand towards collective services. Here we have to establish a hierarchy of determinations, and distinguish well among the crisis's igniting factors and profound modalities. Mandel rightly polemicized against all mono-causal interpretations of the crisis, including the symmetrical theories of a 'profit squeeze'[36] and of the difficulty of surplus absorption à la Sweezy. An analysis of the crisis must combine these explanatory elements – falling rate of surplus-value, overaccumulation, and later falls in productivity rates – in a reading that fits with the configuration of the expansive wave that was drawing to a close.

In hindsight, the most important long-term variable was the slow shift of aggregate demand towards collective services, measured for example by the relative growth of the social wage. This was a sort of anti-Fordism, in two senses. First, workers in the market sector were no longer consuming what they were producing. Instead, they were increasingly consuming the products of the non-market sector. Second, the goods and services that were the concrete bearers of this non-market consumption did not generate sufficiently large productivity increases. 'Fordism' was put out of whack as wages became increasingly autonomous from productivity. The wage increases that were won in the social struggles of the late 1960s thus lowered the rate of surplus-value. The capitalists responded with investments in productivity that did not give the results they counted on, and the rate of profit fell.

The dominant underlying factor is doubtless the exhaustion of the norms of consumption, a fact which highlights the importance of this notion. At least, this is how it appears with the advantage of twenty years' hindsight and the perspective allowed by the current restoration of the rate of profit brought about by wage restraint and capital devalorization. So what is standing in the way now of a renewal of 'Fordist'-type growth? This question is the Regulation School's weak point. In Mandel's work we find the method with which it can be resolved correctly.

Technology

Another way of formulating the question is to ask where in the long wave we are today. Are we seeing the first outlines of a new phase of expansion, notably in the US? In tackling this discussion we need to avoid a certain number of oversimplifications, and Mandel's approach is in this respect an indispensable reference point. First, we need to beware of a mechanical conception of long waves, according to which all you have to do is wait 25 years to see the wave begin again. The only objective basis of such a periodization would be a specific cycle of innovation. But there is no such cycle; and even if there was, there is no reason why the transformation of innovations into productive forces would keep pace with it.

Mandel's long wave theory has nonetheless too often been reduced to a scarcely reinvigorated form of Schumpeter's approach. In a founding text of the French Regulation School, Boyer resurrects this amalgam for his own ends:

> We cannot accept the rather mechanical interpretation put forward by N.D. Kondratieff, recently taken up by E. Mandel, which presents the history of capitalism as a succession of alternating waves of strong and weak accumulation lasting approximately a quarter-century ... There is no teleological principle that could guarantee a mechanical alternation of ascending and descending phases or an automatic transition from a mainly extensive accumulation regime to a predominantly intensive regime.[37]

This is a mistaken reading of *Late Capitalism* (and incidentally of Kondratieff as well), which the Regulation School never rectified. Dockès and Rosier emphasize by contrast that Mandel was 'one of the very first authors identifying with Marx to introduce class struggle explicitly into his explanation of long cycles'[38] – although they reproach him in an almost exactly opposite manner with treating class struggle as an exogenous element, which is also a misreading, albeit of a different kind.

The new 1995 edition of Mandel's *The Long Waves of Capitalist Development* makes short work of this criticism, which strictly speaking was applicable only to Mandel's writings of the early 1960s. But – here his discovery of the *Grundrisse* made its mark – Mandel's later work attributed a growing role to the incapacity of capitalist social relations to realize the full potential of technological progress. In *Late Capitalism*, for example, Mandel cites, in order to refute, the following passage from Habermas:

> So long as the organization of human nature does not change, and we have to sustain our existence by social labour and tools that are labour-substitutes, it is impossible to see how we can ever discard technology, indeed *our* technology, for a qualitatively different one.[39]

Mandel rejects completely this position, discerning in it

> ... the naive or apologetic belief that only the technology developed by capitalism is capable of superseding the inadequacy of simple manual labour ... It remains a mystery why men and women under different social conditions, increasingly liberated from mechanical labour and progressively unfolding their creative capacities, should be unable to develop a technology answering to the needs of a 'rich individuality'.[40]

A few years later Mandel would reaffirm this position once more:

> We have likewise to stress that any idea that present-day 'dirty', nature-destroying or directly life-threatening technology is an 'inevitable' outcome of the inner logic of natural science has to be rejected as obscurantist, a-historical and in the last analysis apologetic for capitalism ... There is nothing new in understanding that technology developing under capitalism is not the only possible technology, but *specific* technology introduced for specific reasons closely linked to the specific nature of the capitalist economy and bourgeois society.[41]

This long wave ...

To analyze the trajectory of contemporary capitalism, it is also better to avoid somewhat hasty historical analogies. Long wave theory must be stripped of its mechanistic tinsel. It must not lead to a vision in which historical and economic ebbs and flows occur according to some grand tide calendar drawn up somewhere in advance. In particular, each 'wave' combines the internal contradictions of capitalism in a different way, follows a specific dynamic, and leads to different conceivable outcomes. Last time the way out was war and fascism, but this scenario

Figure 1   Profit and accumulation in the main industrialized countries

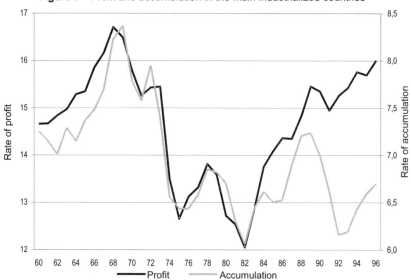

is not the only possible one. It was in fact another, completely different scenario which opened up a new expansive phase at the end of the nineteenth century.[42] We must, finally, steer clear of a conception in which the rate of profit is the alpha and omega, so that once a certain level of profitability is reached a new phase of expansion will take off spontaneously.

In the last quarter-century, capitalism has been enmeshed in a recessive phase, and has put in place a relatively coherent neoliberal system of regulation that is rather new in its history. It is not an expansive phase, since the rates of accumulation and growth have remained modest relative to levels reached in the past. Real wages are growing slowly, and underemployment is spreading throughout the world. But the most novel trait is the restoration of the rate of profit to levels comparable to those prior to the crisis.

Graph 1 shows in detail the different phases of the relationship between these two fundamental quantities, the rate of profit and the rate of accumulation. The data are weighted averages established starting from a sample of the main industrialized countries for which OECD statistics are available: the United States, Japan, Germany, France, Italy, the United Kingdom, Belgium, Denmark, Spain, Greece, Norway, Sweden, Finland and Switzerland. During the 1960s, profit and accumulation advanced hand in hand up to an initial plateau, followed by the first generalized recession of 1974–75. A cycle of recovery then seemed to be taking shape but failed to hold together. There was a second generalized recession in the early 1980s. Starting from this watershed moment, the restoration of the rate of profit began with the generalization of neoliberal policies in all the different countries. But the rate of accumulation did not follow suit. The cycle in the late 1980s seemed to signal a catching-up, but a very clear turning point occurred at the beginning of the 1990s, when the rate of accumulation fell back to low levels roughly comparable to the average for the last twenty years.

It is this disarticulation between profit, on the one hand, and accumulation and growth, on the other, which allows us to speak of the period 1974–98 as the downhill slope of a long wave that world capitalism seems unable to get out of. This inability to return to rates of accumulation comparable to those of the 1960s allows us to reject the idea of a long expansive phase. Examining growth rates clearly leads us to a similar conclusion. But at the same time we must stress the specificities of this neoliberal configuration, joining dynamic profit rates with feeble accumulation. From the point of view of the system's capacity to provide a healthy return to capital, we find ourselves today in a particularly flourishing period. But the surplus-value resulting from this process is less and less able to find suitable sites for accumulation. If we look once more at the graph, the surface area bounded by the two curves represents unaccumulated surplus-value, that is, the growing area occupied by finance. We can even note here how the October 1987 crash had the effect of bursting the financial bubble and bringing the two curves back together. But the two soon diverged once more, and the gap between them has expanded and remained large since then.

In other words, the recessive phase of the long wave is perpetuating itself in the form of a regime of accumulation that unites a growing rate of surplus-value with a constant rate of accumulation. This regime is accompanied by 'financialization', which serves to redistribute unaccumulated surplus-value to social layers whose function is to consume it. Mandel had anticipated quite well this neoliberal hardening of social relations:

> The transition from a 'long wave with an undertone of expansion' to a 'long wave with an undertone of stagnation' is today intensifying the international class struggle. The main objective of bourgeois economic policy is no longer to dismantle social antagonisms but to unload the costs of improving the competitive struggle of each national capitalist industry onto the wage earners employed in it. The myth of permanent full employment fades away ... The struggle over the rate of surplus-value

moves into the centre of the dynamic of economy and society, as it did in the period from the turn of the 20th century to the 30's.[43]

This picture is nonetheless incomplete, because it does not take into account the modalities by which the rate of profit has been restored. The trajectory which followed created an environment with slow growth of sales outlets. The restoration of profitability has been reached by regressive means: the depression of wages rather than the development of social productivity. However, no great defeat has been inflicted on the working class, nor is there any qualitatively new 'exogenous factor' at work. The opening of the Eastern Bloc countries to the world market has been carried out in an extremely selective, regressive way and has not modified the landscape.

Mandel in fact gradually integrated this temporal extension of the cycle of class struggle into his analysis. In 1985, for example, he wrote:

> Precisely because the *organic strength* of the working class (wage labour) is so large at the outset and in the first phase of this depression, the outcome of this intensified class offensive of Capital against Labour is far from certain. The likelihood that the proletariat will suffer a crushing defeat of the type of Germany 1933, Spain 1939 or France 1940 in any of the larger capitalist key countries in a foreseeable future is limited . . . So what is the most likely variant under capitalism is precisely the long duration of the present depression, with only the development of partial automation and marginal robotization both accompanied by large-scale overcapacity (and over-production of commodities), by large-scale unemployment, and large-scale pressure to extract more and more surplus-value from a number of *productive* work-days and workers tending to stagnate and decline slowly, i.e. growing pressure to overexploitation of the working class (lowering of real wages and social security payments), to weaken or destroy the free organized labour movements and to undermine democratic freedoms and human rights.[44]

Mandel's fundamental explanation of capitalism's inability to initiate a new expansive phase comes down, in the end, to another of his central theses: the limits of automation.

Automation and the working day

The influence of Mandel's reading of the *Grundrisse*[45] can be seen in *Late Capitalism*, where he puts forward a central thesis whose full importance is in a certain sense only being revealed today:

> All the historical contradictions of capitalism are concentrated in the twofold character of automation. On the one hand, it represents the

perfected development of material forces of production, which could in themselves potentially liberate mankind from the compulsion to perform mechanical, repetitive, dull and alienating labour. On the other hand, it represents a new threat to job and income, a new intensification of anxiety, insecurity, return to chronic mass unemployment, periodic losses of consumption and income, and intellectual and moral impoverishment. Capitalist automation as the mighty development of both the *productive forces of labour and the alienating and destructive forces of commodity and capital* thus becomes the objectified quintessence of the antinomies inherent in the capitalist mode of production.[46]

Mandel goes even further when he speaks of impossibility:

General automation in large industry is impossible in late capitalism. To await such generalized automation before overthrowing capitalist relations of production is thus just as incorrect as to hope for the abolition of capitalist relations of production through the mere advance of automation.[47]

This position makes it possible to underscore the primary reason why capitalism is getting bogged down, which, as I have tried to show elsewhere,[48] reflects a dual difficulty. Besides social resistance, the defence of legitimate gains won during the years of expansion, capitalism is confronting its own incapacity to bridge the growing gap between its supply of commodities and aggregate demand. It is trying, without succeeding to a sufficient extent, to 'recommodify' a mode of satisfying needs that had been fairly extensively socialized. The many, cumulative technical innovations of the last two decades have not given rise to sufficient productivity increases, due to a lack of growing returns to scale associated with the extension of markets, and also to the very rapid obsolescence of the various products. This is what explains 'Solow's paradox', which states that productivity gains are remaining limited despite technological innovations and transformations of the organization of labour.[49]

It is the lack of commodities suitable for mass production and consumption that stand in the way of a renewal of the 'Fordist virtuous circle'. If this reading is correct, then capitalism is, perhaps for the first time in its history, faced with a systemic crisis. This crisis is challenging capitalism's own criteria of efficiency, inasmuch as capitalism is less and less able to 'translate' the currently most pressing needs – health care, education, housing, quality of life, and above all, by definition, free time – into profitable commodities. If, to use Robert Boyer's words, bad capitalism is driving out good capitalism, this is because the good way of making profits (rapid increases in social productivity) is being

supplanted by the bad, wage restraint in all its forms. To see financialization as the chief characteristic of this configuration is to treat an
effect as the cause, and to stay on the surface, not criticizing capitalism
in a way that goes to the root of its preconditions.[50] In other words,
even if hypothetically the power of the financial markets was brought
under control, this would in no way resolve the fundamental difficulty:
that social needs, as they express themselves historically and concretely
in the most developed societies, cannot be taken into account.

The contemporary response to this difficulty is a regressive one.
Rather than putting in place the conditions for a new expansion,
capitalism's solution is to establish a

> . . . *dual society*, which divides the present proletariat between two antag-
> onistic groups: those who continue to be included (or are newly incor-
> porated especially in the so-called 'third world countries') into the
> process of production of surplus-value, i.e. into the *capitalist process of
> production* (be it for tendencially declining wages); those who are expelled
> from that process and survive by all kinds of other means than the sale of
> their labour power to the capitalists (or the bourgeois state): welfare;
> increase of 'independent' activities; becoming small-scale peasants and
> handicraftsmen; returning to domestic labour (women); 'ludic' com-
> munities, etc. . . .
>
> Capital wants now to reduce its wage-bill to directly paid-out wages
> only, which will then inevitably tend to decline as a result of a hugely
> inflated industrial reserve army of labour . . . It puts new and formidable
> stumbling blocks on the *really emancipatory potential* of new technologies
> and of 'robotism', in as much as it tends to perpetuate in an elitist way
> the subdivision of society between those who receive the necessary leisure
> and potential to appropriate all the fruits of science and civilisation –
> which can only occur on the basis of the satisfaction of elementary
> fundamental material needs – and those who are condemned (including
> who condemn themselves through self-chosen asceticism) to spend more
> and more of their time as 'beasts of burden', to quote again the eloquent
> formula of Marx.
>
> The real dilemma, which is the basic historical choice with which
> mankind is faced today, is the following one: *either a radical reduction of
> work-time for all* – to begin with the half-day of labour, or the half-week of
> labour – or the perpetuation of the division of society between those who
> produce and those who administer. The radical reduction of the work
> time *for all* – which was Marx's grandiose emancipatory vision – is
> indispensable both for the appropriation of knowledge and science by
> all, and for self-management for all (i.e. a regime of associated produc-
> ers). Without such a reduction, both are utopia.[51]

Capitalism: Late or senile?

In an article published in 1968, Mandel admitted that he was not completely won over to the term 'late capitalism':

> The German term, *Spätkapitalismus*, seems interesting, but simply indicates a time sequence and is difficult to translate into several languages. So until somebody comes up with a better name – and this is a challenge to you, friends! – we will stick for the time being to 'neo-capitalism'.[52]

This hesitation, which would finally issue in a different decision, is curious, because the two descriptions have almost opposite connotations. The term 'neo-capitalism' seems to suggest a second youth, whereas 'late capitalism' conveys a feeling of old age. Without wishing to give a disproportionate importance to this terminological debate, it would seem more appropriate to speak of 'mature capitalism'. This capitalism was in fact in full possession of its faculties, and this helps remind us of the exceptional character of its performance between 1945 and 1975. But it was also a capitalism that tended to exhaust itself, to run out of breath, and to reveal its limitations. If we may stretch the metaphor, we could say that today it has been ambushed by senility, and that it is trying in vain to recapture the careless raptures of its youth with the help of neoliberal quack remedies.

In the end the adjectives hardly matter. The essential thing is to understand that Mandel's conception should be resolutely distinguished from the kind of historical determinism that presents 'late capitalism' as 'the final stage', standing on the brink of inevitable collapse. What Mandel says is different. For him, the exceptional performance of postwar capitalism never meant that its contradictions had been irreversibly mastered. On the contrary, they foreshadowed a radical challenge. The successes of 'Fordism' represented the best that capitalism could achieve but, once the parenthesis was closed, the system's incapacity to perpetuate itself by any other means than a great leap backwards became all the more glaring. It is thus time, as Mandel urges us, to reappropriate the most radical Marxist critique of capitalism, and to pose in practice the question of going beyond it.

Notes

1. Ernest Mandel, *Late Capitalism*, London 1978, p. 562.
2. Paul Samuelson, *Economics*, New York 1958, p. 360, and Roy Harrod, *Money*,

London 1969, p. 188, both cited in Mandel, *The Second Slump: A Marxist Analysis of Recession in the Seventies*, London 1978, p. 9n.

3. This citation does not appear in the English edition. L. Stoleru, *L'équilibre et la croissance économique*, Paris 1970, cited in Mandel, *La crise*, Paris 1985, p. 10n.

4. Mandel, *Marxist Economic Theory*, London 1968 [French edition: 1962], pp. 531, 533.

5. Mandel, *An Introduction to Marxist Economic Theory*, New York 1973, pp. 55–6.

6. Ibid., pp. 57–8, 59, 65.

7. Ibid., pp. 74–5.

8. *World Congress of the Fourth International: Documents, Intercontinental Press*, vol. 7, no. 26, 14 July 1969, p. 673.

9. Source: Pierre Villa, *Un siècle de données macroéconomiques, INSEE Résultats*, Paris, no. 303–4, April 1994.

10. Karl Marx, *Capital* vol. 1, Harmondsworth 1976, p. 753.

11. Marx, *Le Capital*, La Pléiade, Paris 1965, Économie I, p. 1111.

12. *Capital* vol. 1, p. 970.

13. Ibid., pp. 971–2.

14. *Late Capitalism*, p. 148.

15. Ibid., p. 24.

16. *Capital*, vol. 3, Harmondsworth 1981, p. 294.

17. Marx, *Grundrisse*, Harmondsworth 1973, p. 92.

18. Mandel, 'Partially independent variables and internal logic in classical Marxist economic analysis', in *Social Science Information*, vol. 24, no. 3, 1985, pp. 487–8 (reprinted in Ulf Himmelstrand, *Interfaces in Economic & Social Analysis*, London 1992).

19. If we call the rate of depreciation 'd', and the accumulated part of new value 'm', then the rate of organic composition tends towards the finite limit m/d. With a rate of depreciation of 10 per cent and a rate of accumulation of 20 per cent of produced value, the rate of organic composition tends towards 2.

20. For a classical presentation, see G.C. Harcourt, *Some Cambridge Controversies in the Theory of Capital*, Cambridge 1972.

21. In order to calculate the number of hours of labour crystallized in the fixed capital invested, we divide the volume of capital (K) by the average productivity of labour in the production of capital goods. Since we are dealing with a conglomeration of goods produced at different times, we must therefore apply, not the current productivity of labour, but the average productivity of these different generations. If the life span of capital is T years, its average age is roughly T/2, so that we can as a first approximation apply the productivity (prod) of T/2 years ago. The value of constant capital is thus $K/prod_{t-T/2}$. The value of the variable capital equals $wN/prod_t$, where w is real wages, N the labour force, and prod is current productivity. The organic composition of capital (O) can be calculated, finally, by the equation $O = [(K/N)/prod_{t-T/2}]/[w/prod_t]$. If the rate of surplus-value $[w/prod_t]$ is a constant, then the organic composition of capital (O) increases only if the technical composition of capital

(K/N) grows more quickly than the average productivity of labour over the period, or prod$_{t-T/2}$.

22. Joan Robinson, *The Accumulation of Capital*, London 1969, p. 99.
23. *Late Capitalism*, p. 572.
24. Ibid.
25. Ibid., p. 531.
26. Ibid., p. 102.
27. Ibid., p. 103.
28. Josef Steindl, *Maturity and Stagnation in American Capitalism*, New York 1976; Paul A. Baran and Paul M. Sweezy, *Monopoly Capital*, New York 1966.
29. *Capital*, vol. 3, p. 368.
30. *Late Capitalism*, p. 31.
31. Ibid., p. 95.
32. Robert Boyer, Alain Lipietz et al., *Approches de l'inflation: L'exemple français*, Paris 1977.
33. *Monopoly Capital*, p. 213.
34. *Late Capitalism*, p. 39.
35. This whole part is strongly influenced by the works of Francisco Louçã, to which Mandel refers in the last edition of *Long Waves*. Besides Louçã's contribution to this volume, see his masterful work, *Turbulence in Economics*, Aldershot 1997.
36. Andrew Glyn and Bob Sutcliffe, *British Capitalism, Workers and the Profit Squeeze*, Harmondsworth 1972.
37. Robert Boyer, 'La crise actuelle: une mise en perspective historique', *Critiques de l'economie politique*, no. 7–8, 1979.
38. Pierre Dockès and Bernard Rosier, *Rhythmes économiques: Crises et changement social, une perspective historique*, Paris 1983, p. 183.
39. Jürgen Habermas, *Technik und Wissenschaft als 'Ideologie'*, Frankfurt 1969, pp. 56–7.
40. *Late Capitalism*, p. 503.
41. Mandel, 'Marx, the present crisis and the future of labour', in Ralph Miliband et al., eds., *Socialist Register 1985/86*, London 1986, p. 449.
42. See Dockès and Rosier, ch. 4.
43. *Late Capitalism*, pp. 472–3.
44. 'Marx, the present crisis and the future of labour', pp. 441, 444.
45. See in particular Mandel's book *The Formation of the Economic Thought of Karl Marx: 1843 to Capital*.
46. *Late Capitalism*, p. 216.
47. Ibid., p. 570.
48. Michel Husson, *Misère du capital: Une critique du néoliberalisme*, Paris 1996.
49. See Michel Husson, 'Du ralentissement de la productivité', *Revue de l'IRES*, no. 22, Fall 1996, as well as *Les ajustements de l'emploi*, forthcoming.
50. See Husson, 'Contre le fétichisme de la finance', *Critique communiste*, no. 149, 1997.
51. 'Marx, the present crisis and the future of labour', p. 447.
52. Mandel, 'Workers under neo-capitalism', *International Socialist Review*, vol. 29, no. 6, Nov.–Dec. 1968, p. 2.

6

Ernest Mandel and the Pulsation of History

Francisco Louçã

Ernest Mandel's *Long Waves of Capitalist Development* was his last major theoretical work. The second edition of the book (1995), which includes two new chapters added to the first English edition (1980) dealing with the current state of the debate, was finished and published very shortly before the author's death in July 1995. This text is the culmination of thirty years of research on a subject which was largely redefined and shaped by Mandel: his arguments, including the polemical tone appreciated by those who knew him, synthesize a broad view of the evolution of capitalism as a civilization, namely of its main economic and social trends, and its interrelation with the political factors in historical perspective.

Mandel's first article on the subject dates from 1964 and was first published in *The Socialist Register*. His general and innovative appraisal of Marxian economics, *Traité d'Economie Marxiste* (in English: *Marxist Economic Theory*) had just been published two years before, but the long periods of the history of capitalism were not considered in that book: business cycles are explained in the *Traité* following Marx's concept of the echo-cycle of investment and no other periods are discussed. The particular feature of the 1964 article was the broadening of that perspective and the consideration of the contributions of three decisive authors who established the preliminary version of the research agenda on long waves: Kondratieff (namely with his 1922, 1924 and 1926 papers and the debate at the Conjuncture Institute of Moscow, published in 1928),[1] Trotsky (namely with his 1921 report to the conference of the Comintern and his 1923 polemic with Kondratieff)[2] and Schumpeter (mainly with his 1939 book *Business Cycles*, but also with some papers published since the end of the twenties).[3]

In 1964, Mandel suggested a new theory based on these contributions, and predicted that the 'thirty golden years' of the post-war boom could be expected to end soon. These two topics then became the most relevant part of his subsequent research. Some time later on, he wrote *Late Capitalism* (published originally in German in 1972), which is the most important piece in the revival of the discussion among Marxists on the Kondratieff waves. It is indeed his magnum opus, comprising a global analysis of capitalism and of its structural changes during the fourth long wave, the one that began after the Second World War. This book was summarized and developed in the Alfred Marshall Lectures delivered by Mandel in 1978 at the invitation of the University of Cambridge, which constitute the first four chapters of *Long Waves of Capitalist Development*.

In 1989, Mandel organized a conference in Brussels, in collaboration with Alfred Kleinknecht and Immanuel Wallerstein, which represented the most important recent effort to synthesize and relaunch the research on long waves. His contribution to that conference, 'The International Debate on Long Waves of Capitalist Development: An Intermediary Balance Sheet', was elaborated in the two chapters prepared for the second English edition of the *Long Waves* book (1995). The historical theory, the definition of the method of research and the critique of orthodox economics were extended in what constitutes a major contribution and a successful challenge to the traditional interpretations of economic and social development and change. The evolution of that research programme is the theme for the following pages.

The origins of the research programme

The research programme on long waves was established simultaneously by several political activists and academic writers who interpreted the distinctive periods of acceleration and deceleration of growth in the nineteenth century: Parvus (main paper, 1901) and Van Gelderen (1913) were active members of the early social-democratic movement, while Bresciani Turroni (1913, 1916), Pareto (1913) and Tonelli (1921) were engaged in academic research. In spite of such diversity, all these authors agreed on two crucial points: the chronology of the long periods of expansion and contraction, and a perspective combining social, political and economic factors. For Pareto, the long cycles were characterized by conflicts inside the ruling elite, namely the succession of periods of domination by speculators and rentiers; for Turroni and

Tonelli, just like for Parvus and Van Gelderen, the social struggles and the schedule of the profit rate were inseparable.

These distinctive features placed the programme on the margin of or in opposition to the new-born neoclassical economics (in which the same Pareto played a major role), since the former was concerned with economic mutations and switches of regimes, and not with some metaphysical gravitation towards equilibrium. In other words, the research programme on long waves was historical by nature and reflected the epistemological requirements of a realist approach to economics, while mainstream economics has been based on the New-tonian properties of an atomist universe where the movements of prices carry all information and encapsulate the natural tendency for equilibrium. Moreover, the idea of convergence and harmony in laissez-faire society described by Mandeville in his *Fable of the Bees* was challenged by the inclusion of political perturbations and social struggles.

Van Gelderen, author of the most precise and complete introduction to the research,[4] insisted particularly on such an articulation of factors, which are to any mainstream economist the definitive proof of the eclecticism and irrelevance of the programme. Kondratieff, who began studying the subject in 1922 and ignored Van Gelderen's contribution, got to the same conclusion and presented a new formulation for an integrated approach of the long periods. Nevertheless, his specification of the 'long cycles' was intensely discussed by two main contenders, Trotsky and Oparin.

Trotsky's speech at the 1921 Comintern conference, acknowledging the existence of different stages and conjunctures of capitalist development, is indeed the first piece of the Russian debate. Having known and cooperated with Parvus, Trotsky was certainly aware of his concept of the *Sturm und Drang* periods of capital expansion and subsequent periods of depression.[5] His intervention was implicitly based on that concept, challenging the ultraleftist position of Bela Kun and the leadership of the German KPD; Kun and the KPD supported the thesis of an imminent revolution and consequently called for offensive action on the basis of the imminent collapse of capitalism.

As Kondratieff's first essay on the 'Long Cycles of the Conjuncture' appeared in 1922, the author was probably convinced that his description and hypotheses were largely shared, and could not hide his surprise when Trotsky sharply criticized his text. In his article of summer 1923, Trotsky used data from the London *Times* to argue that the 'curve of capitalist development' changed abruptly from time to time[6] under the impact of exogenous events, namely revolutions, wars or other political mutations. As a consequence, Kondratieff was criticized for his attempt to endogenize all the political factors, i.e., for ignoring the autonomy of social processes in relation to the economic sphere. In fact, at that time Trotsky was engaged in another political battle, against Bukharin and the idea of a perpetuation or stabilization of the capitalist system. Trotsky rejected the notion that the economy could adjust automatically to upswings and downswings without regard to the strategic dimension – as in Kondratieff. Yet both the 1921 and the 1923 positions were coherent: for Trotsky, major political (exogenous) events determined both the upswing and the downswing of the long wave, which was nothing less than an important change in the trend of the economy. During the maturation of the social conditions of each period, the political factors were supposed to be constrained by the whole dynamic, until the internal contradictions allowed for a new rupture in the 'moving equilibrium'.

Kondratieff was apparently surprised by the critique and in his defence quoted the 1921 speech by Trotsky. Nevertheless, he did not pursue the matter, developing his own positions and trying to avoid any direct political implications. During the 1926 debate at the Institute, such interpretations were scarcely noted. As opposed to Trotsky, Kondratieff argued that the whole dynamic was endogenously determined by the economic contradictions, which indeed included and determined the political factors.

The second main critique was developed by Oparin, a researcher at the Moscow Conjuncture Institute directed by Kondratieff, who presented a counter-report to the 1926 seminar. The main point of that debate concerned the statistical method used to detect long waves. Basically, Kondratieff used several different types of functions to represent the trend line, and considered the trend-deviations as the evidence to be inspected for the existence of long fluctuations. Oparin rightly criticized the arbitrariness of the choice of the functions, but his own alternative was easily dismissed by Kondratieff, since it was based on the assumption of the existence of a number of discrete points of equilibrium and of the existence of a 'natural' rate of growth of gold reserves, as asserted by the early monetarist theory of Cassel.

Shortly afterwards Kondratieff was removed from his position, incarcerated near Moscow and later shot on Stalin's orders. Some of his writings from prison, dealing with general methodological issues, were published in Russia only in 1992 and still await translation. There was then a long interruption in the research, with rare exceptions (e.g., Imbert, Dupriez), until the revival of the research under the influence of Ernest Mandel in the sixties.

Mandel's contributions

When reassessing this debate, Mandel suggested a new hypothesis which was at the core of his research: the internal contradictions of the capitalist mode of production account for the turning point from expansion to depression, but systemic shocks, i.e., exogenous factors propagated through the economy, are needed in order to generate a new phase of expansion.

This is not a synthesis of Trotsky and Kondratieff, but in fact a new and original theory, which is rather distinct from the previous ones. It incorporates the autonomy of the political and social processes and yet does not abandon the requirement for the formulation of economic laws (or tendencies) as the expression of the dialectics of capitalism.

In doing so, Mandel was one of the first authors in the research programme on long waves to consider the necessity for a historically integrated explanation, and in fact to define it as the very condition for the viability of the programme. The large majority of the researchers based their inquiries in smoothing techniques derived from trend-deviation analysis and in transforming data in order to decompose the series in a trend and cyclic movement (like Kondratieff, Oparin, Kuznets, Imbert, Dupriez, Duijn, Kleinknecht, Menshikov, Ewijk, Zwan, Hartman, Metz, Reijnders, et al.). Others abandoned the domain of data analysis and suggested that model simulation could replace the inductive proof (Forrester, Sterman, Mosekilde, et al.). The exceptions have been Gordon (and the first works of the Social Structures of Accumulation school), some of the French Regulationists, Shaikh, Wallerstein, Freeman, Perez, Tylecote, Rosier, Dockès, Kleinknecht and some historians of the phases of capitalist development like Maddison. In this group, Mandel stands as the first researcher to define the modern historical approach to the long waves.

There are two decisive reasons for privileging the historical approach in the analysis, as Mandel did. The first is imposed by the goal itself: long periods of development cannot be supposed to be permanently ruled by the same structural relations,[7] since the changes – the morpho-genetic transformations of the social universe – are a permanent feature of the economies and include such diverse events and factors as technological innovation, modifications of the labour relations, political institutions, dimensions and structure of the market, evolving cultural characteristics or strategies by social groups. In these circumstances, the statistical approaches based on the premiss of equilibrium are doomed to fail: the trend-cycle decomposition which is the basis of the traditional econometric methods assumes independence between the two sets of phenomena and the principle of structural causal stability. Of course, neither of these hypotheses is acceptable in the analysis of real historical series. As a consequence, one must suspect that the inability of the traditional statistics to detect long waves is not a reflection of reality but rather imposed by the very methods used to inspect the data.[8]

The second major factor recommending the use of historical methods of analysis is that economic relations alone cannot completely or exhaustively account for long term changes. As Polanyi pointed out in his *The Great Transformation* (1944), the image of independence and mechanistic functioning of the economic sphere, imposing itself on the society, is an ideological projection of liberalism and a contractarian justification for its imperfect market; the powerful General Equilibrium paradigm is a feature of imagination and has no heuristic power whatsoever. In fact, economic relations are part of the complex social processes.

The whole debate about the endogeneity and exogeneity of the causal factors – which is briefly summarized in Mandel's book – proceeds from such an image and influenced the choice of methods for many researchers. For Kondratieff and for most of the long wave analysts, the perfect model of causality is the one which exhaustively discriminates the endogenous and exogenous variables and attributes the causal determination to the former. Such a requirement was introduced in Kuznets's and Lange's review of Schumpeter's *Business Cycles*,[9] and was later stressed by other critiques of the programme. It is today accepted by most of its practitioners.

Nevertheless, this stance is internally self-contradictory. For if a completely endogenous explanation is presented, it amounts to the excessive claim that some economic function determines the major social events, wars and revolutions, as well as all political forces and the institutional environment itself. Explaining everything amounts to the recourse to an all-inclusive mechanism. As a consequence, the traces and impacts of those factors cannot and should not be meaningfully eliminated from the series, since they are supposedly part of the endogenous mechanism. But the researchers who use the trend-cycle decomposition methods are forced to do so, and mainly to eliminate the variations at the time of the two world wars, in order to detect long waves.[10] In that case the conclusion is contradictory and irrelevant. No claim can be made on reality if the proof is based on the statistical artefact which is a consequence of a procedure that eliminates part of history from the historical series.

On the other hand, the statistical decomposition of the series is inspired by the conception of the business cycle of Ragnar Frisch, who defined in a path-breaking paper of 1933 a model including an impulse system (the non-systematic or random shocks) and the propagation system (representing the systematic behaviour of a damping mechanism).[11] In order to eliminate the excessive deviations caused by the wars in the real series, researchers following this method are forced to equate those events to the random and external forces hereby considered. Of course, this is just the opposite of declaring that those processes are mere consequences of the economic endeavour. Furthermore, in the positivist epistemology implicit in traditional econometrics, causality is defined by the nearer exogenous force, and thus wars or social conflicts should be considered and not ignored as explanatory variables.[12] But since the price of accepting such claims is the rejection of automatic cyclicity, some researchers prefer to live with the contradiction of claiming total endogeneity as the legitimate form of causality, exiling the badly behaved variables to the Purgatory of total exogeneity.

Mandel's work suggests a way out of such self-defeating contradiction: a historical approach to the phases of capitalist development, rejecting the quest for certainty based on the ineffective attempts to prove statistically what traditional statistics are not able to recognize. Since the object is history, this seems to be sound wisdom.

'Parametric determinism' and semi-autonomous variables

Historical analysis can and should be developed in combination with rigorous statistical and formal methods. Beginning in *Late Capitalism*, Mandel argued for a particular articulation to be based on the concept of 'partially independent (autonomous) variables', which represent 'all the basic proportions of the capitalist mode of production',[13] namely the organic composition of capital (including the volume and distribution of capital), the structure of capital (the proportions of the fixed and circulating parts, and their distribution among branches), the rate of surplus value, the rate of accumulation (and the productive and unproductive consumption of surplus), the evolution of the periods of capital rotation, and the structure of the exchange between Departments I and II. This manifold of variables explains the movement of the profit rate, which is the essential cause of both the Juglar cycles and the Kondratieff waves.[14]

This conception involves a thorough reconsideration of the Marxian debates on the issue, since Luxemburg, Hilferding, Grossmann and

Bukharin based their analyses of cycles on the reproduction schemes of *Capital*. Mandel criticized such attempts, which are undermined by the equilibrium properties of the model and by the simplification of those schemes. For Mandel, if the economist is studying the inherent tendency towards ruptures of the equilibrium, the crucial interdependencies between causal factors as well as their partial autonomy may only be comprehensible in a concrete framework. In other words, history must be reconciled with theory: theory without history is mute and history without theory is blind.

Kalecki addressed a similar problem in one of his last papers, published in 1968, suggesting the concept of 'semi-autonomous variables' in order to represent forces which are exogenous from the point of view of the current mathematical models, but which are still in the framework of what should be explained by the theory.[15] Those variables explain in Kalecki's model the growth and the eventual changes of the economy, i.e., represent history. Abandoning the ambitious programme for the complete endogenization of causality, Kalecki's argument implies that no simple model with a small number of variables can faithfully represent reality. The study of the complexity of social relations requires flexible, partial and limited models, but also a general theory of the economic process in which those models and results are interpretable. But Kalecki did not develop the insight, although it is clear that many of the crucial variables in some of the most important economic models are of that kind.[16]

This is why Mandel's concept of the 'partially independent variables' is so important, since it develops for Marxism the central condition for the incorporation of history. Instead of the simplistic guess-work involved in formal models of three or four dimensions, history is assessed in its organic totality – processes and not equilibrium, change and not continuity, dialectics and not causal invariance, concrete and total determinations and not abstract and totalitarian determinism, are at stake.

In a biographic sketch prepared for the *Biographical Dictionary of Dissenting Economists* in the last years of his life, Mandel argued that one of his main contributions was the concept of 'dialectical (parametrical) determinism' as opposed to 'mechanistic determinism',[17] which characterizes general equilibrium economics and traditional econometric methods. This rupture is evidently inspired by his life-long opposition to unilinear and positivist Marxism, but incorporates as well the attempt to synthesize the system in which those semi-autonomous variables are modelled. Humanity poses the problems it is able to solve, and in those determinate boundaries occurs the conflict for control, for co-ordination and for power.[18]

This theme was already dealt with by Mandel in 1985, in a paper where he discussed the distinction between endogenous and exogenous variables. In his view, endogenous variables, from the economic point of view, are those describing the automatic processes flowing from the system's structure:

> These can determine the speed, direction, degree of homogeneity/ heterogeneity of the development. They cannot alter the nature of the system or overturn its general historical trends . . . Besides the inner logic of the system, exogenous factors are at work, which partially co-determine the system's development, at least at short- and medium-term ranges . . . [19]

So far this is Mandel's standard explanation by Mandel. However, the paper added an important insight: the inner logic of the system is constrained by a parametric structure describing its possible trajectories, and that only major systemic events can change those settings.

> Hence any interaction between endogenous and exogenous forces is always limited by these parameters, by these constraints, it reaches its limits when it threatens to eliminate basic mechanisms of the system . . . [20]

In this sense, the exogenous forces are not really independent and would be better described as 'partially autonomous variables', or, if we follow Kalecki's definition, as semi-autonomous. Both these contributions are, in my opinion, major contributions to the critique of the orthodox approaches to fluctuations, irregularities and cycles in historical processes, which are limited to the inquiry into equilibrating mechanisms disturbed by non-informative and meaningless 'white noise' shocks. Kalecki's and Mandel's views suggest that the analysis of complex phenomena is indeed irreducible to simplicity and that the reductionist approach is doomed to fail. Semi-autonomy, referring to non-linear interactions and modelling, incorporates what linear mathematics and formalization is unable to recognize – the constitutive complexity of social processes.

This unveils part of the enigma of long waves, which are very obvious specific periods of the history of capitalism. The traditional theories and statistical methods cannot detect those periods of structural change, since they are only suited to describing continuity, convergence and equilibrium, i.e., to ignoring history. The massive amount of empirical evidence included in *Late Capitalism* and summarized in *Long Waves of Capitalist Development* is instead a tour de force presenting the case for the systemic changes which are the very process of evolution of capitalism, namely its successive 'systems of machines', technological revolutions and social contradictions.[21] From that point of view, Mandel's research was a decisive scientific achievement.

Complexity and history

Mandel stressed the closeness of his own theory and that of Maddison, who studied the 'phases of capitalist development', although some differences remain in the adopted chronology. Both indicated that 'systemic shocks' are needed in order to create momentum for a new expansive wave,[22] but Mandel was particularly concerned with the fact that some of these 'systemic shocks' imply the upswing and others the downswing.[23] From that point of view, it is evident that a strictly deterministic technological explanation is inaccurate, since the acceleration of technological innovation is not the single relevant factor in the increase in the organic composition of capital. The mismatch between the techno-economic system and the socio-institutional one may prevent or extend the systemic impact of those changes, and social relations are therefore the ultimate determination of the process of undulatory development.

This vindicates again the incorporation of history into real life economics, i.e., political economy (or economics as a 'moral science') in the classical sense. Mandel's work was an example of such an approach, which he clearly presented as the project of exploring the integrated totality including internal economic factors, exogenous environmental changes and the mediation through socio-political developments. He was aware that such was the condition for the inquiry into the concrete dialectics of objective and subjective factors. The historical approach was thus reaffirmed: 'We can therefore accept the idea that the long waves are much more than just rhythmic ups and downs in the rate of growth of the capitalist economies. They are distinct historical periods in a real sense.'[24]

Mandel's theory, since it is based on the 'historical reality of the long wave [as] an integrated "total" character',[25] allows for a comprehensive explanation of those processes. There is indeed a trade-off between very simple and formal models which have a mathematical representation and therefore may be parametrized, and historical explanations or general theories which cannot be exhaustively modelled. Choosing the first avenue, many of the researchers become hostages of the available statistical methods, namely of the linear specifications which are needed to solve the equations, because normally even a very simple non-linear system cannot be solved. But only non-linear systems can mimic the real complexities of economies, such as the dynamic stability and simultaneous structural instability of these dissipative systems. The common methods of econometrics are based on an epistemological mistake and not only cannot explain but also cannot detect long waves or any type of historical processes.[26] The choice of the second option is therefore a sign of theoretical wisdom, and Mandel fought for such an alternative.

Quantitative and empirical research in the framework of the research programme on long waves is still in its infancy. Contradictory results on the long-term movement of the profit rate, such as those of Entov, Poletayev, Moseley, Duménil, Altvater or Shaikh, indicate that the methods are not robust, that there is a lack of information, and that the hypotheses are still being defined. Of course, the difficulties are immense, since conventional statistics is not suited to measurement in line with the Marxian concepts, and the theory is still not sufficiently developed to produce the conjectures to be tested. Some of these results are presented in Mandel's last book, and confirm at least that economies cannot be studied merely as an aggregate sum of factors, but that differences between branches are crucial in order to understand the evolution of profitability, the impacts of technological change and the profile of the mismatch between the social and economic subsystems.

In particular, Mandel's theory – and other models of the long waves based on the same type of assumptions – is centred on the concept of power or, more generally, of the coordinating aspect of economies and societies, which is at the heart of the pulsation of history, and this concept cannot be quantified. As a consequence, different combined methods are needed in order to understand real economies.

Capitalism may then be explained by two main tools: political economy, i.e., history, and the complexity approach, i.e., the formalization of the nonlinear, structurally unstable and creative relations in economies. Both methods challenge the certainties of neoclassical economics and attack its equilibrium mystique. Their combination is needed in order to develop both the programme's analytical capacity and its ability to explain real evolutionary processes. Ernest Mandel's work is one of the building blocks for such a coming-together.

Notes

1. The main articles by Nikolai Kondratieff, his whole statistical tables and technical comments and indications have been published in French by

Louis Fontvieille (N.D. Kondratieff, *Les Grands Cycles de la Conjoncture*, Paris 1992). An English edition, including a large collection of Kondratieff's works on other topics as well, is forthcoming, from Pickering & Chatto.

2. Leon Trotsky's report to the Comintern is published in *The First Five Years of the Communist International*, New York 1945, vol. 1, pp. 174–226. His critique of Kondratieff titled 'The Curve of Capitalist Development' can be found in *Problems of Everyday Life*, New York 1973, pp. 273–80.

3. Joseph Schumpeter, *Business Cycles*, New York 1939.

4. Van Gelderen only wrote one series of articles about long waves: 'Springvloed – Beschouwingen over Industrieele Ontwikkeling en Prijsbeweging' (1913) *Die Nieuwe Tijd*, no. 4, 5, 6, Amsterdam 1973. His ideas were developed later on by his friend De Wolff, but both wrote in Dutch and were generally unknown to their own and to the next generation of researchers. After publishing the paper, Van Gelderen did not write any more on the subject, and later on a tragic destiny interrupted his work (he committed suicide in 1940 when the Nazis invaded his country) and even the diffusion of his writings. Kondratieff and the other participants in the 1926 debate at the Moscow Conjuncture Institute did not know about the paper, which was not translated from Dutch and was published in English for the first time in Christopher Freeman, ed., *Long Wave Theory*, Aldershot 1996.

5. Alexander Parvus (1901), 'Die Handelskrisis und die Gewerkschaften' (Auszug), in Parvus et al., *Die langen Wellen der Konjunktur*, Berlin 1972.

6. His chronology of those changes in the trend was the following one: 1781–1851, 1851–1873, 1873–1894, 1894–1913, 1913– . . . This corresponds closely to the chronologies by previous authors, namely the Italians or Van Gelderen, probably unknown to Trotsky. The coincidence of so many authors on the chronology, although working independently, suggests the distinctive features of the historical developments of nineteenth-century capitalism.

7. It is interesting to note one of the previous (and unrelated to the present theme) discussions on structural stability and the applicability of multiple correlation methods to real historical data. At the end of the thirties, John Maynard Keynes sharply criticized Jan Tinbergen for his use of econometric methods for a ten years series, 1922–33, since those methods suppose some form of structural stability during the period studied. One may add that those arguments are still more relevant if the hypothesis of structural stability is extended to two hundred years.

8. In normal economic series, there are reasons to expect non-stationarity (from the general growth and changes in mean and in variance), and also auto-correlation (from the historical features of the series) and heteroscedasticity (the variation of variance from the structural changes represented by different regimes). The traditional way to deal with these characteristics, in order to allow for statistical tests, are punitive methods against data: transformations in order to eliminate non-stationarity and auto-correlation, and some weighting procedure in order to eliminate variations of variance. These methods are inadequate, lead to spurious results and contradict the evidence from historical analysis of real events.

116   THE LEGACY OF ERNEST MANDEL

It is also significant that the two men who shared the first Nobel Prize (1969) in economics, Ragnar Frisch and Jan Tinbergen, awarded for their decisive contributions to the foundation of the econometric programme, both accepted and supported the hypothesis of long waves in spite of the inability of the traditional econometric methods to prove their existence. History was considered therefore an alternative and authoritative proof.

9. Simon Kuznets, 'Schumpeter's *Business Cycles*', in *American Economic Review* 30, 1940, pp. 257–71; Oskar Lange, 'Schumpeter's *Business Cycles*', in *Review of Economic Statistics* 23, 1941, pp. 190–93.

10. See the example of Metz, who most emphatically declares that the world wars are 'outliers' of the statistical series and should be eliminated and ignored (Rainer Metz, 'A Re-examination of Long Waves in Aggregate Production Series', in Kleinknecht, Mandel and Wallerstein, eds., *New Findings in Long Wave Research*, London 1992, p. 110).

11. Ragnar Frisch, 'Propagation Problems and Impulse Problems in Dynamic Economics', in K. Koch, ed., *Economic Essays in Honour of Gustave Cassel*, London 1933, pp. 171–205.

12. From this point of view, there is a contradiction between mainstream economic models (referring causality to the endogenous mechanism generating equilibrium, i.e., generating no events at all) and the positivist foundation of the programme (which refers causality to the exogenous variables). This paradox is evident in Schumpeter's work on cycles and long waves. He tried to solve it with an eclectic combination of historical insights on the creation of novelty, emerging from path-breaking innovations and challenging the state of equilibrium, and traditional concepts on the convergence to equilibrium. Therefore, change is endogenous to the working of the capitalist system in the Schumpeterian scheme.

13. *Late Capitalism*, London 1975, p. 42.

14. In a private letter to the author (3 March 1995), Mandel argued that those 'partially autonomous variables' reflected the uncertainty and complex determination of social evolution, under historical constraints. Therefore, the set of variables includes some political factors as well as those economic factors which are by themselves part of the social conflict and real history.

15. Michael Kalecki, 'Trends and Business Cycles Reconsidered', in *Economic Journal* 78, 1968, pp. 262–76.

16. It is obviously the case of Marx's rate of profit, of Schumpeter's concept of innovation, or still of the three 'psychological laws' of Keynes (preference for liquidity, propensity to consume, the determinations of the marginal efficiency of capital). In orthodox macroeconomics the problem is also present, for instance under the form of the dual specification of investment as autonomous (exogenous) and induced (endogenous), therefore challenging the positivist requirement for unequivocal determination.

17.
Thus Mandel tries to develop a unified theory of economic and social/political science, based upon a dialectical (parametrical) concept of determinism as opposed to a mechanistic one. Such a concept of determinism integrates into the economic and social processes the possibility, nay the inevitability, of choice – but choice within certain

given constraints and choice, in the last analysis, determined by social interests which will remain conflicting ones unless a classless society can one day be established.

Mandel, in Arestis, Sawyer, eds., *A Biographical Dictionary of Dissenting Economists*, Aldershot 1992, p. 340.

18. Neither the origin nor the content of this concept are very clearly stated. In a private letter to the author (9 September 1994), Mandel presented the concept as the expression of the uncertainty of the fight for social power. Presumably, the concept was influenced by some important contemporary researches in biology and thermodynamics. Writing in the early eighties, Levins and Lewontin argued that the stability of an evolutionary system depended on the balance of the feedback processes and the parameters governing the rate of evolution and defining its boundaries. At the same time, Prigogine and Stengers argued that the evolution of the parameters of a system could create chaos and complexity, and therefore new forms of order. Both notions are inspired by the early work of Poincaré on nonlinear systems, and an attentive reader of Mandel should notice the importance of those concepts for social sciences. The introduction of complexity, time, uncertainty, order and disorder, destroys the linear and equilibrium world of traditional economics, where convergence to equilibrium is presented as the desirable property of the system, in spite of representing its entropic death. 'Parametric determinism' stresses the nature of the causation and the boundaries of social evolution, and argues for new research methods. The importance of Mandel's contribution, applied to the study of historical economic processes, derives evidently from the fact that it anticipated these works.

19. 'Partially Independent Variables and Internal Logic in Classical Marxist Economic Analysis', first published in *Social Sciences Information* 14(3), 1985, pp. 485–505; reprinted in Himmelstrand, Ulf, eds., *Interfaces in Economic and Social Analysis*, London 1992, pp. 33–50. Quotes from 1992, p. 37.

20. Ibid., p. 39.

21. Like any anticipatory and global analysis, Mandel's has some flaws. Several critiques have pointed out that he considered the 'third technological revolution' (beginning after the Second World War) to consist of nuclear energy, the automation process and electronics (*Late Capitalism*, pp. 120–21), whereas it is evident today that the first generations of electronics were not as important as the diffusion of consumer durables. Today (micro)electronics is preparing the ground for a new long-wave transition. But, of course, *Late Capitalism* was published just one year after the creation of the micro-processor, and the economic impact of the latter was clear only in the eighties or nineties. On the other hand, Mandel keeps the date of 1968 as the end of the phase A of the fourth long wave, implying a priority for the political criterion, since the crisis of the international monetary system and the general recession marking the end of the postwar boom only occurred some years later.

22. Angus Maddison, *Dynamic Forces in Capitalist Development*, Oxford 1991; Mandel, *Long Waves of Capitalist Development*, London 1995, p. 141, n. 19.

23. *Late Capitalism*, p. 139.
24. *Long Waves*, p. 82.
25. Ibid., p. 76.
26. Francisco Louçã, *Turbulence in Economics*, Aldershot 1997.

7

Ernest Mandel and the Marxian Theory of Bureaucracy

Charles Post

The emergence and growth of bureaucracy, the non-propertied offi-cialdom of various organizations, over the last two hundred years has been the subject of considerable discussion among social scientists. Conventional, bourgeois sociology argues that bureaucratic hierarchies are an unavoidable feature of modern societies, whose size and com-plexity preclude any possibility of popular democratic control over political, economic and social life. Max Weber saw bureaucracy as the most rational and effective mode of organizing the activities of large numbers of people because it ensured decision-making according to general rules rather than the whims of officials, cultivated trained 'experts', and reduced the possibilities of corruption and nepotism.[1] Robert Michels extended Weber's theory of bureaucracy, originally developed to analyze the officialdom of the capitalist state, to the study of the mass working-class parties and unions of the early twentieth century.[2] The 'iron law of oligarchy', today embraced by social demo-crats and neo-Stalinists, asserts that the growth and usurpation of power by a layer of full-time officials are inevitable features of mass working-class parties and unions under capitalism and of any post-capitalist social order.

Ernest Mandel's work provides a powerful Marxian alternative to Stalinist, social-democratic and bourgeois theories that deny the possi-bility of democratically organized workers' struggles and workers' power in the modern world. In a series of works,[3] Mandel presents a complex, coherent and empirically well grounded response to the notion that the arrogation of power by a minority of officials and experts is the 'inevitable' result of complex, large-scale, modern social organization. Mandel argues that bureaucracy is the product of specific, historically limited relations among human beings and between human beings and the natural world – of specific social relations and material forces of production. Mandel's theory of bureaucracy provides a contemporary defence, extension and deepening of the classical Marxist discussion of bureaucracy, in particular the work of Rosa Luxemburg and Leon Trotsky.

For Mandel, the emergence of bureaucracies in both the mass working-class parties and unions under capitalism and in the post-capitalist societies is rooted in the reproduction of the social division of labour between mental-supervisory and manual labour. Whether the product of the episodic character of working-class struggle under capitalism or of profound material scarcity in the case of twentieth-century post-revolutionary societies, the persistent division between 'head' work and 'hand' work gives rise to a layer of full-time officials who administer either mass parties and unions or the post-capitalist state apparatus. This layer, in most circumstances, evolves into a distinct social layer with its own material interests, politics, and ideology. The development of the bureaucracy does not enhance the 'efficiency' and effectiveness of mass workers' organizations under capitalism or of centrally planned economic life in the post-capitalist societies. Instead, the officialdom's monopoly of power *undermines* the ability of the working class either to defend its most immediate interests under capitalism or to build a viable alternative to capitalism. Mandel's theory of bureaucracy is one of the central scientific foundations of the revolutionary political project of working-class self-activity, self-organization and self-emancipation.

My discussion of Mandel's theory of bureaucracy is divided into three parts. In the first, I examine Mandel's analysis of the origins and role of the labour bureaucracy in capitalist social formations, and his theory of the revolutionary workers' organization as an alternative to bureaucratic reformism. I also assess Mandel's attempt to explain why, contrary to revolutionary Marxists' expectations, no truly mass revolutionary parties have emerged in the advanced capitalist countries since the 1920s. In the second part, I review Mandel's attempt to update and refine Trotsky's analysis of the bureaucracy in the post-capitalist societies. Specifically, I grapple with the issue of whether the bureaucracy's relationship with the working class constitutes a new mode of production, and whether these regimes can be understood as 'workers' states' in any meaningful, Marxian sense. I conclude with a discussion of the political importance of Mandel's theory of bureaucracy.

1. The labour bureaucracy in capitalist social formations

The classical Marxist discussion of the labour bureaucracy began as an attempt to explain the growth of reformism within the mass socialist parties of the early twentieth century. The leaders of the revolutionary left-wing of European socialism did not merely criticize the theory and practice of the mainstream of social democracy, but attempted to uncover the social and material roots of the labour movement's conservatism and ultimate capitulation to their national capitalist classes during the First World War. Given the Bolsheviks' practical revolutionary success, it was not surprising that Lenin's thesis on the degeneration of social democracy became, in Mandel's words, 'the "dogma" for revolutionary Marxists for nearly half a century'.[4] According to Lenin, the growth of reformism in the labour movement in the advanced capitalist countries was the ideological expression of the 'labour aristocracy,' a privileged minority of the Western working class whose superior standard of living came from a share of the 'super profits' extracted by the imperialist bourgeoisie in the colonies and semi-colonies. This layer of workers supported the 'petty-bourgeois intellectuals' in the party and union apparatus who propagated reformist and 'social patriotic' politics before and during the First World War.[5]

Mandel was the first thinker in the revolutionary Marxist tradition to reject explicitly the validity for the contemporary world of Lenin's notion of the 'labour aristocracy'. Mandel cites three important reasons for jettisoning the notion that a layer of workers in the imperialist countries share in the 'super-profits' extracted from workers in the 'third world'. First, the multinational corporations' total profits from their direct investments in Africa, Asia and Latin America cannot account for the wage bill of even the best paid, unionized workers in the industrialized countries. Put simply, workers in the 'third world' do not produce sufficient surplus value to 'bribe' a significant sector of the working class in Europe, the US or Japan. Second, the gap between the workers' wages in the 'North' and 'South' is much greater than wage differentials among workers in the 'North'. In other words, the entire working classes of Europe, the US and Japan are potential 'labour aristocracies'. But, Mandel points out, these global wage differentials are the result of the greater capital intensity (organic composition of capital) and higher productivity of labour (rate of surplus value) in the advanced capitalist social formations, not some sharing of 'super profits' between capital and labour in the industrialized countries. Put simply, the better paid workers of the 'North' are *more exploited* than the poorly paid workers of the 'South'. Finally, Mandel points out that some of the best paid workers in Europe, the US and Japan, especially those in the metal working industries, were among the most militant and radical proletarians, providing the mass base of the revolutionary Communist parties of the 1920s and early 1930s.[6]

Mandel found a more fruitful Marxian discussion of the labour bureaucracy under capitalism in the work of Rosa Luxemburg.[7] Luxemburg, well before either Lenin or Trotsky, understood that the emergence and development of the trade union and party officialdom was the key to German social democracy's growing conservatism.[8] In the wake of the Russian revolution of 1905, Luxemburg encountered opposition to her advocacy of the 'mass strike' as a tactic for the German workers' movement from both the openly 'revisionist' wing of the SPD led by Bernstein, and from the 'orthodox Marxist' leadership of the party around Kautsky and Bebel. She concluded that the full-time party and union officials' hegemony over the SPD, not simply the influence of middle-class intellectuals, was the root of the entire leadership's refusal to countenance any activities other than election campaigns and routinized collective bargaining. For Luxemburg, this bureaucracy, once consolidated in the mass working-class institutions, placed greater importance upon the preservation of the party and union apparatus than on any attempt to deepen and extend the workers' struggles.

Mandel located the origins of the labour bureaucracy in the episodic and discontinuous character of working-class struggle under capitalism. For Mandel, the necessary condition for the development of class consciousness is the self-activity and self-organization of the workers themselves. It is the experience of mass, collective and successful struggles against capital and its state in the workplace and the community that opens layers of workers to radical and revolutionary political ideas. When workers do not engage in mass struggle or suffer defeats, they become open to conservative and reactionary ideas as one section of the class makes a futile attempt to defend their particular sectional (national, occupational, racial-ethnic, gender) interests against other sectors of the working class. In sum, it is the level of class militancy and independence, not cultural influences like suburbanization, television, films and the like, that determines the basic parameters of class consciousness under capitalism.[9]

The working class cannot be, as a whole, permanently active in the class struggle. The entire working class cannot consistently engage in strikes, demonstrations and other forms of political activity because this class is separated from effective possession of the means of production and is compelled to sell its labour power to capital in order to survive. The 'actually existing' working class can only engage in mass struggles *as a class* in extraordinary, revolutionary or pre-revolutionary situations, which, because of the structural position of wage labour under capitalism, must be of short duration. Most of the time, different segments of the working class become active in the struggle against capitalism at different times.

In the wake of successful mass struggles, only a minority of the workers remain consistently active. Most of this 'workers' vanguard' – the layer of workers which 'even during a lull in the struggle . . . does not abandon the front lines of the class struggle but continues the war, so to speak, "by other means" '[10] – preserves and transmits to newer workers the traditions of mass struggle in the workplace or the community. However, a minority of this 'militant minority', together with middle-class intellectuals who have access to cultural skills from which the bulk of the working class is excluded, must take on responsibility for administering the unions or political parties created by periodic upsurges of mass activity. Mandel recognized that 'the development of mass political or trade-union organizations is inconceivable without an apparatus of full-timers and functionaries.' However, he points out that the emergence of a layer of full-time officials brings with it:

> . . . risk that working-class organizations will themselves become divided between layers exercising different functions. Specialization can result in a growing monopoly of knowledge, of centralized information. Knowledge is power, and a monopoly of it leads to power over people . . . if not checked, [this can] mean a real division between new bosses and the bossed-over mass.[11]

During the unavoidable lulls in the class struggle, when the vast majority of the working class is passive, the potential for bureaucratization is actualized. Especially during 'long waves' of capitalist growth, when most workers' living standards and working conditions improve without tumultuous, mass struggles, the officialdom of the mass workers' organizations can separate itself from the rest of the working class. Those workers who become officials of the unions and political parties begin to experience conditions of life very different from those who remain in the workplace. The new officials find themselves freed from the daily humiliations of the capitalist labour process. They are no longer subject to either deskilled and alienated labour or the petty despotism of supervisors. Able to set their own hours, plan and direct their own activities, and devote the bulk of their waking hours to 'fighting for the workers', the officials seek to consolidate these privileges and create new ones, in particular incomes substantially higher than those of the workers they purportedly represent. In defence of their privileges, which become quite substantial as the unions and mass working-class parties gain a place in bourgeois society, the labour bureaucracy excludes rank-and-file activists in the unions and parties from any real decision-making power.

The consolidation of the labour bureaucracy as a social layer distinct and separate from the rest of the working class under capitalism gives rise to its distinctive political practice and world-view. The preservation of the apparatus of the mass union or party, *as an end in itself*, becomes the main objective of the labour bureaucracy. The labour bureaucrats seek to contain working-class militancy within boundaries that do not threaten the continued existence of the institutions which are the basis of the officials' unique lifestyle. Thus the 'dialectic of partial conquests', the possibility that new struggles may result in the destruction of the mass organizations of the working class, buttresses the labour bureaucracy's reliance on electoral campaigns and parliamentary pressure tactics ('lobbying') to win political reforms, and strictly regimented collective bargaining to increase wages and improve working conditions. Any and all discussion, not to speak of attempts to promote the tumultuous self-activity and self-organization of working and oppressed people in the forms of militant workplace actions, mass political strikes or the like, must be quashed.[12] At this point, the bureaucracy's organizational fetishism (giving priority to the survival of the apparatus over new advances in the struggle) grows into a substitutionism that demands the workers' unquestioning obedience to leaders who claim they know 'what is best for the workers'.

As Mandel never tired of pointing out, the reformist substitution of electoral politics and routinized bargaining for mass struggles ignores 'the *structural character* of the basic relations of production and of political and social class power'.[13] In other words, the politics of the labour bureaucracies in the capitalist social formations are *utopian* in the most negative sense of the word.[14] The labour bureaucracy's attempts to broker the struggle between capital and labour, modifying very gradually the relationship of forces in favour of the workers, constantly flounders on capitalism's unavoidable crises of profitability and the resulting intensification of the class struggle. The history of both the classical social-democratic parties and the Communist parties after 1935, when they began their transformation into reformist parties,[15] sadly confirms the thoroughly unrealistic character of the bureaucracy's gradualism. During revolutionary and pre-revolutionary crises, like those in Italy in 1920, Germany during 1918–23, Spain and

France in 1936–37, and Chile in 1970–73, the social-democratic and Stalinist parties successfully disorganized the workers' struggles and organizations (workers' councils, factory committees and the like) in the name of preserving bourgeois democracy and the past conquests of the workers' movement. Unfortunately, the derailing of mass revolutionary struggles did not merely waste opportunities to seize state power and begin the construction of a new democratic and socialist order, but opened the road to the forces of reaction. The Italian fascists' victory in 1921, the Nazis' seizure of power in 1933, Franco's military victory in 1939, the collapse of the French Third Republic in 1940, and Pinochet's coup of September 11, 1973 were all the products of the working class's inability to seize power when the opportunity presented itself. In sum, the labour bureaucracy's attempt to 'self-limit' the workers' struggles within the boundaries of capitalist democracy facilitated the consolidation of dictatorial and repressive forms of capitalist rule.[16]

The reformist substitution of electoral campaigns, parliamentary pressure politics and bureaucratized collective bargaining for working-class and popular mass action has led to profound disorganization and passivity in the ranks of the labour movement in the West since the Second World War. While such bureaucratic forms of 'struggle' were able to 'deliver the goods' in the form of higher wages, improved benefits, stabilized working conditions and an expanding 'welfare state' during the 'long wave' of expansion of the 1950s and 1960s, this strategy proved completely inadequate during the 'long wave' of stagnation that began in the late 1960s. As the crisis of capitalist profitability deepened, reformism's substitutionism gave way to *realpolitik* – adapting to the new 'reality' of declining living and working conditions. As Mandel points out:

> . . . the underlying assumption of present-day social-democratic gradual-ism is precisely this: let the capitalists produce the goods, so that governments can redistribute them in a just way. But what if capitalist production demands more unequal, more unjust distribution of the 'fruits of growth'? What if there is no economic growth at all as a result of capitalist crisis? The gradualists can then only repeat mechanically: there is no alternative; there is no way out.[17]

Eschewing militancy and direct action by workers and other oppressed people, the labour bureaucracy and reformist politicians in the West have *no choice* but to make concessions to the employers' offensive and to administer capitalist state austerity. The spectacle of reformist bureaucrats shunning the struggle for reforms has been repeated across the capitalist world in the last two decades with tragic results: from the Italian Communist party's embrace of austerity, to the concession bargaining of the US AFL-CIO officials, to the Mitterrand regime's budget cuts, privatization and deregulation, to the subjugation of an ANC-COSATU-led government in post-apartheid South Africa, to what some have called the 'sado-monetarism' of the IMF and World Bank. Again, even the most moderate forms of social-democratic grad-ualism prove to be profoundly utopian – unable to defend the workers' past gains no less win significant new reforms during the crisis of capitalist profitability.[18]

Given its roots in the necessarily episodic character of mass struggle under capitalism, is the bureaucratization of the mass organizations of the working class inevitable? Clearly, Mandel's theory of the labour bureaucracy in the capitalist social formations leads us to the con-clusion that reformism will continue to be a problem in the workers' movement until capitalism is overthrown internationally. However, Mandel's theory also identifies countervailing social forces to, and safeguards against, the bureaucratization of the political parties and trade unions. In perhaps his greatest political-theoretical contribution, his elaboration and clarification of the Leninist theory of organiz-ation,[19] Mandel demonstrates how the same episodic process of class struggle that creates the environment for the growth of the labour bureaucracy provides the human material for a mass, revolutionary workers' party. Out of the ebbs and flows of the class struggle, a *workers' vanguard* is precipitated. The ability of a revolutionary socialist nucleus to organize and eventually fuse with the most active, militant and radical workers creates a variety of potential counter-weights to the labour bureaucracy.

In non-revolutionary periods, non-socialist organizations of 'advanced workers' in organized and unorganized workplaces – what in the US we call 'rank-and-file' currents – play an important role in keeping alive traditions of militancy and solidarity in the workers' movements and fighting for effective, democratic safeguards (election of officials, reduction of salaries, free debate and discussion of compet-ing positions, and so forth) in the unions and popular organizations. Often such organizations are able to displace the party and union bureaucracies and lead important successful day-to-day struggles that develop workers' political and ideological self-confidence. Even in non-revolutionary periods, relatively small revolutionary socialist groups play a crucial role in organizing these 'rank-and-file' currents and in educating the most radical workers in Marxian theory and politics. In revolutionary and pre-revolutionary conjunctures, the effective fusion of revolutionary nuclei with the broad vanguard of the class into a real revolutionary workers' party could open the possibility of socialist revolution. A mass revolutionary party with significant roots in the workers' movement can help promote the formation and centralization of organs of working-class power (councils in the neighbourhoods, workplaces, schools), pose a practical alternative to the reformist bureaucrats' attempts to limit the struggles within limits compatible with capitalist profitability and political power, and lead a successful seizure of power.[20]

The question remains, despite the evident inability of the bureaucracies in the unions and reformist parties to organize even the most elementary, defensive struggles against the employers' offensive and the capitalist austerity drive, why have we not seen the emergence of truly mass revolutionary parties since the 1920s? In the late 1930s, Trotsky and his supporters in the Fourth International believed that the Second World War would lead to a terminal crisis of bureaucratic rule in the USSR and a rapid collapse of the Stalinist Communist parties in capitalist Europe, opening the road to building new, mass revolutionary workers' organizations. Again in the late 1960s and early 1970s, with the beginning of the 'long wave' of economic stagnation and the tumultuous rise of workers' struggles across the capitalist world, revolutionary socialists inside and outside the Fourth International expected their relatively small organizations to grow rapidly and become rooted in the insurgent layers of the working class. Ernest Mandel was certainly not immune to the enthusiasm of this period:

> The essential function of the period from 1968 to the present day [c. 1977] has been to allow the far Left to accumulate sufficient forces to enter this revolutionary period with the realistic possibility of winning over the majority of the working class.[21]

The revolutionary left's optimism, often bordering on triumphalism, was sorely disappointed as the wave of mass strikes and pre-revolutionary upsurges of the early 1970s turned into the uninterrupted retreat of the working class across the industrialized world in the 1980s and early 1990s. As the capitalist offensive proceeded with few challenges, most of the generation of students and young workers radicalized in the late 1960s and 1970s abandoned revolutionary politics, and the promising revolutionary organizations of the earlier period stagnated or went into decline. The massive public-sector workers' strike in France, anti-austerity strikes in Canada, still fragmented industrial actions like the Dayton autoworkers' strike in the US, and other struggles during the past two years are examples of a possible new combativeness on the part of the working classes of advanced capitalism. However, these struggles must be weighed against the continuing success of the capitalist offensive across the capitalist world. They should not lead socialists to renewed predictions of imminent revolutionary upsurges.

Mandel in the late 1970s offered some tentative explanations for why the upsurge of the late 1960s and early 1970s had not transformed the European revolutionary left into organizations of several tens of thousands of worker revolutionaries. On the one hand, he pointed to what he saw as a temporary disorientation of the new 'militant minority' that had arisen in the European labour movement since 1968. The global recession of 1974–75 and the beginnings of the employers' offensive and austerity drive, coinciding with the defeat of the Portuguese Revolution,

> ... caught the working class unaware and unprepared ... I mean the bulwark of the working class, the vanguard, the organizing cadres, the shop stewards – all those comrades who have been in the forefront of the proletarian struggle in the past period. These comrades were well seasoned and experienced in mounting struggles to defend real wages against inflation, but they were not at all prepared for a fight against massive unemployment. This lack of experience was compounded by the total capitulation of the bureaucracy – the Communist Party in Italy and Spain, Social Democracy in most other countries – to the ideological and political aspects of the bourgeois offensive on this front ...[22]

However, Mandel believed that this working class 'has now been thrown onto the defensive temporarily'.[23] With nearly twenty years of hindsight, it is quite clear that Mandel gravely underestimated the setback suffered by the European workers' movement.

On the other hand, Mandel was aware of some of the cumulative effects of the transformation of the Communist parties into reformist organizations in the 1950s and 1960s. In particular, Mandel noted:

> ... the disappearance of an anti-capitalist tradition is a relatively recent phenomenon, one which accompanied the definitive turn of the Communist Parties in the industrially advanced countries at the end of the Second World War, and especially at the end of the Cold War. This sort of anti-capitalist education had continued even during the Popular Front ... Today, Social Democratic and Stalinist reformism are joining forces to keep the working class a prisoner of bourgeois and petty-bourgeois ideology. But any vision of the class struggle that focused exclusively on this aspect of reality would underestimate the almost structurally anti-capitalist mainsprings inherent in the class struggle during any phase of pronounced instability.[24]

Ultimately, the obstacles to the construction of a mass revolutionary party after 1968 were, in Mandel's opinion, of an extremely transitory character. In a relatively short period of time, he believed revolutionary organizations would be able to sink roots in the activist workers' vanguard and establish small mass parties with tens of thousands of members in the major capitalist countries.

As the 'temporary' setback of the workers' struggles in the late 1970s turned into the prolonged capitalist offensive of the 1980s and 1990s, Mandel's political co-thinkers in the Fourth International began to look at more long-term obstacles to the building of mass revolutionary parties in the advanced capitalist countries. In documents adopted at the last three World Congresses of the Fourth International there has been a recognition that the 1950s and 1960s saw a profound break in the history of the workers' vanguard. The notion that revolutionaries merely had to win over already militant, anti-capitalist workers from the existing bureaucratized parties has been replaced by a perspective that envisioned a gradual recomposition of the workers' vanguard through new mass defensive struggles. In the words of a resolution of the most recent World Congress of the Fourth International:

> . . . a new accumulation of mass experiences, partial victories and radical-
> ization of new generations is needed to bring together all the conditions
> for a new leap forward in building vanguard organizations that will be
> both revolutionary and internationalist. The crisis of the revolutionary
> vanguard can in fact no longer be posed in the terms of the 1930s. Today
> it is not only a matter of changing the bankrupt leaderships. The
> necessary recomposition will not be limited to a change in the balance of
> power within the organized workers' movement as it exists today. It has
> to go through the gradual reorganization of the different emancipatory
> social movements internationally. This will be a long process, which may
> be accelerated by certain big events in the world class struggle.[25]

Mandel's theory of bureaucracy and his analysis of the social and political transformation of the Western Communist parties actually hold the key to explaining the virtual disappearance of a massive layer of radical and revolutionary workers. Mandel, following Trotsky, saw the Seventh World Congress of the Communist International as the turning point in the evolution of the Stalinist parties in the advanced capitalist countries.[26] The 'Popular Front' strategy transformed the Communists parties politically and sociologically. Politically, the CPs adapted the traditional strategy of reformism – the defence of bourgeois democratic institutions as the best guarantors of the 'historic gains' of the labour movement. Sociologically, the 'Popular Front' helped launch a long process which culminated in the crystallization of labour bureaucracies closely enmeshed with the top leadership and much of the cadre of the Communist parties in France, Italy and (later) Spain. In other words, the CPs were transformed from parties of rank-and-file worker militants who actively organized in their workplaces against both the bureaucrats and the employers, into recruiting grounds for trade union and party functionaries. Combined with the effects of the long wave of economic expansion in the 1950s and 1960s, the social transformation of the Communist parties all but destroyed the traditions of militancy, solidarity, democracy and anti-capitalist radicalism defended by the mass workers' vanguard since the late nineteenth century. This new situation poses new and difficult tasks for revolutionary Marxists in the West. While continuing revolutionary socialist propaganda and education aimed at recruiting and training worker activists as Marxists, they must also play an active and leading role in reorganizing a workers' vanguard, around a 'class struggle', but not explicitly socialist, programme of militancy, solidarity, democracy and political independence.[27]

2. The bureaucracy in the post-capitalist societies

Mandel's theory of the Stalinist bureaucracies in the post-capitalist societies deepened Trotsky's pathbreaking Marxist analysis of the origins and contradictions of the bureaucratic rule of the Soviet Union.[28] The bulk of the Bolshevik leaders in the 1920s viewed the growth of the full-time officialdom in the post-revolutionary party and state, in Mandel's words, 'as a purely power-political, institutional . . . administrative problem' because of their 'substitutionist concept of the party-worker relationship: the dictatorship of the proletariat is exercised by the party under the leadership of its Leninist Central Committee.' In other words, most Russian revolutionaries saw the problem as one of 'bureaucratism' – inefficient administration and bad decision making by incompetent officials. In 1923, Trotsky was the first Marxist to understand

> . . . the transformation of . . . [the Soviet] bureaucracy into a specific
> social layer with its own particular material interests. The party apparatus
> defended its monopoly of political power as a means of defending and
> extending its own material interests.[29]

For Mandel, Trotsky's understanding of the *material* roots and character of the Stalinist officialdom enabled him to develop both a rigorous Marxian analysis of the dynamics and contradictions of the bureaucratized Soviet society, and a consistent political strategy, based on workers' revolutionary self-organization and self-activity, to oppose bureaucratic rule.

Mandel and Trotsky's theory of the bureaucratization of post-capitalist societies begins from Marx's assertion of the necessity of a phase of transition between capitalism and socialism.[30] To move immediately after the global (no less than a merely national) overthrow of capitalism (an economy of generalized commodity production and growing inequalities within and between societies) to socialism (an economy of democratic planning by the 'freely associated producers' where social inequality and the state are 'withering away') is impossible because capitalism prevents the even and steady development of labour productivity to its fullest potential. While the application of science and technology to the production process on a global scale in the late twentieth century would allow all humans' basic needs to be met relatively quickly and painlessly, this would require

> ... a *restriction of needs to the most elementary ones:* men would have to be content with eating just enough to appease their hunger, dressing quietly, living in a rudimentary type of dwelling, sending their children to schools of a quite elementary kind and enjoying only a restricted health service.[31]

In order for the entirety of humanity to enjoy a standard of living and, even more importantly, *a reduced working day* that will allow them to develop their fullest potential, eliminate economic inequalities and promote the 'withering away' of the state, a further development of the global productive forces is necessary. This, in turn, requires the preservation of certain norms of 'bourgeois distribution' – to each according to their *labour*, rather than their *needs*. The wage form, money, markets for certain consumer goods, and a state apparatus that ensures that all will work are necessary features of a society in transition to socialism. While the classical Marxist tradition believed that workers' democracy was possible and necessary to a successful transition, they also recognized that the maintenance of the state and 'bourgeois norms of distribution' carried with it the possibility of the development of new forms of social inequality and conflict. However, revolutionary Marxists before the mid-1920s believed that a rapid victory of a world socialist revolution, especially its spread to the most industrially advanced capitalist societies, would greatly reduce these dangers.[32]

The actual development of the world revolution in the twentieth century, the historic 'stalemate in the international class struggle'[33] that developed after 1923, confronted the revolutionary Marxist movement with a completely unexpected situation. Rather than beginning the global transition to socialism in a number of countries, including the more industrialized ones like Germany and Italy, the revolution was isolated in the most economically backward part of Europe, the former Russian empire. Russia's economic backwardness was compounded by the devastating effects of the civil war – the death of much of the generation of revolutionary workers who had made the October revolution, extensive destruction of the country's meagre industrial base and the dispersal of the bulk of the industrial proletariat to the countryside. The failure of the German and Italian revolutions, for which the social-democratic bureaucracies bear major responsibility, created a situation in Russia where all of the inherent contradictions in a transitional society – between socialized production and bourgeois distribution – were intensified.

The absence of the two main preconditions for a successful transition to socialism – material abundance and a large and concentrated proletariat – created the environment for the growth of the Soviet bureaucracy. A layer of full-time state and party officials separate from the mass of workers emerged first to administer the distribution of scarce goods and services among the population. During the civil war, the number of state and party officials began to grow, as the Soviets requisitioned grain from the peasants to feed the urban workers and Red Army, and attempted to organize the shrinking state-owned industries for war production. The party and state bureaucracy mushroomed in the 1920s under the New Economic Policy, which allowed for the revival of commodity production and circulation in both the cities and countryside. In the late 1920s and 1930s, the Soviet bureaucracy deepened its grip over the state institutions and state-owned means of production with the disastrous collectivization of agriculture and the creation of the 'command economy'. The bureaucracy, through its purge of the party and state apparatus in the late 1930s, dispersed and disorganized all opposition, particularly from the working class and peasantry, and consolidated its political power and enormous material privileges.[34]

Like Trotsky before him, Mandel emphasized the objective, material sources of the bureaucratization of the Soviet Union. On the one hand, the need for an agency 'above society' to distribute goods in a situation of extreme material scarcity provided a fertile environment for the growth of the party-state officialdom. On the other, the dispersal of the industrial proletariat through unemployment undermined the activist social base of Soviet democracy.[35] However, both Mandel and Trotsky recognized that the Bolsheviks made important subjective political errors that contributed to the victory of the Stalinist bureaucracy, particularly after the revolutionaries' victory in the civil war. Trotsky and Mandel argued that the decisions of the Tenth Congress of the Communist Party in 1921 – the blanket prohibition on all opposition parties from participation in the Soviets and the ban on opposition factions within the ruling party – 'hindered rather than promoted the self-activity of the Russian workers.'[36] These decisions undermined the ability of the Soviet workers, even the most politically active party members, from organizing themselves against the emerging bureaucracy, and gave these bureaucrats a potent ideological weapon against any and all opposition within and without the ruling party. As Trotsky recognized in 1937:

> The prohibition of parties brought after it the prohibition of factions. The prohibition of factions ended in a prohibition to think otherwise than the infallible leaders. The police-manufactured monolithism of the party resulted in a bureaucratic impunity which has become the source of all kinds of wantonness and corruption.[37]

In the last years of his life, Mandel forthrightly confronted the presence of unmistakably *substitutionist* elements in the politics of Lenin and Trotsky during the 'dark years' of 1920–1921.[38] While clearly embracing Marcel Liebman's characterization of pre-revolutionary Bolshevism as a stridently anti-substitutionist 'libertarian Leninism',[39] Mandel revealed how the Bolshevik leaders transformed violations of workers' democracy *necessitated* by the civil war into *political virtues*. Specifically, Lenin and Trotsky argued that temporary bans on opposition socialist parties, limitations of peasant and bourgeois suffrage, and empowering the *Cheka* to arrest, try and execute accused counter-revolutionaries without any political oversight were *necessary* and *desirable* features of proletarian rule. In numerous writings, both Lenin and Trotsky defended a clearly substitutionist conception of the relationship of the party and the working class. In *Terrorism and Communism* (which Mandel correctly declared 'his worst book'[40]) and his polemics against the Workers' Opposition, Trotsky proclaimed that the working class was a 'wavering mass' incapable of exercising its rule directly and democratically. In the same years, Lenin repeatedly described the mass of workers as hopelessly divided, with sectors (the 'labour aristocracy') corrupted by capital. In 1920–21, both proclaimed the party as the only force – even against the wishes and desires of the working class – capable of building socialism. Mandel did the revolutionary Marxist movement a great service by recognizing and *rejecting* this aspect of its tradition.

As in the case of the labour bureaucracy in the capitalist countries, the ruling officialdoms in the former Soviet Union and the other bureaucratic societies developed their own, substitutionist world-view and political practice. The 'dialectic of partial conquests' led the ruling bureaucracies in the East to embrace their particular version of 'organizational fetishism' – the belief that the preservation of existing state-party institutions took priority over self-organization and self-activity of the working class. Internally, the Stalinist and neo-Stalinist bureaucrats' substitutionism privileged the 'leading role of the party'. The ruling Communist parties were the sole legitimate representatives of the working class. They alone could defend the 'historic interests' of the working class against all enemies, including 'dissidents' and 'deviationists' from within the ranks of the working class itself. The substitutionist ideology of the ruling bureaucracies provided ready-made justifications for the brutal repression unleashed against the working class during the Soviet purges of the 1930s, the uprisings in East Germany, Poland and Hungary in the 1950s, the 'Prague Spring' in 1968, the mass strikes in Poland in 1971 and 1981, and the students and workers in Tiananmen Square in 1989. For the bureaucratic regimes, only the party, not the workers, was the ultimate guarantor of the 'true interests' of the proletariat.[41]

Externally, the ruling bureaucracies sought to subordinate the struggle of working people in other countries to the 'defence of socialism in one (choose your favourite) country'. Mandel extended Trotsky's analysis of the disastrous results of giving priority to the defence of some 'socialist fatherland' abroad over the actual struggles of the workers and oppressed at home. The Communist parties in Germany in 1933, France and Spain in 1936–37, Greece after the Second World War and in Indonesia in 1965 paid an extremely high price – massive repression and hundreds of thousands of militants murdered – for placing the diplomatic needs of the post-capitalist bureaucracies ahead of the needs of the class struggle in their own countries. Subservience to the ruling officialdoms in the East created the conditions for the gradual transformation of the French, Italian and Spanish Communist parties into reformist parties, and led to the collapse of much of the revolutionary left of the 1960s that looked to the Maoist bureaucracy for political guidance.[42]

Ultimately, the post-capitalist bureaucracies were incapable of consolidating a prosperous, attractive and stable alternative to capitalism. One of Mandel's major contributions has been his elaboration of Trotsky's insights into the limits of bureaucratic central planning:

The progressive role of the Soviet bureaucracy coincides with the period devoted to introducing into the Soviet Union the most important elements of capitalist technique ... It is possible to build gigantic factories according to a ready-made Western pattern by bureaucratic command – although, to be sure, at triple the normal cost. But the farther you go, the more the economy runs into the problem of quality, which slips out of the hands of a bureaucracy like a shadow ... Under a nationalized economy, *quality* demands a democracy of producers and consumers, freedom of criticism and initiative – conditions incompatible with a totalitarian regime of fear, lies and flattery.[43]

Mandel theoretically refined and empirically documented this thesis with extensive research.[44] By substituting the party-state officialdom for the democratic decisions of workers and consumers, the Stalinized command economies were (and are in the case of China) left without any mechanism for insuring the long-term and continuous development of labour productivity. The post-capitalist bureaucracies were capable of organizing *extensive* growth, forcing millions of uprooted peasants to labour in plants that reproduced the labour processes of the capitalist West, producing a 'one-time-only' increase in labour productivity. However, they floundered when faced with organizing *intensive* growth, the continuous replacement of labour with new technologies and production of new items of consumption. The bureaucracy lacked either the 'whip of competition' that ensures that each capitalist firm continuously reduces necessary labour through mechanization, or the democratic control over economic decisions by the 'freely associated producers and consumers' with an interest in reducing their labour time and insuring quality items of individual and collective consumption. As a result, the bureaucratic economies were under no economic or political compulsion to develop new techniques or economize on the use of resources. The result was 'a general lack of responsibility, and indifference to the factory's performance is therefore a characteristic feature of the system and threatens the USSR with stagnation and decline.'[45] The fate of the bureaucratic command economies in Eastern Europe and the former USSR tragically confirmed Mandel's and Trotsky's theses.

Unlike Trotsky, who confined himself to a general call for the restoration of soviet democracy through an anti-bureaucratic workers' revolution, Mandel presented a detailed model of democratic centralist economic planning. A global 'self-administered' economy would be founded upon democratic councils of producers and consumers. The officials of these councils would be elected by the entire adult population, would be subject to immediate recall and would be paid the average salary of a skilled worker. These democratic institutions of workers' power, created through anti-capitalist revolutions in the West and anti-bureaucratic revolutions in the East, would be articulated at the international, national, industrial and office, factory or neighbourhood level.

> Decisions should be taken at the level at which they can most easily be implemented. And they should be taken at the level where the greatest percentage of people actually affected by them can be involved in the decision-making process.[46]

Put simply, international and national bodies would be empowered to draw up the basic outlines of the economic plan, while industrial, regional or plant-office bodies would decide how to implement their particular parts of the plan in consultation with those who would consume their products.[47]

In order for democratic 'self-administration' to be effective, the working class must be able to express its needs and desires in the planning process and there must be mechanisms for the correction of social and economic miscalculations. According to Mandel, *political pluralism* is required to allow the working class, in all its heterogeneity, to effectively control the planning process. Without the right of all political currents (including ideologically pro-capitalist tendencies) to organize political parties, have access (in proportion to their numbers) to the media and to organize demonstrations and other non-violent actions to advance their particular viewpoints, central planning will not be able to utilize productive resources efficiently and raise the productivity of labour. Mandel also recognizes that formally democratic institutions and the rigorous guarantee of political rights for all sectors of the population, while *necessary* conditions for democratic socialist rule, are not *sufficient*. There are also crucial social and economic conditions, most importantly the radical reduction of working time for the mass of the population so that all 'have the time to administer the affairs of their workplace or neighbourhood'.[48] Such a reduction of the working day would allow most of humanity to spend three to four hours a day in the production of goods or provision of services and another three to four hours a day in the work of social self-administration. In order to abolish the division between mental and manual labour, the basis of bureaucracy, there must be generalized access to education, culture and literacy, which assumes a high level of material abundance and labour productivity. This, Mandel asserts, will only be possible when not only bureaucratic rule has been replaced in the East, but capitalism has been overthrown in a number of advanced industrial societies and their vast productive potential freed.[49]

Mandel, like Marx and Trotsky before him, recognizes that commodity production and circulation, the market, will survive for a considerable period after the overthrow of capitalism on a world scale. Mandel agrees with Alec Nove, the most sophisticated theorist of 'market socialism', that 'the radical suppression of residual market relations' in any of the post-capitalist societies was not 'presently desirable or practical'. In fact, Mandel sees elements of Nove's model of 'feasible socialism' as similar to his own conception of the combination of market and plan in a democratically ruled society in transition to socialism.[50] Mandel's disagreement with the 'market socialists' is with their claim that commodity production was a permanent and unalterable feature of economic life. For Nove, the complexity of economic decisions in an industrialized economy and the 'unlimited wants' of human beings makes the abolition of scarcity, the foundation of commodity production, impossible.

The withering away of the market is possible for two reasons according to Mandel. First, a system of 'articulated self-management' could allocate most of the thousands of decisions necessary to a planned economy to different democratically organized bodies, overcoming the problem of 'too many decisions'. Second, it is possible to envision a 'saturation of demand' for goods and services once basic material needs are satisfied. Mandel rejects the simplistic notion of 'human nature' that underlies both neo-classical economics and the theories of 'market socialism':

> The continual accumulation of more and more goods . . . is by no means a universal or even predominant feature of human behaviour. The development of talents and inclinations for their own sake; the protection of health and life; care for children; the development of rich social relations as a prerequisite of mental stability and happiness – all these become major motivations once basic material needs have been satisfied. One has only to look at how the upper reaches of the bourgeoisie conduct themselves with regard to food, clothing, housing, furniture or 'cultural goods' to note that for those who already 'live under communism', rational consumption takes the place of a restless pursuit of more.[51]

Mandel, responding to the rise of the environmental movements of the last twenty-five years, incorporates a detailed discussion of the relationship of different forms of social and economic organization to the natural environment. He addresses two objections to the Marxian vision of socialism raised in the 'Green' analysis of the rape of the environment in both capitalist and bureaucratic economies. Various 'Green' theorists argue that the Marxian vision of a future society based upon the abolition of material scarcity would place an unbearable strain on the physical resources of the planet and lead to an ecological disaster. Mandel points to the scale of socially wasted resources under both capitalism and the bureaucratic command economies. The immediate abolition of the arms industry alone would free up tremendous resources for socially useful production (based upon renewable energy sources, environmentally safe technologies, and so forth) that could provide an adequate standard of living for the bulk of the world's population without thrusting new demands upon the finite capacities of the planet. As the basic, material needs for physical security and gratification (food, clothing, shelter, medical care, education) are met, priority could be given to meeting the non-material needs for 'self-actualization' (cultural, political, intellectual and personal development), needs whose satisfaction do not require utilizing finite natural resources.

The second 'Green' critique of Marxism, based upon the experience of ecological disaster in the former USSR and Eastern Europe, claims that centrally planned economies are no more ecologically friendly than market-capitalist economies. For Mandel, the destruction of the environment in the East flowed from the same bureaucratic mismanagement that gave rise to systematic waste of labour power and other resources. In other words, the absence of any democratic accountability on the part of central planners and industrial managers allowed them to systematically befoul the physical environment in the East. By contrast, a democratically planned economy has the potential to avoid the ecological disasters that characterize both capitalism and the bureaucratic command economies. Workers and consumers actively involved in formulating and implementing an economic plan have a compelling interest in developing labour processes that will neither destroy the health of those directly involved in production, nor foul the air and water that all must breathe and drink. In addition, the possibility of democratic 'self-correction' would minimize environmental damage that might ensue from workers attempting to raise their standard of living without consideration of its effects on future generations.[52]

Mandel's elaboration and extension of Trotsky's theory of the post-capitalist bureaucracies not only provides a powerful alternative to liberal, social-democratic and Stalinist theories of bureaucracy, but to other Marxian theories as well. In particular, Mandel has produced an extensive critique of the theory that the former USSR, Eastern Europe and China were 'state capitalist' social formations.[53] The notion that economies where the main means of production are allocated according to conscious planning decisions, however bureaucratically mismanaged, and not according to differential profit rates and prices of production; where labour power is no longer a commodity and a state monopoly of foreign trade mediates the effects of global capitalist competition on the planned economy are capitalist is theoretically and empirically untenable. This theory, as Mandel pointed out numerous times, does violence both to the Marxian theory of capitalist accumulation and the empirical reality of the bureaucratic economies.[54]

Mandel's critique of the other major alternative Marxian theory of the bureaucratic regimes, the theory of 'bureaucratic collectivism', is not as rigorous as his dissection of the theory of 'state capitalism'. For Mandel, like Trotsky, the bureaucracy in the post-capitalist societies is a *caste*, a social layer that, unlike a social class, plays no necessary role in social production. The 'parasitic' relationship between the bureaucracy and the planned economy deprives these post-capitalist societies of the social coherence of an established mode of production. Since the late 1930s, various Marxist critics of Stalinism have challenged this theory, arguing that the bureaucracy was a new exploiting class that organized a new, post-capitalist mode of production in the former USSR and the Eastern bloc countries.[55] The theory of 'bureaucratic collectivism' has been held by a wide variety of revolutionary socialists, including many prominent anti-bureaucratic activists in the former Eastern bloc.[56] Its theoretical attraction is not surprising. On the one hand, it avoids the problems of the theory of 'state capitalism'. On the other it avoids the complexities and ambiguities of Mandel and Trotsky's theory of a 'transitional society' by situating the bureaucracy and the command economy in the familiar Marxian categories of class and mode of production.

Mandel offers two different criticisms of the theory of bureaucratic collectivism. The first and, in my opinion, the weaker response points to the survival of commodity production and circulation in the bureaucratic economies. The survival of the wage form, the impact of the world market, and so forth are features of *any* transitional society, and run counter to the logic of planning. Thus, these economies are:

> . . . a *hybrid combination* of an allocative and a commodity-producing economy, in which the law of value operates but does not hold sway. And this influence of the law of value *ultimately sets immovable limits to bureaucratic despotism.* This is what theorists of 'bureaucratic collectivism' . . . fail to see . . . *For a 'new', 'bureaucratic' non-capitalist mode of production to emerge,*

the Soviet bureaucracy would have to have liberated itself once and for all from the influence of the law of value.[57]

This line of argument is open to several important criticisms. First, Mandel and Trotsky's notion that the bureaucracy's privileges and power are derived primarily from the survival of 'bourgeois norms of distribution' is problematic. Much of the bureaucracy's substantially higher standard of living compared to the working class was not derived from their superior incomes and market access to commodities. It was instead based upon their political power, derived from their command of the state apparatus and the state-owned means of production, to gain preferential *non-market, non-commodity* access to consumer goods through special stores and 'jumping the queue' for relatively scarce consumer goods like cars, housing, and so forth.

Second, and more importantly, there have been numerous societies where non-capitalist modes of production coexisted with quite extensive commodity circulation and where '*the privileges of the dominant classes . . . are mainly confined to the realm of private consumption, [and] they have no long-term interest in a sustained increase in productivity.*'[58] European feudalism, slavery in both classical antiquity and the so-called 'new world', and the various 'Asiatic' societies all allowed for, and in some cases promoted, extensive commodity production, although not the generalized commodity production possible only under capitalism. These same modes of production were dominated by exploiting classes whose privileges were confined to private consumption, and who were unable to organize the labour process of their direct producers in a manner that allowed for sustained increases in productivity. In fact, it is only under capitalism that the ruling class's privileges extend to *real possession* of the means of production – the ability to organize the labour process. Thus, the bourgeoisie is the first ruling class in world history to be both capable of and compelled to continually raise the productivity of labour through mechanization.[59]

The introduction of 'market mechanisms' into the bureaucratic command economies during the past twenty-five years has demonstrated the possibility of combining 'market' and 'plan' without undermining bureaucratic privilege and power. The ruling officialdom in Yugoslavia, Poland, Hungary, China and the former USSR all introduced 'market reforms' at different points in the last forty years in attempts to overcome the chronic stagnation of labour productivity in the Eastern bloc. As we know, these reforms were singularly ineffective in either stimulating intensive economic development or lessening bureaucratic despotism. If anything, market mechanisms enriched the bureaucracy and sharpened its antagonism with the working class and peasantry without forcing productive units to introduce new labour processes or use materials more efficiently.[60] In sum, while the combination of planning and commodity production is a *necessary* feature of every society in transition from capitalism to socialism, the combination of plan and market is not a *sufficient* basis for rejecting the notion that a new mode of production developed in the former USSR, Eastern Europe and China.

Mandel's second and stronger critique of the bureaucracy as a 'new ruling class' points to the profound contradiction between bureaucratic power and the logic of effective economic planning.[61] First, the bureaucracy has a 'parasitic' relationship to economic planning – it is theoretically unnecessary to a planned economy. The working class could quite as easily organize a planned economy without a privileged layer of officials, although at least initially not without specialists and technicians. By comparison, one cannot conceive of an economy of generalized commodity production without capitalists.

Second, the bureaucracy's attempt to enrich itself undermines the effectiveness of the planning process. At every level of the command economy, bureaucrats systematically hide resources, whether labour power, raw material or machinery, in order to meet production targets and obtain bonuses in the form of cash or access to better housing, vacations and the like. Bureaucratic secrecy makes effective economic planning impossible. Without realistic information about resources and productive capacity it is impossible to set realistic production targets. By contrast, the bourgeoisie's efforts to enrich itself deepen the conditions of capitalist competition as each capitalist attempts to undercut all others and increase market share by lowering costs. The individual self-interest of the capitalist *coincides* with the operation of the law of value, but the individual self-interest of the bureaucrat *runs counter* to the logic of economic planning.

Finally, the contradictions between the privileges of the bureaucracy and the logic of planning deprives the bureaucratic economies of any *internally generated dynamic of crisis and recovery*. When the bureaucracy's privileges undermined the effectiveness of planning, leading to declining rates of growth in the 1970s and 1980s, there was no mechanism internal to the bureaucratic economy that could resolve the crisis. Only a profound shift in the relationship of social forces politically, either a workers' anti-bureaucratic revolution or capitalist restoration, could establish the conditions for renewed growth. Capitalism's inherent drive to replace human labour generates declining profit rates and periodic 'long waves' of economic crisis. However, capitalism generates its own solution to these prolonged crises. The massive destruction of inefficient capitals and 'redundant' labour during an economic collapse restores the conditions of profitable accumulation and sparks a new 'long wave' of expansion.[62] Thus, there are no 'terminal crises' of capitalism. The rule of capital, like that of the feudal aristocracy and other ruling classes rooted in modes of production, must be *overthrown*. The strongest historical validation of Trotsky and Mandel's thesis that the former USSR and Eastern European regimes were not rooted in a new mode of production was the rapidity with which they collapsed in 1989–91. Bureaucratic rule in these societies was not overthrown by either the working class or imperialism, but *imploded* as a result of chronic economic stagnation. Not surprisingly, the social formations that emerged in Eastern Europe and the former Soviet Union have yet to make a successful transition to capitalism.

While Mandel and Trotsky's theory of the 'transitional' character of the post-capitalist societies remains convincing, their claim that these regimes were 'bureaucratized' forms of the proletarian dictatorship is open to question.[63] Through the early years of the Russian revolution, revolutionary Marxists generally equated the workers' state with highly democratic forms of popular participation and power, in particular with the Paris Commune of 1871 and the workers', soldiers' and peasants' councils that had arisen in Russia, Germany, Hungary and Italy between 1917 and 1921.[64] The defeat of the central and western European revolutions and the devastation of the civil war undermined the viability of the Russian soviets as organs of popular power. For Lenin and Trotsky, the working-class character of the Russian state was preserved in the Communist party, which organized the most active and radical workers. However, the 'rule of the party' proved an inadequate basis for preserving even an indirect form of workers' self-government. The decline of party democracy after the 1921 ban on factions and the consolidation of the party-state bureaucracy in the late 1920s transformed the Soviet Communist party into the political instrument of the Stalinist officialdom.

By the late 1930s, Trotsky argued that the Soviet Union remained a workers' state, despite the 'political expropriation' of the working class, because the bureaucracy continued to defend the social and economic 'conquests of the October Revolution' – nationalized property, central planning and a state monopoly on foreign trade. The Soviet regime was a form of 'bonapartism', similar to both feudal absolutism, where the aristocracy ceded power to a royal bureaucracy that preserved feudalism, and fascism, where the bourgeoisie ceded power to a petty-bourgeois faction that safeguarded the conditions of capitalist accumulation. Thus, the mainstream of the Trotskyist movement, including Mandel, saw the USSR, and later Eastern Europe, China and Vietnam, as 'bureaucratized workers' states' where the working class *ruled* but did not *govern*.[65]

There are compelling theoretical reasons for maintaining the theory of the 'bureaucratized workers' states'. Most importantly, the traditional Trotskyist conception is consistent with the fundamental Marxian axiom that every society torn by social conflicts, no matter how unstable and transitional, is ruled by a single social class. As Perry Anderson argued, Trotsky's interpretation of Stalinism

> . . . provides a theory of the phenomenon of Stalinism in a long *historical* temporality, congruent with the fundamental categories of classical Marxism. At every point in his account of the nature of the Soviet bureaucracy, Trotsky sought to situate it in the logic of successive modes of production and transitions between them, with corresponding class powers and political regimes, that he inherited from Marx, Engels or Lenin . . . Because he could think of the emergence and consolidation of Stalinism in a historical time-span of this epochal character, he avoided the explanations of hasty journalism and improvised confections of new classes or modes of production, unanchored in historical materialism, which marked the reaction of many of his contemporaries.[66]

These strengths, however, conceal profound problems with the concept of a 'workers' state' where the workers rule, but do not govern. The analogy with feudal absolutism and capitalist dictatorships tends to obscure the *differentia specifica* of the transition to socialism. First, neither the feudal nor capitalist modes of production emerged from the struggles of classes self-consciously attempting to create new forms of society. Instead, feudalism and capitalism arose out of the struggles of already propertied classes to consolidate and extend their class domination. Socialism, by contrast, is the first form of society created in a conscious struggle by a *propertyless* social class, the working class. Further, both feudalism and capitalism are reproduced through a 'blind economic logic' that operates 'behind the back' of both the economically dominant classes and the direct producers. The feudal aristocracy and the bourgeoisie can remain socially dominant without directly dominating the state. Socialism is the first form of society based on conscious and deliberate planning of economic development. These profound differences between socialism and all previous forms of social labour led Mandel to argue in his last major work:

> *There is no way in which the working class can rule without governing.* It has to exercise power simultaneously within enterprise and branch, municipality

and region, as well as at the aggregate levels of the state and the national economy, if it is to 'rule' in any real and direct sense of the word: to take the key decisions about economic, social, and cultural priorities in the allocation of scarce resources. Thus, the functional division of the proletariat, between those who "professionally exercise power" and the mass of the class, sets in motion a social process which suppresses the direct collective rule of the class as such.[67]

Here Mandel provided compelling reasons for rejecting the analogy between absolutism, fascism and bureaucratic rule upon which he and Trotsky had based their notion of a 'bureaucratized workers' state'.

In other writings, Mandel attempted to defend the 'bureaucratized workers' state' theory by arguing that the Stalinist bureaucracy was a privileged layer of the working class which had usurped power from the rest of the class. First, he claimed that the bureaucracy derived most of its privileges in the form of wages:

> . . . the bureaucracy, since it does not own the means of production, participates in distribution of the national income exclusively as a function of remuneration for its labour-power. This entails many privileges, but it is a form of remuneration that does not differ qualitatively from remuneration in the form of a salary.[68]

This claim is open to two criticisms. First, as we have already seen, the bureaucracy secures much of its greater levels of consumption through *non-wage, non-market* access to consumer goods. The officialdom's access to special stores, *dachas* and the like derives from its political power – its domination of the state apparatus and control over state-owned means of production. Second, the wage form, while a *necessary* characteristic of the working class, is not *sufficient* to define a social group as part of the proletariat. In the capitalist social formations, top- and middle-level corporate executives receive salaries. Even when these executives do not own stock (although most do), they are part of the capitalist class because they command the labour power of others and dispose of the means of production. Similarly, it can be argued that a much larger layer of wage-earners – low-level supervisors, technicians and professionals – are not part of the working class in advanced capitalism. Many contemporary Marxists view these groups as forming a new middle class, produced by the concentration and centralization of capital and the systematic application of science to production under capitalism.[69]

Mandel also argues that the post-capitalist bureaucracy is a layer of the working class because of the ease by which individual workers move into the bureaucracy.

> For it is absolutely certain that a good number of today's bureaucrats, in
> this broad and real sense of the term, are not merely the sons and
> daughters of workers but even former workers themselves . . . The particu-
> lar structure of society in the Soviet Union enables the bureaucracy to
> absorb the sons and daughters of workers, and even workers themselves,
> into the apparatus. Not into the summits of the apparatus, but into
> positions much higher than those of the so-called middle classes in the
> advanced capitalist countries.[70]

Granting much higher, but clearly slowing, rates of upward social
mobility between the working class and the bureaucracy in the East
than between the working and capitalist classes in the West,[71] this
argument remains theoretically unconvincing. From a Marxian perspective, classes are defined by their objective relationship to social
production, not the social origins of their members. Put simply, contemporary capitalist societies could experience a significant increase in
social mobility – the wholesale proletarianization of the bourgeoisie
and the bourgeoisification of a small minority of the working class –
without altering the structural relationship between capital and wage
labour. The fact that many, or even most, post-capitalist bureaucrats
came from the working class did not make the officialdom part of the
proletariat.

This discussion of the post-capitalist bureaucracy leaves us in a
difficult theoretical position. On the one hand, there is little theoretical
or empirical basis for the notion that the bureaucracy is a new social
class based in a new mode of production. The post-capitalist command
economies were transitional societies, whose progress toward socialism
was blocked by the rule of an officialdom whose power and privileges
made effective economic planning impossible. On the other hand, it is
extremely difficult to argue that the bureaucratic regimes were
'deformed' forms of the proletarian dictatorship. The working class in
the East neither ruled nor governed, and the bureaucracy was not a
'layer' of the working class. This leaves us unable to identify what class
ruled the former USSR, Eastern Europe and China. At best, it could be
said that these societies were 'historical abortions', the product of the
'global stalemate of the class struggle' in the twentieth century. They
were highly unstable, transitional societies governed by bureaucracies,
who excluded the working classes from any real or formal social and
political power, but were not themselves ruling classes. Their rapid
implosion in 1989–91 demonstrated their profound instability and the
bureaucracy's thoroughly 'parasitic' character. This is the best understanding Marxists can have of these societies based upon the experience of their actual historical evolution. Further theoretical

clarification would require the emergence of new bureaucratized transitional societies, which would bring additional 'raw material' to this theory. For that reason, we have reason to hope this is a theoretical issue that will never be settled decisively.

3. Conclusion: the necessity of working-class self-emancipation and workers' democracy

Mandel, working from the foundation provided by Luxemburg and Trotsky, has provided us with the most theoretically rigorous and empirically well-founded Marxian discussion of bureaucracy to date. Mandel's analysis of the labour officialdom under capitalism and the ruling bureaucracy in the post-capitalist social formations is a powerful alternative to the liberal, social-democratic and Stalinist theories that claim that the rule of a full-time corps of non-propertied officials is an unavoidable feature of modern society. Rather than an unavoidable development in human history, bureaucracy is the product of specific and historically transitory social relations and material forces of production.

Mandel does much more than demonstrate that democratic self-organization of the working class in both capitalist and post-capitalist societies is *possible*. His theory of bureaucracy, together with his investigations into the dynamics of capitalist accumulation in the twentieth century, points to the *necessity* of working-class self-emancipation as the only basis for human liberation and survival. The notions that the labour bureaucrats can defend the gains of workers under capitalism or that the ruling bureaucracies can construct a viable alternative to capitalism have proven to be thoroughly *utopian*. The material position and self-interest of the reformist bureaucracies in the West have led them to disorganize and demobilize the working class and surrender, practically without a struggle, most of the hard-fought-for gains of the past half-century. The material position and self-interest of the ruling bureaucracies in the East have led them to undermine the planning process and waste precious human and natural resources. In short, the failure of bureaucratic strategies for gradually reforming capitalism or building an authoritarian alternative to it has necessarily floundered on the *social position of the bureaucracies in both the capitalist and post-capitalist social formations*.

Mandel's theory of bureaucracy is one of the central *scientific* foundations of the revolutionary socialist political project in the late twentieth century. The contention that the self-activity and self-organization of the working class provide the only *possible* basis for stemming the current capitalist offensive, overthrowing the rule of capital and constructing an alternative collectivist social order flows directly from Mandel's theory of the social-democratic and Stalinist bureaucracies. Not good will, democratic idealism or a commitment to an egalitarian morality alone, but a *scientific understanding of the role of the officialdom of the workers' movement and post-capitalist societies* is needed to defend working-class self-emancipation as the only *practical* alternative to capitalist barbarism.[72]

Notes

1. Max Weber, *Economy and Society: An Outline of Interpretative Sociology*, Berkeley 1979, vol. 2, chapter XI.
2. Robert Michels, *Political Parties: A Sociological Study of the Oligarchical Tendencies of Modern Democracy*, New York 1962 (originally published in German in 1911).
3. For our purposes, the three most important works are: *Marxist Economic Theory*, vol. 2, chapter 15; 'What is the Bureaucracy?' in T. Ali, ed., *The Stalinist Legacy: Its Impact on 20th Century World Politics*; *Power and Money: A Marxist Theory of Bureaucracy*.
4. 'What is the Bureaucracy?', p. 75.
5. Lenin's theory of the 'labour aristocracy' flows from his theory of 'monopoly capitalism'. See: V.I. Lenin, *Imperialism: The Highest Stage of Capitalism: A Popular Outline*, chapter 8 in *Selected Works*, vol. 1, Moscow 1970.
6. Mandel's critique of Lenin's theory of the 'labour aristocracy' is found in 'What is the Bureaucracy?', pp. 75–76. Mandel's thinking on the roots of wage differentials between workers in the 'third world' and the industrialized capitalist societies underwent considerable evolution. In *Marxist Economic Theory* (New York 1970, vol. 2, pp. 453–9), Mandel argued that the low wages of workers in the underdeveloped capitalist countries account for the low organic composition of capital and low rate of exploitation in these societies. In *Late Capitalism* (London 1975, pp. 359–64) Mandel argued, correctly in my opinion, that the uneven development of fixed capital and labour productivity is the cause of global wage differentials.

   More recent discussions of the theory of the 'labour aristocracy' and wage differentials have rejected the idea that 'monopoly' or 'oligopoly' – the absence or limitation of competition – is the root of wage differentials. Instead, wage differentials are the result of real capitalist competition, which necessarily gives rise to different degrees of capital intensity within and between branches of production. See Samuel Freidman, 'The Theory of the Labor Aristocracy', *Against the Current* (Old Series) 2,3, Fall 1983; and 'Structure, Process and the Labor Market', in William Darity Jr., *Labor Economics: Modern Views*, Hingham (MA) 1983; Howard Botwinick, *Persistent Inequalities: Wage Disparity Under Capitalist Competition*, Princeton 1993.

7. 'What is the Bureaucracy?', pp. 72–5.

8. Luxemburg's most important work in this regard is *The Mass Strike, The Political Party and the Trade Unions*, New York 1971.

9. Mandel's theory of class consciousness is presented at length in 'The Leninist Theory of Organization: Its Relevance for Today' in S. Bloom, ed., *Revolutionary Marxism and Social Reality in the 20th Century: Collected Essays of Ernest Mandel*, Atlantic Highlands (NJ) 1994, pp. 80–91. A similar argument is made in J. Brenner and R. Brenner, 'Reagan, the Right and the Working Class', *Against the Current* (Old Series) 1,2, Winter 1981, pp. 29–35.

10. 'Leninist Theory of Organization', p. 85.

11. *Power and Money*, p. 60.

12. Clearly, the labour bureaucracy is not monolithic. Mass struggles have led to splits among the leaders of the unions and reformist parties in which a wing of the officialdom attempts to take leadership of a wave of working class struggles. However, this realignment of a sector of the officialdom is generally a response to independent organization and initiatives 'from below' (rank and file currents in the unions, and so forth) often led by radicals and revolutionaries. The 'rebel' bureaucrats attempt to intervene in these struggles to contain them within the boundaries of reformist politics. This was clearly the case with John L. Lewis's role in the emergence of mass industrial unionism in the US during the 1930s. It may also have been the likely background to the role of Carl Legien and other social-democratic union officials in arming and mobilizing German workers to defeat the Kapp Putsch in 1920. On the US case see A. Preis, *Labor's Giant Step: Twenty Years of the CIO*, New York 1964, Part 1; M. Davis, 'The Barren Marriage of American Labor and the Democrats', *New Left Review* (hereafter NLR) 124, November/December 1980, pp. 46–54. On the German case see C. Harman, *The Lost Revolution: Germany, 1918 to 1923*, London 1982, chapter 8.

13. *Power and Money*, p. 235 (emphasis in the original).

14. I am using 'utopian' in the same sense that Marx and Engels used it in relationship to the pre-Marxian socialists, and Trotsky used it in relationship to the Stalinist notion of 'socialism in one country': a strategy for social change that is not based on a realistic, *scientific* understanding of the dynamics of the capitalist mode of production and the class struggle.

    Mandel did recognize there was a positive aspect to 'utopianism': the ability to imagine a better, more democratic, egalitarian and collectivist social order as a spur to revolutionary struggle. See *Power and Money*, pp. 232–5. See also Michael Löwy, *On Changing the World: Essays in Political Philosophy from Karl Marx to Walter Benjamin*, Atlantic Highlands (NJ) 1993.

15. On the social-democratization of the Western European Communist Parties, see Mandel, *From Stalinism to Eurocommunism: The Bitter Fruits of 'Socialism in One Country'*, London 1978, chapter 1.

16. See F. Claudin, *The Communist Movement: From Comintern to Cominform*, vol. 1, New York 1975.

17. *Power and Money*, p. 236.

18. Mandel discusses this dynamic in detail in 'The PCI and Austerity' in *From Stalinism to Eurocommunism*, pp. 125–49. For a similar analysis of the contra-

dictions of reformism, see Robert Brenner, 'The Paradox of Reformism', *Against the Current* 43, March–April 1993.

19. 'The Leninist Theory of Organization.'
20. One of the best presentations of this strategy, despite its grossly over-optimistic estimation of the short- and medium term possibility of revolution in Western Europe in the late 1970s is Mandel, 'Socialist Strategy in the West', in *Revolutionary Marxism Today*, London 1977, chapter 1.
21. 'Socialist Strategy in the West', p. 42.
22. Ibid., pp. 48–9.
23. Ibid.
24. Ibid., p. 61.
25. 'Building the Fourth International Today', *Documents of the 14th World Congress of the Fourth International*, Special Issue, *International Viewpoint*, Spring 1996, p. 58.
26. *From Stalinism to Eurocommunism*, pp. 17–22.
27. This argument is presented in much greater detail in C. Post and K.A. Wainer, *Socialist Organization Today*, Solidarity pamphlet, Detroit (MI) 1997.
28. The most complete statement of Trotsky's mature analysis of the Soviet bureaucracy is *The Revolution Betrayed: What is the Soviet Union and Where Is It Going?*, New York 1977 (originally published 1936). For an excellent overview of the development of Trotsky's theory of the Soviet bureaucracy, see Perry Anderson, 'Trotsky's Interpretation of Stalinism', in Ali, ed., *The Stalinist Legacy*, pp. 118–28.
29. Mandel, *Trotsky As Alternative*, London 1995, p. 41.
30. Marx's discussion of the necessity of a transitional phase between capitalism and socialism is contained in his brief 'marginal notes' on the 1875 programme of the German Workers' Party, *Critique of the Gotha Programme*, New York 1938. Trotsky's more elaborate discussion of the transition is found in *Revolution Betrayed*, chapter 3. For Mandel's contribution to this discussion, see *Marxist Economy Theory*, vol. 2, chapter 16.
31. Mandel, *Marxist Economic Theory*, vol. 2, p. 608 (emphasis in the original).
32. On the near unanimity of the leadership of the Communist International, prior to 1923, on the impossibility of constructing 'socialism in one country', see Trotsky, 'The Draft Program of the Communist International – A Criticism of Fundamentals' in *The Third International After Lenin*, New York 1970 (first published 1936), pp. 3–73.
33. Mandel, *Trotsky as Alternative*, p. 47.
34. Mandel's analysis of the material roots and development of the Soviet bureaucracy in *Power and Money*, chapter 2, and *Trotsky as Alternative*, chapter 3, closely follows that of Trotsky in *The Revolution Betrayed*, chapters 2, 4, 5. Mandel provides a very powerful reply to various social democrats and former Stalinists who claim that Stalin merely implemented Trotsky's economic proposals, albeit in a 'barbaric form', in the late 1920s and 1930s. In *Trotsky as Alternative*, chapter 4, Mandel demonstrates that Trotsky continued, until his death in 1940, to advocate a democratically controlled economy that combined a dominant state-owned, planned sector with market mechanisms.

35. Samuel Farber (*Before Stalinism: The Rise and Fall of Soviet Democracy*, London 1990), despite many important insights, tends to underestimate the weight of these material factors as he highlights the Bolshevik mainstream's subjective underestimation of democratic institutions and rights. For a good discussion of the strengths and weaknesses of Farber's work, see David Mandel, 'The Rise and Fall of Soviet Democracy', *Against the Current* 37, March–April 1992, pp. 48–9.

36. Mandel, *Trotsky as Alternative*, p. 82.

37. Trotsky, *The Revolution Betrayed*, pp. 104–5. Trotsky's most lengthy discussion of these issues is *Stalinism v. Bolshevism*, New York 1974 (originally published 1939). Mandel presents these points at length in several works: 'What is Bureaucracy?' pp. 83–5; *Power and Money*, pp. 117–18; *Trotsky as Alternative*, pp. 81–2, 84–6.

38. *Power and Money*, pp. 118–25; *Trotsky as Alternative*, pp. 83–4.

39. Marcel Liebman, *Leninism Under Lenin*, London 1975. See also Paul Le-Blanc, *Lenin and the Revolutionary Party*, Atlantic Highlands (NJ) 1993.

40. *Trotsky as Alternative*, p. 83.

41. *Power and Money*, pp. 104–9.

42. See *From Stalinism to Eurocommunism* and *Revolutionary Marxism Today*, *passim* for Mandel's discussions of the disastrous effects of 'socialism in one country' on the world labour movement.

43. Trotsky, *The Revolution Betrayed*, pp. 275–6.

44. *Marxist Economic Theory*, vol. 2, chapter 15; *Beyond Perestroika: The Future of Gorbachev's USSR*; *Power and Money*, chapter 1.

45. *Power and Money*, p. 42. One can see similar patterns of wasted resources and low quality to consumers in the services provided by the capitalist state (health care, post and telecommunications, transport, and so forth). Again, the absence of either the 'whip of competition' or producer-consumer control of these services leads to bureaucratic waste and inefficiency. This is the material foundation for much working- and middle-class support for 'privatization' of government services in the advanced capitalist countries.

46. Ibid., p. 213.

47. 'In Defence of Socialist Planning', *NLR* 159, September/October 1986, pp. 5–38.

48. *Power and Money*, p. 202.

49. Ibid., pp. 197–214.

50. 'In Defence of Socialist Planning', pp. 9, 31–4.

51. *Power and Money*, p. 206. These arguments were first developed in Mandel's debate with Alec Nove in *NLR*: Mandel, 'In Defence of Socialist Planning'; Nove, 'Markets and Socialism', *NLR* 161, January/February 1987, pp. 98–104; Mandel, 'The Myth of Market Socialism', *NLR* 169, May/June 1988, pp. 108–21.

52. *Power and Money*, pp. 209–10, 240–46.

53. Tony Cliff, *State Capitalism in Russia*, London 1975 (originally published in 1955); P. Binns, T. Cliff and C. Harman, *Russia: From Workers' State to State Capitalism*, London 1987.

54. Most of these themes are contained in Mandel's debates with Chris Harman

and other members of the British 'International Socialist' current, in *The Inconsistencies of State Capitalism*, IMG Publications, London 1969.

55. Max Shachtman, *The Bureaucratic Revolution: The Rise of the Stalinist State*, New York 1962; Jack Trautman, ed., *Bureaucratic Collectivism: The Stalinist Social System*, Detroit (MI) 1974.

56. Jacek Kuron and Karol Modzelewski, 'Open Letter to Members of the Warsaw Sections of the United Polish Workers' Party and the Union of Young Socialists', in G.L. Weissman, ed., *Revolutionary Marxist Students In Poland Speak Out (1964–1968)*, New York 1968, pp. 15–90.

57. *Power and Money*, pp. 28–30 (emphasis in the original).

58. Ibid., p. 32 (emphasis in the original).

59. Robert Brenner, 'The Origins of Capitalist Development: A Critique of Neo-Smithian Marxism', *NLR* 104, July/August 1977, pp. 25–92.

60. See Catherine Samary, *Plan, Market and Democracy:*, Notebooks for Study and Research, nos. 7–8, IIRE, Amsterdam 1988; R. Smith, 'The Chinese Road to Capitalism', *NLR* 199, May/June 1993, pp. 55–99.

61. *Marxist Economic Theory*, vol. 2, pp. 572–4, 584–99; *Beyond Perestroika*, chapters 1 and 3.

62. A. Shaikh, 'The Current Economic Crisis: Causes and Implications', *Against the Current* Pamphlet, Detroit (MI) 1989; 'The Falling Rate of Profits and the Economic Crisis in the US' in R. Cherry et al., eds., *The Imperiled Economy*, vol. 1: *Macroeconomics from a Left Perspective*, New York 1987, pp. 115–26; Mary C. Malloy, 'Finance and Industrial Capital in the Current Crisis: On Brenner's "Politics of U.S. Decline"', *Against the Current* 57, July–August 1995, pp. 27–32.

63. I use, as did Marx, the terms 'proletarian dictatorship' and 'workers' state' interchangeably. See Hal Draper, *Karl Marx's Theory of Revolution*, vol. 3: *The 'Dictatorship of the Proletariat'*, New York 1986.

64. Marx, *The Civil War in France* in *The First International & After*, Random House, New York 1974; V.I. Lenin, *State and Revolution* in *Selected Works*, vol. 2; *The Proletarian Revolution and the Renegade Kautsky* in *Selected Works*, vol. 3.

65. The best statement of this position remains Trotsky, *In Defense of Marxism*, New York 1970 (originally published 1940). See also Mandel, *Revolutionary Marxism Today*, pp. 141–50.

66. Anderson, 'Trotsky's Interpretation of Stalinism', pp. 123–4.

67. *Power and Money*, pp. 74–5 (emphasis in the original).

68. *Revolutionary Marxism Today*, p. 142.

69. For a summary of the arguments about the new middle class, see C. Post, 'The New Middle Class?', *Against the Current* (Old Series) 2,4, Winter 1984, pp. 35–41.

70. *Revolutionary Marxism Today*, p. 143.

71. Mandel discusses the literature on the slowing rate of upward mobility in the USSR in *Beyond Perestroika*, chapters 3 and 4.

72. I would like to thank Mary C. Malloy and the discussants and participants in the Amsterdam seminar on 'The Contribution of Ernest Mandel to Marxist Theory' for their comments on an earlier draft of this chapter.

8

Mandel's Views on the Transition to Socialism

Catherine Samary

This article discusses three organically linked debates: 1) on socialist society as such; 2) on the notion of a 'transition to socialism'; and 3) on the nature of the (formerly) 'actually existing socialist' countries – and the transformations they are now undergoing.

First I will summarize Ernest Mandel's consistent approach to these questions over the years. Then I will look at some of the main debates in order to assess the strengths and weaknessses of Mandel's contributions. In light of the ongoing process of capitalist restoration, many of his positions on the so-called socialist countries can be rethought or better formulated today. In conclusion I will look back at the debate on the broader, now the central question: the fight for a socialist society.

Introduction: Ernest Mandel's consistency

Ernest Mandel often stressed (especially in his teaching – and I learned this from him) the limits of Marxist thinking on building a socialist society: that is, on transitional societies between capitalism and socialism. While Marx could develop his concepts in *Das Kapital* on the basis of his knowledge of the most advanced capitalist societies of his time, he refused to dream up any 'model' of socialism. Marxists in the twentieth century had to theorize about the society in transition from capitalism to socialism 'as they went along', and always in poor rather than developed countries. Stalinism added additional theoretical difficulties, besides repressing critical Marxist analysis from within. Thus, according to Mandel, Marxists trying to understand Eastern European countries faced 'a basic problem: the theoretical framework required to analyse societies moving from capitalism to socialism does not yet fully exist ... [Therefore] it is extremely difficult to decide which developments are due to bureaucratic degeneration and which are historically inevitable'. He added: 'We know Marx's ideas on socialism and, while it is difficult to define closely what socialism is, we know quite well what it is not.'[1]

Mandel's view of what socialism was not was completely determined for almost his whole life by his conviction that socialism meant direct self-organization, *without the need of money*. Subsequent debates on socialism have shown that this 'negative definition' was not as clear as he imagined.

1) Ernest Mandel consistently upheld a classic interpretation of Marx's and Engels's writings on socialism, as a society based on the 'direct association of producers' who would use their own direct judgement in allocating resources and organizing production and distribution. The abolition of the social relationships concealed by commodity relationships in the capitalist market is obviously a goal of an emancipatory socialist project. This goal was often defined by Mandel as a withering away of commodity categories linked with increasing abundance and increasing self-organization. In his debate with Alec Nove, Mandel centres his argument around the feasibility of what he claims to be 'the goal of Marxist policies – socialism without commodity production'.[2] He associates the possibility of achieving such a goal with the development of productive forces.

Socialism was therefore understood by Mandel in the Marxist tradition: the product of worldwide resistance by workers against the most developed capitalism as an articulated world system. The fact that a socialist revolution had been victorious at capitalism's periphery, and was not aided by revolutions in developed capitalist countries meant that the post-capitalist society could not be 'socialist'. This was not the result of Stalinist degeneration but of underdevelopment and isolation (which themselves were key conditions for Stalinism).

2) Mandel's notion of a 'society in transition to socialism' lies in the continuity of the Bolshevik approach in the 1920s. The concept was first introduced after the October revolution. It was therefore somewhat different from the notion of socialism as a 'transition to communism' that can be found in Marx. It was organically linked to the idea that taking power in Russia was only the first step in a global process of

resistance to international capitalist domination. For the Bolsheviks, the revolution and the new society were 'socialist' in their objectives – not in their social reality. Classes, different forms of ownership, the market and underdevelopment could not be abolished from one day to the next nor without the help of socialist victories in developed countries. Socialism 'in one country' and in conditions of underdevelopment was impossible. But breaking the weakest link of the 'imperialist chain' could encourage more resistance and make it possible to begin a socialist transformation of the Soviet Union.

In such a framework, the Soviet Union was conceived as a hybrid society, whose dynamic was towards socialist transformation under a workers' state. The initial formulations used by the Bolsheviks had a descriptive tendency; presenting a juxtaposition of 'sectors' related to different relations of production and ownership ('socialist', capitalist, small private property), all subject to state control. The plan itself had the label 'socialist'. Preobrazhensky developed a comprehensive vision of the conflicting logics of transitional societies in the context of a very productive capitalist environment. He formulated it as a conflict between the law of value and the 'law of socialist accumulation'. The main historical tasks that the society in transition towards socialism had to carry out were the development of productive forces and the transformation of social relationships. The programme of permanent revolution expressed, at the national and international level, those tasks to be accomplished, beginning from the initial conditions of the revolution and laying the material, economical and cultural basis for a future socialist society.

Mandel developed his own analysis in this theoretical framework, facing the bureaucratization of Soviet society and Stalin's proclamation that socialism could be (in fact by 1936 had been) built in one country.

The main feature Mandel stressed to illustrate the non-socialist character of (existing) transitional societies, besides the total denial of any decision-making power to workers, was the persistence of money and commodity categories. By contrast, he linked limits to the rule of the law of value and the non-commodity substance of Soviet planning with the non-capitalist character of those societies.

Instead of merely juxtaposing aspects of different relations of production, Mandel insisted more and more on the necessity of analyzing the 'specific relations of production' of the transitional societies as such:[3] as relations that were 'neither capitalist nor socialist'.

That transitional context, where commodity categories and some market relations would continue to exist, was not considered by Mandel as something short-term, or even limited to underdeveloped countries.

It was fundamentally linked with the underdevelopment of productive forces in comparison with the needs still to be satisfied at a world level.

Mandel insisted therefore, along the same lines as Preobrazhensky, on enduring *conflicting logics* as long as there is no abundance. He expressed it more often under the formula of a conflict between the logic of planning and that of the still existing markets (world market, consumer goods markets, and so forth); or a conflict between 'the bourgeois norm of distribution' (to each according to his labour) and the logic of the plan.

Because the problems of socialist transformation were not (and will not be) posed only in the short term (in the revolutionary period), Mandel insisted on the necessity of material incentives, while stressing the contradictions that monetary incentives could produce.[4] Therefore he emphasized those incentives which could stimulate collective behaviour, improvements in the conditions of work, education and responsibility.

3) The degeneration of the October Revolution led Mandel to try to understand another source of exploitation and alienation linked with the bureaucratization of the workers' state: planning itself could conceal social relationships of exploitation and alienation. Such relationships did in fact exist in those spheres of production analyzed by Mandel as subject to direct planning (without the active role of money). Mandel's analysis of the bureaucracy emphasized the effects of the delegation of power and the division of labour in underdeveloped societies, exacerbated by political conditions. The analysis of the bureaucratization of the workers' state reinforced his theoretical views and political conclusions. He stressed that only workers' self-activity and self-organization can make possible both the withering away of the state and that of the market as preconditions to any socialist future.

The limits to overcoming both commodity relationships and bureaucratic domination were rooted, according to Mandel's strong 'materialist' convictions, in the underdevelopment of productive forces. But Mandel's political standpoint resisted linear and fatalistic versions of 'historical materialism'. Underdevelopment of productive forces did not mean that it was impossible to resist bureaucratic degeneration, or that market relations would 'necessarily' predominate. He opposed Charles Bettelheim on those grounds, on the basis of a concrete and theoretical analysis of the relations of production of those specific societies: that is, social relations of production not only at the level of each factory but also between factories.[5]

Like Preobrazhensky, Mandel (like Brus later on) made a fundamental *distinction between the existence of 'market categories'* (prices, wages, etc.) *and the domination of the law of value,* the first not being the 'proof' of the second. He therefore developed an analysis of the role of the money (and of prices) in different spheres of the economy, arguing that labour had a directly social character in the planning system in spite of its bureaucratic features and waste. He argued this mainly on the basis that there was no market 'sanction' (bankruptcy, unemployment) for bad planning. The main feature of bureaucratic planning was the poor quality or under-production of use-values.

Trotsky's prediction

Marxist debates on the nature of the Soviet Union and similar societies developed along these lines. They also had to assess Trotsky's forecast that there would be no historical place for a specific bureaucratic mode of production. Although he left open the hypothesis of the bureaucracy transforming itself into a class if it could destroy workers' capacities for resistance, Trotsky posed the fundamental alternatives as either a socialist, anti-bureaucratic revolution or a capitalist restoration: one or the other was supposed to occur rapidly.

The geographic expansion and relatively long duration of bureaucratic rule gave credibility to analyses that maintained either that the bureaucracy was the direct instrument of world bourgeois domination or that it could crystallize (or had crystallized) into a new class.

Mandel consistently rejected such arguments, on the grounds that bureaucratic degeneration – and even counter-revolution – did not abolish (and even reinforced) non-capitalist features of those societies and could not destroy workers' resistance to the bureaucratic dictatorship. It meant that Trotsky's fundamental alternatives were still posed, even if the decision hung in the balance for several more decades. Mandel tried to analyze why it could hang in the balance so long. But he often repeated that a few decades were not so long a period in historical time (the time needed for classes to consolidate themselves); and he argued that a capitalist counter-revolution would have to dismantle the state and undermine the workers, neither of which occurred before the 1980s.

At an international level, Mandel stressed the specificity of the Second World War, which ended in partial defeats for the working class but in the general framework of the defeat of fascism, extension of the revolution (to Yugoslavia and China) and growing working-class activity. Workers' capacities for resistance were not destroyed, even if they lacked the subjective ability to impart a consistent socialist dynamic to the class struggle. The alliance of the 'democratic bourgeoisie' and Stalinism against fascism consolidated both regimes for a period of time, but under strong working-class pressures. This had to be taken into account both by the postwar capitalist system and by the bureaucracies of the workers' states. This played a key role in Mandel's understanding of both late capitalism and of bureaucratic reforms.

These specific features strengthened, in Mandel's analysis, the theme of working-class resistance on two fronts: the thesis of a 'triangular struggle' against both capitalism and bureaucracy. But there was no symmetry: the extension of Soviet-type societies was still analyzed in the conceptual framework of *transitional societies,* even if the transition towards socialism was considered blocked. In Mandel's definition of transitional societies, the main feature was not the dynamic (transition towards what?) but the 'neither/nor' character of those societies: their indeterminacy in terms of class domination. Mandel considered them to be still neither socialist nor capitalist nor stabilized. That is to say, the fundamental class confrontation between consistent logics of production, between the world bourgeoisie and the workers, was still at stake despite the hybrid nature of those societies: there would be *either a capitalist restoration or a 'political revolution'.*

What would that 'political revolution' be? The 'ambiguity' of the idea, Mandel said,

> ... lies not in the term 'political revolution' but in the peculiarity of a political revolution in a workers' state, which, by definition, even if it is bureaucratized, is a state whose economic weight is exceptional. As a result, even a revolution that is 'purely political' (an absurd concept in any event) will obviously have socio-economic effects infinitively greater than those of a bourgeois political revolution. The latter at most replaces one faction of the bourgeoisie in power by another ... [while in a bureaucratized workers' state] a political revolution would be simply this: a take-over of the management of the state, the economy and all spheres of social activity by the mass of producers and the toiling masses, in the form of the power of democratically elected workers' councils, soviets.[6]

The formula 'political revolution' was therefore linked with the characterization of the ruling bureaucracy and of the state.

The formula 'degenerated workers' state' was developed by Trotsky in his analysis of the 'revolution betrayed'. It expressed a contradictory reality combining several features:

1) Stalinism had been a 'political counter-revolution' which had consolidated not merely or mainly Stalin's rule, but the crystallization of a bureaucratic layer defending its own specific material interests

through the party/state; the state 'degenerated bureaucratically'. The socialist transformation of the society would be blocked unless a new workers' upsurge, an anti-bureaucratic 'political revolution', occurred.

2) But the state was still characterized as working-class, first because there had not been a social counter-revolution, a capitalist restoration, and second because the bureaucratic caste had not stabilized an independent position in a specific mode of production. It ruled on the workers' behalf – and at their expense.

Mandel's analysis of the social nature of the Soviet state was developed in this framework. It was linked to his analysis of the bureaucracy of that state – and to his evaluation of the situation of the working class. According to Mandel, the bureaucracy included 'all the layers in the Soviet society which are privileged in one way or another'. The bureaucracy 'since it does not own the means of production, participates in distribution of the national income exclusively as a function of remuneration for its labour-power'. Finally, the bureaucrats 'are not merely the sons and daughters of workers but even former workers themselves.' They were 'a fraction of the working class'.[7]

The workers, far from having been undermined under the bureaucratic dictatorship, developed both numerically and qualitatively (increasing their skill levels). Therefore Mandel stressed

> ... a fundamental paradox of this situation: the fact that the working class, which is proclaimed as the ruling class in all official propaganda, is in reality devoid of all political rights. At the same time, although the working class does not participate in the management of the economy and the state, it nevertheless does command de facto powers and rights.[8]

Power to control the rhythm of work and cultural and social rights were workers' gains, making possible a pseudo-Marxist legitimization of the bureaucratic rule as 'socialist'.

Finally, according to Mandel,

> ... the formula 'bureaucratized workers' state' refers to criteria of the Marxist theory of the state. For Marxism there is no such thing as a state that stands above classes. The state is in the service of the historic interest of a given class ... Up to now this state has prevented the restoration of capitalism and the power of a bourgeois class ... It is only in this sense that we use the adjective 'workers'' ... There is a very big difference between, on the one hand, maintaining certain socio-economic structures historically linked to the interests of a particular social class and, on the other, defending the immediate, daily interests of a social class in the sense of what it itself sees as – and wants to be – its place in society.[9]

But the domination of the bureaucracy was not stabilized. In his analysis of the 'law of development' of those societies, Mandel stressed a fundamental contradiction between the potential of development rooted in the abolition of capitalist domination and in the establishment of planning on the one hand, and bureaucratic conservatism on the other. The latter was viewed as a growing obstacle to the development of productive forces. Whatever the attempts at reform and stabilization of its rule, the bureaucracy could never overcome the characteristics of 'extensive accumulation'. That was linked to two main contradictions often stressed by Mandel:

> First . . . it is impossible to forge a rational link between the material self-interest of the bureaucracy and the optimization of economic growth. Second, there is no way to overcome the relative indifference to production on the part of the direct producers themselves.[10]

The first 'stumbling block' could only be overcome by capitalist privatization; the second, by a workers' political revolution.

Mandel, like Trotsky, stressed the fact that part of the bureaucracy, 'especially its "managerial" wing', was trying to stabilize its privileges through capitalist restoration.

> But before all these tendencies could lead to an actual restoration of capitalism, they would have to overcome the resistance of the key sectors of the state apparatus that oppose this whole trend. This, incidentally, is the objective justification for our use of the scientific formula 'degenerated workers' state' to describe the USSR, in spite of all anti-working-class measures and the total lack of direct working-class power, or even political rights. Even more important though, they would have to overcome the resistance of the proletariat itself, which has a lot to lose through such a process of capitalist restoration, particularly what is undoubtedly the major remaining conquest of October from the standpoint of the workers: a qualitative higher degree of job security than exists under capitalism.[11]

There was an obvious error of prediction in Mandel's analysis. But where was the error? How does it relate to his overall understanding of what Stalinism was? In other words, was the bureaucracy since Stalin a state bourgeoisie or a new class after all? Or was there an historical turn in the dynamic of class struggles *in the 1980s*? To what extent did the crisis of the system and of all the revolutionary experiences in that specific international context change the way in which workers and bureaucrats tried to defend their interests? If that was under- (or badly) estimated (as I think it was), then something was also unclear or wrong in the way the concept was presented. These are the points to be discussed below.

Most of the debates on the dynamics of Soviet society that Mandel participated in can be directly evaluated in light of the transformations now under way. Others go beyond the scope of this test, even if they are obviously deeply influenced by it. They concern the socialist project itself. It is possible to draw up a balance sheet of the major debates, assessing Mandel's strong and weak points.

1. Debates over the 'transitional societies': the test of capitalist restoration

The collapse of the so-called socialist countries and the process of 'transition to the market', as it is called, has much to tell us. It should help to overcome somewhat the sclerosis of previous debates, and perhaps make better formulations possible. In spite of (or because of) the disastrous social effects of neoliberal policies and the terrible legacy left by Stalinism, we must take advantage of the short distance we have travelled so far, more than six years after the fall of the Berlin Wall, in the 'transition towards capitalism'.

It would go beyond the scope of this contribution to produce a systematic analysis of the ongoing process of capitalist restoration.[12] That would require citing figures on the present situation and taking a comparative approach towards all the countries concerned, while the main debates Mandel took part in and most discussions of the nature of the so-called socialist countries have centred on the former Soviet Union. Here the present will be used only to clarify the past, and the discussion will centre mainly on the Soviet Union.

Nonetheless, it is worth stressing some common features and difficulties, in order to summarize what is at stake.

At the end of the 1980s one could have the impression that the collapse of the single-party system and capitalist restoration was an incredibly easy process. The idea that those populations had nothing to lose was reinforced. Workers did not defend the 'bureaucratized workers' state' – and neither did the bureaucrats. The dominant layers of the former nomenklatura, contrary to what Mandel had expected, even played a decisive role in the turn towards privatization.

Six years later, the picture is somewhat more complex, and very differentiated. But the dominant lesson is that capitalist restoration is a *difficult* process. There is no longer any doubt about the fact that the population had a lot to lose along the way. Where the transition is the most 'advanced' and 'successful' – Lithuania, Poland, Hungary, Bulgaria – the population has freely expressed its disillusionment by voting for those parties which represented some continuity with the past. However, there is no question of going back to the past. The 'ex-communist' neo-social democrats in Poland or Hungary are not prepared to stop their countries' integration into the world capitalist system. Even the conflicts for power in Russia have more to do with what type of capitalism – for whose benefit – than with genuinely counterposed projects. But if we look back at the whole process, popular democratic fronts of different sorts did exist against the single-party system but there was nowhere any revolution from below in support of an explicit restorationist programme. The only partial exception was German unification. But there is no West Germany that can integrate the whole of Eastern Europe into the capitalist order and pay the bill.

'Privatization' is more or less declared accomplished, be it in the Czech Republic or in Russia. Behind those declarations, however, there is a lack of capital and of a social basis for the restorationist process. It is not an organic process based on an already existing bourgeoisie.

This means that we are facing an absolutely new historical experience. This has to do with the specificity of these societies as they were. Some analysts refused to call them 'post-capitalist' because there were elements of 'pre-capitalist', quasi-feudal forms of non-market protection. But, first, unlike the period of bourgeois revolution against feudalism, there is today a powerful world capitalist system, with its institutions as a global framework. That is a key element in the restorationist process today. Second, in the Soviet Union, industry represented the largest share of the national product. It employed huge concentrations of workers who enjoyed job security. All those features were closer to a 'post-capitalist' reality than to any feudalism.

These remarks are aimed at avoiding excessively abstract debates. Whatever concept is used to describe the former Soviet Union, there was – and still is – a need to look behind the concept, behind the economic categories, behind the plan, as in the West we need to look behind the market, in order to see the real social relationships. This is my concern here. Only on such a basis can we clarify the usefulness of different concepts.

I will deal with the following questions about the ongoing 'transition towards the market' and the debates on the nature of these societies: (1) the theory of state capitalism in light of the experience of capitalist restoration; (2) 'new class' theories; (3) reasons for the historic turning point of 1989–91; (4) the 'soft' counter-revolution; and (5) the social nature of the state in transitional society. After that I will turn to the problem of rethinking and reformulating the debates on socialism.

1.1 Debates around the theory of state capitalism and the economic categories of Soviet-type societies[13]

In spite of the fact that the 'state capitalist' theory has no difficulty in explaining why key elements of the old nomenklatura play a leading role in the ongoing process ('it was already a bourgeoisie'), that approach does not help us understand the specific non-capitalist features of the former system. Therefore it does not help us understand what is at stake; it does not clarify the historical turning point we are facing. The paradox, by the way, is that it does not help us understand why the most probable form of capitalist restoration is *state capitalism*. Such a concept has to have something to do with the main features, social relationships and mechanism of exploitation of a capitalist system. That is what is being introduced today through the necessary (from a bourgeois point of view) destruction of the former system. That is what the world bourgeoisie (through its 'experts' and institutions: the World Bank, the IMF and the European Union) is consciously doing. What the world bourgeoisie is discovering is the difficulty and the cost of this project.

The reality of capitalist restoration today

Nationalizations in capitalist countries (e.g. in France after the Second World War) helped increase profitability in the private sector; they were never meant to limit the rights of private property. That was not the dynamic in the Soviet Union. Moreover, in 'actually existing capitalist societies' privatizations of nationalized sectors of industry occur when and where it is efficient for private capital under conditions of existing market competition. At all events, whether in developed capitalist countries or in their periphery such as Latin America, privatizations occur in market economies where there are capital markets, capitalist financial institutions, and so on. That is simply not the case in the former Soviet Union. What is at stake in Eastern Europe and especially in the former Soviet Union is the privatization of the whole of industry (whose dominant sectors are unprofitable under market conditions), the creation of a capital market and the transformation of workers into 'free' wage earners. In other words, what is at stake is *(re)establishing all the social relationships and institutions that enable money to become capital, and capitalist market criteria and discipline to function.* State capitalist theory does not make it possible to explain that.

Tony Cliff's main argument in the past was that the world capitalist market dictated the logic of Soviet investments. The reverse is true. The Soviet Union could protect itself for decades from the world market – and it was partially forced to do so by forms of boycott that prevented it from buying strategic technologies. Import policies were shaped by the COMECON division of labour and the opening of Eastern European countries – though not the Soviet Union – to foreign credits and imports *in the 1970s*. The debt crisis in these countries in the 1980s (softened for a time by the support of the Soviet Union and by the COMECON system of prices) and the direct impact of the arms race on the Soviet Union qualitatively increased the effect of world capitalism on these societies, at a moment when the internal contradictions of their own system were increasing. Russia opened its economy to direct world market pressure mostly as part of the restorationist government's 'shock therapy'. This foreign debt increased dramatically in the 1990s.

In other words we can speak today, in a restorationist context, of the direct role of the world market in the Russian economy. This was not true from the time Stalin consolidated power up until the 1980s. The result of opening Russia to the world market (as is also the case for other Eastern European countries) has been a disaster. This allows us to evaluate to what extent that pressure was *not* effective before, contrary to 'state capitalist' claims.

But this is not the end of the story. To define a society as capitalist only on the basis of the pressures of world capitalism is obviously insufficient. One must make a concrete analysis of the existing internal mechanisms, social relations and market institutions through which this pressure is exercised and capitalist relationships can be analyzed. Capitalist exploitation is not the only historical form of exploitation, i.e. of appropriation of the surplus by specific social layers or classes. In a capitalist system appropriation of surplus must take the form of surplus-value, of profit: money must be able to make more money through specific relations of production and ownership.

Was this the case in the Soviet Union? If the bureaucracy was already a bourgeoisie, why is it so difficult to establish market rules and a capital market in the former Soviet Union? Why is outside pressure from world capitalism (and bourgeois institutions) not sufficient to re-establish the domination of the law of value? For the moment it is still not functioning properly in Russia.

The explicit programme of the 'transition to a market economy' speaks volumes about what prevented capitalist rules from orienting investments in the Soviet Union:[14]

- In the planned sector, money was a (bad and rather passive) instrument which only served as an accounting unit (even if it was called a 'rouble', you could not buy anything with it except when it was distributed as wages).
- There were no real factory accounts before the 1980s, because there was no measurement of real 'costs'.[15]
- Managers (or other private persons) could not buy or sell means of production, raw materials or factories.
- Factories could not go bankrupt.
- There was no capital market, no banking system functioning on the basis of private capital and profit.
- Workers were broadly 'socialized' in huge factories which gave them not only jobs and wages, but all kinds of goods and services, flats, childcare, even hospitals, schools and vacation centres. Those social links were (and are still) major obstacles to the mobility of a 'free' labour force. They were introduced by managers in order to keep the labour force they needed whatever the cost. Often a whole town if not region was built around those huge combines.
- Prices were set according to the social or economic goals of the planning authorities, and did not reflect costs or the pressure of supply and demand.
- There were 'no real owners'. Bureaucrats' behaviour was consistent with the fact that they were neither collective nor private 'owners' of the means of production. They produced at whatever cost in order to maintain their own privileges. Neither were the workers 'real owners', with rights of control and decision-making. Irresponsibility was the price paid for this kind of alienation.

As the well-known advocate of 'shock therapy', Harvard's Jeffrey Sachs, clearly said, privatization was meant to break a non-capitalist system and impose new social relationships suited to market discipline.

The greatest strengths of Mandel's analyses are here: the non-commodity nature of the means of production in the former Soviet Union, the dominant feature of planning as based on use-values, the 'passive role of money' in the planned sector. This is all still visible in the very limited restructuring produced by changes in prices. Barter relationships between big factories, huge inter-factory debts, limited unemployment in a context of a dramatic decline of production: these are all significant ways to escape from the pressure of the credit system, and from the social relationships associated with the law on value. The main difficulty in the privatization process is the *lack of capital* – which also means the lack of a 'real bourgeoisie' bringing in capital. That is the main reason why privatizations are often juridical (in Russia the most common tactic has been to transfer ownership to factory 'collectives', including managers), without restructuring and without real changes in behaviour and relationships between managers and workers.

This is confirmed by the concrete analysis given by people like Jacques Sapir (a former supporter of Bettelheim's positions) of the still predominantly 'non-market' reality of Russian society (in 1995):

> In Russia, the lack of economic flexibility includes the labour force, because the firms are sites of social integration. The wage-earners' social gains must be financed by the firms and constitute a total fixed capital. . . . From 1988 on, the disintegration of central control over the wages fund fostered the assertion of wage-earners' power within the firms. By the end of 1991 the real average wage had doubled relative to its 1987 level.[16]

Later he adds:

> The underdevelopment of market infrastructures, whether material or institutional, stops the mechanisms of mediation from functioning, or saddles them with counterproductive dynamics . . . The emergence of a payments crisis reflects the existence of major technical and institutional rigidities: the productive system cannot adapt to the instantaneous transformation of the rules of the game.[17]

Finally under the heading 'absence of any element of market discipline', Sapir comments:

> Another factor that weighs heavily given the lack of conditions for market discipline resides in the social role attributed to firms in the old Soviet system. Firms are not simply places where one works and collects a wage; they play a major role in social programmes and contribute decisively to local social infrastructure (housing, childcare centres, dispensaries). Not only does all this constitute a drag on their finances, it makes individual or collective layoffs very difficult . . . The spontaneous decomposition of the system creates the conditions for solidifying relationships between firm managements and local elites . . . As a result it becomes impossible, at least in the short term, to implement any sort of bankruptcy law . . .[18]

Differences between regions and industries (but also between different Eastern European countries) give indications of the varying degree of real restoration of market laws. But it is interesting to stress very similar problems of restructuring and the deep weakness of the banking system behind the so-called 'mass privatization' in the 'most advanced' country in the process of transition towards capitalism: the Czech Republic. An analysis published by Banque Paribas says that the

> ... idyllic picture of a successful transition nonetheless hides a certain number of major structural problems, having to do with the delay in restructuring firms and the weakness of the banking system . . . Beginning from a virtually nonexistent private sector, the privatization process launched in 1991 has increased the private sector's share of GDP from 4 percent in 1990 to almost 70 percent today . . . But often only the formal part of the process [the 'big privatization', which in two different waves allowed Czech citizens to become shareholders] has been accomplished. Once the shares were divided among investment funds, these funds often failed to exercise any real control over the firms. At the same time the big state-owned banks, which most often administer the investment funds (through which they control almost 70 percent of stock issued) find themselves in the position of being simultaneously shareholders and creditors of the privatized firms, which explains the small number of bankruptcies. In addition the economic reform has often not gotten under way, and numerous firms have not really begun the process of restructuring. At the same time privatization contracts have often included 'anti-layoff' clauses . . . The banking sector incidentally is where the traces of economic planning are still most visible: doubtful loans are massively present in their institutional balance sheets.[19]

The uneven development of market discipline results from variations in the former structure of the economy, in the role of small commodity production, in the size of the factories, in the positions of different industries in market competition, and so on. The methodological distinctions used by Mandel to stress that the existence of 'commodity categories' like wage and prices was not the proof that market laws were functioning are still useful to analyze the uneven degree of capitalist restoration.

The 'bureaucratized workers' state' formula responds to the main 'criticisms' that have been made of the old system by supporters of the restorationist process:

1) *'Too much protection', 'workers' privileges', 'egalitarianism', 'lazy workers'*. This has something to do with the abolition of market discipline, the limits of the bureaucratic form of exploitation, the specificity of bureaucratic rule on behalf of the workers but at their expense, a wage structure more favourable to miners than to doctors, workers' control over rhythms of work – but also with irresponsibility, alienation, and so forth.

2) *'No real owner'*.

a) The population and especially the workers have always reacted

strongly against 'nomenklaturist privatization', which they see as rob-
bery, as an illegal appropriation. They never considered the bureaucrats to be owners; even the state was not considered the owner.
Property was supposed (and considered) to be 'social'. One of the
goals of 'mass privatization' was to respond to the popular call for
justice in the privatization of social ownership. How can you explain
and understand that, if the bureaucrats were real 'collective owners'?
There were no shares, no property for the bureaucrats to transmit to
their sons and daughters. That is why they want privatization.

b) Liberal theories of 'property rights' confirm what Mandel said
about the rationality of bureaucrats' behaviour given the absence of
real rights of ownership (control, transmission of property, and so on).
The neoliberal conclusion is the need for privatization; ours is the
need for real socialization, that is social control. But the diagnosis is
the same: because bureaucrats were not real owners (they had no right
to private accumulation, no freedom to hire and fire workers, no right
to buy or close a factory), they had no interest in efficient production.
Their only interest was in better access to scarce products and services
– that is consumer logic.

*But there were also weak points in Mandel's polemics – and a forecasting error
that requires explanation.*

1) Because he wanted to avoid giving credibility to a class analysis of
the bureaucracy, Mandel often refused to recognize that bureaucrats
did have privileges (specific forms of private appropriation of part of
the surplus) linked to their position in the relations of production. In
fact there was a specific connection between their function in the
productive sphere and their privileges. It was a partial, incomplete,
uncertain form of real ownership (and control), in the context of a
non-market form of control over implementation of the plan.

Bureaucrats could not invest profits. So their income took the form
of wages and access to specific goods, shops, cars, flats, trips, and so
on. But those material privileges were of course linked with their
function in the productive process. That function was not a capitalist
one, but it did exist. They could protect and improve their positions
and privileges if they met the planned targets (or surpassed them) –
with no workers' unrest; they depended on political criteria for appoint-
ment. Because bureaucrats had no legitimate ownership rights and
were ruling on behalf of the workers, they were much more afraid of
workers' unrest (despite the lack of any rights to self-organization)
than any bourgeoisie is of real trade unions. If they were considered
responsible for unrest they could be simply fired and lose everything

from one day to the next. That is why, even without any right to strike, workers' unrest and strike threats were so effective.[20] This led to the bureaucrats' obsession with formal fulfilment of the plan – and their bargaining to have as many resources as possible (especially in order to maintain the number of workers), to minimize the official targets, to hide those resources they might need (and could not buy) for the productive process, and so on.

Bettelheim (like other supporters of the 'state capitalist' theory) was right to stress the increasing 'bargaining power' that local (sectoral, regional) managers gained in the process of planning. It did not mean that there were 'independent' units of production linked by a market, that is to say by market rules and constraints (there, Mandel was right). But it did mean increasing gaps between what was planned and what was produced, and increasing costs and waste.

In this case, to say that everything that was planned was 'directly recognized as social labour', as Mandel argued, was correct but insufficient. Correct, because there were no bankruptcies, no changes in prices automatically linked to waste, acting as an *ex post facto* determination of the amount of 'private labour' considered as 'socially necessary'. But a planned system needs in fact an equivalent of the category of 'socially necessary labour'.[21] In the Soviet Union, it did not exist.

2) Above all, Mandel's views on the resistance to capitalist restoration from key sectors of the bureaucracy were adequate to describe what occurred in past decades. First Stalinist consolidation, then changes and reforms of the bureaucracy's mode of domination were made on the basis of a non-capitalist system. Partial use of the market and partial privatizations were always subordinated to non-capitalist relations of production. The logic of earlier bureaucratic reforms (from Stalin's forced collectivization to the Gorbachev reforms, at least at the beginning of Gorbachev's rule) was to try and improve the efficiency of the system, not to change it – unlike today. These were bureaucratic reforms: they used partial market mechanisms but not democracy. Those inconsistent features always produced differentiations within the bureaucracy. This had all been analyzed by Mandel.

But this was not enough to foresee the turning point. In the ongoing process of restoration, leading sectors of the nomenklatura have been directly acting in favour of privatization for their own benefit and no significant part of the former apparatus is really opposed to the restorationist process. Differentiation can occur between 'comprador' as opposed to domestic bourgeoisies, state capitalist strategies as opposed to immediate (impossible) systematic privatization, those who are more or less opposed to foreign domination, and so on. The difficulties are real; I will come back to them later. But if there is still a triangular struggle, its base has changed. The bourgeois side has been consolidated and broadened at the expense of the bureaucratic one, which has lost its coherence. The workers' side of the triangle, on the other hand, has been the weakest throughout the process. (I will discuss the reasons for this in section 3.)

1.2 The 'new class' debate

Mandel's 'bureaucratized workers' state' (BWS) approach did make it possible to stress that no reform had stabilized the rule of the bureaucracy. Its specific domination on behalf (but at the expense) of the workers did not give the bureaucracy an independent position in the relations of production, through real ownership. The bureaucracy was unable to launch a class offensive on the basis of its hybrid non-capitalist relations of production. If there was a 'new class' it was therefore both historically very young (if it was born after the revolution) and very fragile. The 'new class' theory has to explain *why key sectors of the bureaucracy turned towards becoming real bourgeois*, while the 'state capitalist' approach does not make it possible to understand that there was a turn at all. From this point of view, the BWS formula is more adequate than either alternative.

Mandel was correct to say that the abolition of capitalist rule in the factories and the economy made social gains possible for the workers. This was part of the programme of a proletarian revolution. However, that was not the end of the story.

Mandel's understanding of the BWS formula had two built-in, linked biases. On the one hand he presented all gains as 'long-term results of the October revolution' (whereas Stalin, Khrushchev and others introduced some of them). On the other hand, he underestimated the limits of those gains, due precisely to the bureaucratic context of their introduction: full but bad employment; free services but of more and more disastrous quality; increases in education and skills, but without freedom of thought; and so on.

The consequence of a crystallized bureaucracy for the 'transitional society' was that it really *blocked* any development towards socialism. Therefore, if he had taken seriously his own criteria for the Marxist theory of state (the defence of the historical interests of a class), Mandel should have stressed that the anti-worker content of the Soviet state was dominant, both weakening the workers' capacity to resist capitalist restoration and favouring a bureaucratic turn towards capitalism. That reality explains why, when he had to clarify the content of what a

'political revolution' would be, Mandel (as I quoted him in the introduction) in fact described a new phase of a real socialist revolution, not only
the 'social dimensions' of a political revolution. This was consistent with
his overall analysis of the historical meaning and limitations of the
October revolution as one step in the global tasks of the permanent
revolution. It was true that capitalist rule had not been re-established.
But preventing the return of capitalism was only one of the tasks of the
proletarian socialist revolution. The others had been blocked by the
crystallization of the bureaucracy. A social revolution was still needed.[22]

Finally, one should stress that there was (at least in the Soviet
Union) a real sociological trend towards self-reproduction of the
bureaucracy. Upward mobility by workers into the apparatus tended to
stop under Brezhnev's strongly conservative rule. Increasingly sons and
daughters of bureaucrats had a better chance to go to university and
become bureaucrats than others. That is to say, there was a dynamic
for the bureaucracy to attempt to stabilize itself as a class, even if it did
not succeed.

1.3 The reasons for a historical turning point:
changes in the 'triangular struggle'

Mandel did not draw the conclusions of his own analysis: the bureaucracy's inability to reconcile its own material interests with any efficiency
of the plan or to break workers' increasing passivity. Bureaucratic
behaviour and choices (for a non-capitalist form of rule or capitalist
privatization) have of course nothing to do with ideology and everything to do with pragmatism. The crisis of the BWS and its bureaucratic
rulers must be understood historically, based not on permanent features of the 'nature' of the bureaucracy but on the changing concrete
historical conditions in which it tried to maintain its privileges. The
bureaucracy could have a specific non-capitalist source of privileges up
to a certain moment, and then find it in its interests to switch to a
different logic in a new context.

Up until the mid-1970s, the gap between the transitional societies
and the developed capitalist ones decreased. After that it increased.
From the mid-1970s on, the system's inability to shift from extensive to
intensive forms of production was more than just an obstacle to further
development of productive forces. It expressed itself through increasing imports into Eastern Europe in the 1970s (backed by the Soviet
Union), leading to a debt crisis in the 1980s.

While the capitalist system was itself launching a strong offensive
against the workers through neoliberal policies and a radical technolog-

ical revolution, bureaucratic conservatism was unable to impose greater 'discipline' on workers or to maintain social gains, even less to make any technological revolutions. The gap with the developed capitalist countries widened again. Pressures from the world imperialist system increased still more thanks to the arms race, higher interest rates, the direct and visible hand of the IMF, and so on. The ideological offensive against any form of welfare state had a decisive impact on the Soviet and Eastern European intelligentsia because of 1) the failure of successive reforms; 2) the repression of independent socialist movements and activists; and 3) an incentive system that was much more favourable to middle-class layers in a capitalist society than in a Soviet-type society.

The bureaucracies of the transitional societies could stabilize their own privileges on the basis of a non-capitalist system of production *only under conditions of economic growth.*

The absence of a workers' anti-bureaucratic revolution

Although Mandel was right about some descriptive aspects of workers' strength, he had too 'objectivist' a view of workers' ability to play an independent role against the bureaucracy and the restoration process simultaneously. Even on the 'objective' level, not enough attention was paid to the effect of the specific relations of production analyzed.

This failure was encouraged by what had been the dynamics of workers' struggles in the past: 1956 in Hungary and Poland was always taken as proof that the spontaneous logic of workers' struggle, in spite of a total lack of rights or organization, was to build workers' councils. Workers' self-organization, self-confidence, and demands to become the factories' real owners were stimulated by the ideology of the system and by its relations of production: bureaucrats were not legitimate owners, they were ruling in the name of the workers. Only repression of all kinds – and workers' passivity – could maintain that situation. But in periods of crisis, when differences appeared openly in the party leadership, workers' demands could suddenly increase. Mandel was right to stress a strength linked with huge concentrations, rising skills and education, and increasing demands once elementary needs were satisfied. The dynamic of the struggle was not the restoration of capitalism, in spite of the official justification for sending in Soviet tanks. It was social control of the factories. Perhaps Mandel overestimated this dynamic. True, there had been massive self-organization. But the fact that it had been crushed by Soviet tanks or by bureaucratic rulers had an effect. That was not taken into account in Mandel's – or any of our – optimism.

His optimism was even reinforced by Solidarnosc in Poland, which in fact represented a turning point. It began as a very impressive working-class mobilization. But Mandel accepted a very rosy picture of it, underestimating the subjective weaknesses and internal conflicts in the movement (between the self-management current and the unionist one, and between pro-market experts and socialist ones). Privatization was not Solidarnosc's programme. But it was significantly confused on the question of the market. Was the market favourable to the workers? To self-management? Or on the contrary, was it an instrument of division and fragmentation of the working class, as it had been in former Yugoslavia?

At all events, repression was once more destructive for the main positive aspect of the Solidarnosc experience: massive self-organization. Poland had been the only society where there was an accumulation of working-class experience of mass struggles.

In sum, Mandel underestimated several aspects of the overall situation and their effect on workers' consciousness, especially in the Soviet Union:

1) The big enterprise as a form of socialization of workers' daily life, and the effect that conflictive alliances that workers and management established at that level against 'the centre' had on workers' consciousness and capacity for 'class' struggle.

2) The lack of accumulated experience of workers' independent struggles – not only because of direct repression, but precisely because the main form of workers' resistance in the system had been through the control of the rhythm of work and job security at the level of the factory. Poland was a different situation because of the possibility of an accumulation of workers' experiences without comparable repression, and because the market reform of prices suddenly unified the working class against those who, at the centre, were responsible for the decision to change the price system.

3) The attraction for workers of the market and of forms of collective privatization at the level of enterprises (both seen as means of resisting the central bureaucratic powers).

4) The crisis itself, which increased the difficulty of collective struggle. How could workers fight against inflation, increasing unemployment and increasingly divergent situations in different regions, industries and factories? How could they struggle when they were often obliged to work two or three jobs in order to have some income?

5) The illusion that there was nothing to be lost through privatization and the market, which encouraged 'wait-and-see' attitudes towards new policies. Social gains linked with the non-capitalist forms of

production had deteriorated considerably in the 1970s and 1980s. The market and privatization were supposed, according to neoliberal propaganda, to bring efficiency and freedom, not unemployment and poverty. When the experiment was completed, it was already late.

6) The international context of a crisis or failure of all revolutionary experiments combined with a bourgeois offensive against the workers.

7) A 'subjective difficulty' that has been underestimated (probably linked to some aspects of the debate on socialism). Working-class resistance to different forms of exploitation does not in itself give the workers the capacity to organize the production/distribution process better simply on the basis of direct democracy. A social alternative is a complex system that has to be invented. Workers need (and sense that they need) more than a radical political vanguard in order to be able to resist the capitalist environment and to participate in another mode of production.

1.4 The 'soft' counter-revolution

Mandel's statement that capitalist restoration required breaking the existing state was true. It was true that the repressive apparatus had to be (more or less) purged. The single party had to be broken as a key instrument of state domination, and the legal framework of the system and of all economic institutions had to be changed. It was also true that there was often 'witch-hunting', and that the new bourgeois governments tried to find new personnel for their apparatus.

. . . *But all this occurred without a violent counter-revolution.*
There were several reasons:

- For all the reasons analyzed previously (the crisis of the system of bureaucratic domination once economic growth came to an end), substantial parts of the bureaucracy were ready to stabilize their privileges through privatization in their own interests, or ready to serve the cause of capitalist restoration. The single-party system covered up the bureaucracy's heterogeneous composition. The nomenklatura was only one part of it; and it was the only part for which a party card was an absolute precondition for upward mobility and a career. Many 'ex-bureaucrats' switched sides with relative ease. The huge amount of money and the international bourgeois institutions that were exercising pressure on the system helped to give credibility to such a strategy.
- The workers were also, for reasons analyzed previously, not in a

position to resist this process, which presented itself on the ideological (propagandist) level as anti-bureaucratic, pro-freedom and pro-efficiency. Market and privatization were abstract things. Resistance was scattered, concentrated at the factory level.

Yet the restorationist process lacks a social base. This illustrates in a very specific way some of Mandel's views on the nature of those societies.

The general scenario has been: 1) a shift in the governmental sphere, where the programme defended shifted from reforming the system to 'systemic change', 2) an initial transformation of state institutions, legislation and the repressive apparatus, with the aim of 3) changing the socio-economic logic: abolishing planning, price reforms, privatizations, all under international pressure from the IMF (armed with the growing foreign debt).

For the mass of workers the development of market rule means social regression. When they discover this, it is already too late. This does not make those in power who have advocated these changes (and lied about their effects) any more popular.

Bureaucrats have no objection to capitalist restoration if it helps them to stabilize their own power or social position. But it is not enough for bureaucrats to *want* to transform themselves into bourgeois to be able to do it, for several reasons:

- The bureaucrats (except for some mafiosi) could not carry out a 'primitive accumulation of capital'. This is now under way, thanks to changes in the function of the money (the possibility of investing and speculating). Meanwhile there is a general lack of capital relative to what has to be privatized: thousands of factories in each country, often huge ones, which taken together generally account for the majority of GNP and of the labour force. The amount of savings in each of these countries represents ten to twenty per cent of the value of the plants to be privatized, assessed at the lowest possible level. Nor does the fact that people have savings mean that they are necessarily prepared to invest them in crisis-ridden factories. This is why, even if all the bureaucrats would like to become bourgeois, there is still a general absence of a bourgeoisie (except where it existed with capital 'of its own', as in West Germany or the Chinese diaspora).
- Bureaucrats could find various ways of 'selling' the factories they managed to themselves at very cheap prices. But this was neither popular nor secure. Furthermore, even such a 'nomenklaturist

privatization' does not give bureaucrats the means (money and legitimacy and therefore power) to transform, restructure and modernize their factories in order to become competitive. As a result, capitalist restoration does not mean stability and social security for all bureaucrats. Under pure market conditions most of the factories would have to close. So some bureaucrats resist privatization pragmatically when their market conditions are poor.

- They are ready to become 'comprador bourgeois'. But foreign capital is not rushing in. While $150 billion has been invested every year by the German bourgeoisie in its new Länder, in 1995 only about $20 billion has been invested in the whole of Eastern and Central Europe – half of it in Hungary – and about $2 billion in Russia. Credits exist, but nothing like the Marshall Plan. Many bureaucrats can sell their knowledge (in particular their knowledge of the system). But this does not ensure everyone a job.

- Mass privatization was a way of overcoming the shortage of money and the unpopularity of nomenklaturist privatization – up to a point. It made it possible to change the juridical status of factories and to legitimize privatization by giving everyone 'vouchers': 'part of the social property' in the form of a piece of paper with a small nominal face value, with which people could buy shares. But in the Czech Republic, for instance – the 'most advanced' country in the transition – privatization through vouchers has not up until now been accompanied by a restructuring of the factories. The law on bankruptcy has not been implemented; huge interfactory loans and bad debts have destabilized the banking system, and there is no clear 'owner' of the privatized factories (except, behind the banks, the state). Even the concentration of shares in the hands of a bank or of a manager of a big factory does not give them the strength to restructure it, when this would mean not only the loss of a job, but also of a flat, kindergarten, health care and so on for thousands of workers.

- The state is used to impose market discipline, but has no power to impose it in Russia, because both managers and workers resist it. That does not mean that managers are against capitalist restoration as such. They are only against its restoration *at their expense*. So they will bargain with the state to protect the industry they are running – while increasing their power for the future. That is why, behind old forms and curious alliances, a new real '*state capitalism*' can develop – under the real pressure of the world market, and with a real bourgeois state changing the role of money and the role of the private sector and putting pressure on the public sector itself to restructure.

This whole restorationist process conceals an *asymmetry between Stalinist counter-revolution and the capitalist restoration,* which explains the difficulty of restoration in spite of all the factors in its favour. The Stalinist radical suppression of the private sector and of the rule of the market was accompanied by vast upward social mobility. This made the system popular, in spite of the bloody repression and the political and social costs. The restorationist process needs to improve the social position at least of a significant part of the population in order to stabilize itself. Since this has not so far been the case (on the contrary), there is governmental instability, a multiplicity of political parties without stable parliamentary majorities, growing abstention rates, and so forth. The difficulties are not the same in Poland as in Rumania or the same in Hungary as in Russia. But political disillusionment expressed itself in the 'most advanced' restorationist countries in elections. And the sway of the market has still not been completely imposed. Capital requires money and a financial and credit system. This is the weakest point of a capitalist restoration that is not rooted in an organic primitive capitalist accumulation.

This difficulty does not suffice to create a socialist alternative, however. On the contrary, the international weakness of a socialist alternative helps the restorationist dynamic to persist.

1.5 Once again on the social nature of the state in the transitional society

Mandel may not have been right to speak of a general Marxist theory of the state. In any event no such theory exists on the state in transitional society. Mandel introduced quite convincingly the idea that in spite of the fact that the transitional society is not (by definition) a stable 'mode of production', it does have 'relations of production'. These relations of production cover very hybrid forms of ownership and of class conflict, as a rule *without the stable domination of any class.* The specificity of the proletarian revolution is that the proletariat (and its peasant allies) are not dominant classes before they take power.

The theory of permanent revolution – i.e. of the tasks of socialist transformation after the seizure of power – could be an adequate framework for developing a theory of the state in a society in transition towards socialism, including the risks of restoration and of bureaucratic crystallization.

In such a framework, it is necessary to analyze the contradictory class content of the 'transitional state'. The only 'sure' feature is that the bourgeoisie is no longer dominant, because if it were, or if it became dominant again, the society would no longer be transitional. But 'bourgeois aspects' of the transitional state do exist. Trotsky stressed some of them: the very fact that a state exists as a separate apparatus, and formal legal equality (but this last point should be discussed). The state will certainly give some protection to private property, and so on. We can also analyze the tendency of the state towards bureaucratization (in ownership, in the functioning of workers' parties, in the planning system, in the institutions, and so forth).

The socialist dynamics can only be ensured when the 'proletarian dimension' of the state prevails over both bourgeois and bureaucratic anti-worker dimensions. What then is the criterion for the proletarian nature of the state? In Mandel's approach it is centred on the anti-capitalist dimension (nationalizations and abolition of the dominant role of profit). But that is not the end of the story. The proletarian revolution is fighting for socialization of ownership, withering away of the state and of classes; it should fight against all forms of oppression.

All those transformations, all those aims (to be discussed) are *tasks of the permanent revolution*. They express the historical function of the transition from the point of view of the socialist revolution. All accomplishments of these tasks represent a strengthening of the proletarian dimension of the state (in the sense I have given to it) – including, paradoxically, the withering away of that state – and a strengthening of the proletariat.

These transformations can be analyzed at the governmental level (nature of the political parties in power and their programmes); at the level of state institutions (withering away of the state through the development of self-organization and self-administration); at the level of the social relations of production; at the level of the socialization of ownership (development of real social control in whatever form), and so on.

Advances and retreats and conflicting class logics can exist at all levels. Taking power can give birth to a very fragile workers' state if there are not sufficient possibilities for transformations at other levels (e.g. socio-economic). But it becomes a 'workers' state' as soon as it fights clearly against bourgeois domination. In a parallel way, if bourgeois parties in government are not there as a compromise in the framework of a workers' state, but are able to change the institutional framework in a restorationist direction, it is already a bourgeois state. It may be a fragile bourgeois state if it cannot quickly find a social basis and cannot impose the domination of profit criteria. I tend to think that the existing Eastern European states are more or less fragile bourgeois states. But they are strongly helped by the strength of the bourgeoisie internationally (whatever its difficulties) and the weakness of the workers' movement.

2. Rethinking and reformulating the debates on socialism

Words like 'socialism' have been robbed of their meaning. But human values and needs have not. The ongoing capitalist 'globalization' shows in a clearer way what is at stake behind 'isms' that people do not like: either the logic of profit (more and more opposed to the satisfaction of basic needs) or the logic of satisfaction of human needs (against that of profit).

For pedagogical reasons, but also for purpose of clarity, we should dispense with formulas that present social projects in terms of *means* rather than *ends*. The ends of the socialist project can be radical and clear today (even if it is an open project). The means (the 'model' of organization, how to attain those aims, the degree of nationalization, the role and the form of the plan, the role of money and the market) can and must be *discussed* in relation to the ends, experience and context.[23]

The issue must be: how can needs be satisfied? The answer is a bit more complex than foreseen by Marxists. But Marx left sophisticated guidelines underscoring that each society has its own way of measuring 'time' and organizes time according to its objective, so as to make production take place in accordance with the totality of its needs.

In Mandel's classical approach to socialism, two features are often used to characterize that society (as distinguished both from the notion of 'transition to socialism' and from 'communism': first, a mode of distribution 'to each according to his or her labour'; and second, the direct organization of the economy, interpreted as the withering away of commodity categories. Both of these criteria require discussion.

Mandel developed his argument on the second question (the role of market and commodity categories) in a systematic way in *New Left Review* in 1986–88, in opposition to Alec Nove's book *The Economics of Feasible Socialism*.[24] I do not claim here to give a systematic review of that very important debate, in which three dominant logics are expressed: 1) Nove develops a model of 'market socialism', starting from his belief that *none* of Marx's remarks on socialism are useful (worse, they are utopian and misleading) in building a 'feasible socialism'. Nove takes as a point of departure for his own proposals the analysis of 'actually existing socialist societies' and of capitalism. His model is pragmatic, with minimal 'criteria' that define it as socialist:

strong limitations on private property and a limited plan. Its regulator is a market. 2) Mandel defends a radical model of socialism without money, in a socialized economy based on self-organization. 3) Diane Elson puts forward a model of socialization of the market, in which socialist relations are developed as a means to control and use the market.

As a matter of fact, Mandel later shifted the axis of the debate – as we will see – in a text written in 1990. So the two periods have to be distinguished.

The 'socialist mode of distribution'

In certain debates,[25] Mandel had stressed that the survival of commodity categories in the transitional period was organically linked to the impossibility of organizing distribution on the basis of the slogan 'from each according to his or her ability, to each according to his or her needs', generally presented as associated with the abundance that characterizes 'communism'. He also stressed the destructive effect of monetary incentives based on individual productivity.[26] He insisted then on material incentives linked to collective results and avoiding any increase in monetary distribution: reduction of labour time, improvement in conditions of work, increasing social consumption, and so forth.

Several aspects should be discussed here.

First, the normative 'definition' of the mode of distribution in the transitional period and in socialism is anything but convincing. The formula 'to each according to his or her labour' is neither a dogma, nor a precise one. How to 'measure' labour: according to its quantity? its quality and results? its skill level?

In the Soviet Union and Eastern Europe, in general, both for practical and ideological reasons, compensation was paid for unpleasant and difficult manual work. This seems reasonable from a socialist point of view. The slogan 'to each according to his or her labour' has also been implemented 'according to the level of responsibility' (in fact bureaucratic position); this should certainly be criticized, with strict ceilings on bureaucrats' wages. Finally in the market reforms, the formula was interpreted 'according to the result of labour' as measured on the market. This meant that for the same input of labour you could receive very different wages, according to the position of your factory or industry on the market; this increased unacceptable inequalities and conflicts.

In addition, a criterion of *distribution according to needs*, disconnected from labour, has taken on growing importance in many capitalist societies, as well as under Khrushchev in the Soviet Union and elsewhere. There is no reason not to broaden it.

In fact, in a seldom-quoted letter, to which Roman Rosdolsky drew attention, Engels shed an interesting light on Marx's views on this question. 'The question has been approached very "materialistically" in opposition to certain idealistic phraseology about justice', Engels said. 'All one can reasonably do, however, is 1) to try to discover the method of distribution to be used *at the beginning*; and 2) to try and find the *general tendency* of the further development.'[27] This is a far cry from a normative vision of socialism 'defined' as a society in which the mode of distribution is already determined.

Our conclusion takes the form of a paradox: *if the socialist future is not present in the immediate post-capitalist society, there will be no socialist future at all.* The socialist (communist) transformation should be (once more) understood as a global emancipatory movement, not as a society precisely distinguished from the 'transitional' one. Therefore the needs to be satisfied do not have to 'obey' a determinist, economistic logic; they have to fit in with priorities that make it possible to consolidate the popular support given to such a project.

Means must be consistent with ends

Shortening the working week, eliminating the most tenuous and strenuous jobs, allowing time for training, education, management tasks and leisure, providing men and women with the means to control the conditions that affect their lives, can be forms of nonmonetary material incentives – along with the development of a taste for decision-making for its own sake. These wellsprings of energy and creativity have not been tapped, even when self-management made them a real possibility.

Wouldn't it be better to take the goal itself – transforming social relations and raising productivity to reduce the work week – as an incentive? Reuniting the worker with his or her labour, encouraging the free public expression of needs and promoting a debate on the incentives themselves, would help to discard inadequate solutions to the problems.

Democratic management of distribution networks could link rises in monetary income to increases in the general productivity of the system; this would incite workers to disseminate all advances achieved in their particular location, stimulating those with the 'highest performance' to associate with others and pass on their know-how . . . This raises once again the question of what is the best time/space set in which the workers/consumers can judge these advances and improvements. Should they measure it in the opaque, compartmentalized dimension of value? Or in the dimension of the entire chain of social labour and use value?[28]

This raises the broader question of the regulation of the system as a whole.

The role of the market: the Mandel/Nove debate

In the debate with Nove in *New Left Review*,[29] Mandel begins his argument by presenting as '*the goal of Marxist politics – socialism without commodity production*'. Then how should production and costs – 'socially necessary' labour – be measured? Mandel's implicit answer is that this can be done 'directly'. This would mean direct organization of production and distribution in terms of use-values or concrete labour – i.e. without money and prices.

It is interesting to note Trotsky's views on such an attempt at direct and comprehensive planning of the whole of the production and distribution. In 'The Soviet Economy in Danger', he wrote that there is no 'universal mind' able to 'draw up a faultless and exhaustive economic plan, beginning with the number of acres of wheat down to the last button for a vest.'[30] This is not a 'short-term' statement, limited to situations of relative scarcity or of underdevelopment of productive forces. Nor was his criticism of the Stalinist attempt to plan everything in detail based on an analysis of bureaucratic behaviour. It was based on the impossibility of such a project, and on the necessity for a planned economy to react to the market expression of demand. One could even argue that complexity would increase further with development, and that socialization of the economy does not eliminate the need for economic measurement in terms of prices.[31] In fact Trotsky's argument is reinforced by the most recent advances in science, which demonstrate that even with the best information about a system's resources and laws of development, the results could still be unpredictable.

Trotsky also stressed the fact that in its concentration of decision-making power, the bureaucracy had 'fenced itself off from intervention by concerned millions'. This raises another aspect of the problem: the possibility of different choices. He counterposed to the Stalinist suppression of the market the idea that 'the plan is checked and, to a considerable degree, realized through the market.' A 'firm monetary unit' was for him indispensable to avoid chaos. In the concrete conditions of the transition in the Soviet Union, Trotsky considered that 'only through the interaction of these three elements, state planning, the market, and Soviet democracy, can the correct direction of the economy of the transitional epoch be attained.'[32]

Mandel takes quite a different approach in his debate with Nove. The following example shows how he sees direct democracy as a substitute for any kind of market in the socialized economy: as the general mechanism to solve any question including the colour and number of shoes each person will be allowed to get.

> In factories manufacturing consumer goods, the product mix would flow from previous consultation between the workers' councils and consumers' conferences democratically elected by the mass of the citizens. Various models – for example, different fashions in shoes – would be submitted to them, which the consumers could test and criticize and replace by others. Showrooms and publicity sheets would be the main instrument of that testing. The latter could play the role of a 'referendum' – a consumer, having the right to receive six pairs of footwear a year, would cross six samples in a sheet containing a hundred or two hundred options.[33]

This type of procedure is supposed to determine production and distribution among factories and between factories and consumers in the socialized sector. 'Commodity exchange transacted in currency should essentially be limited to the inter-relations between the private and co-operative sectors on the one hand, and the individual consumer or the socialized sector on the other.'[34] Even if one accepts Mandel's argument that there is considerable waste in existing capitalist shops, that not everyone has to decide everything, and that there is a substantial number of products for which standard quantities and qualities could be planned in advance, this still leaves a vast proportion of your daily time that is taken up in meetings instead of shopping or consulting a catalogue or computer.

The argument is not convincing:

- The worst thing about it is that it weakens Mandel's fundamental and convincing defence of the need for direct democracy. Too many meetings and votes on details would inhibit participation in really necessary collective decision-making about key choices.
- The use of money and of ordinary buying and selling does not contradict the efficiency of a plan. It can be a tool used for its elaboration and implementation and to check that it does satisfy needs, whether of consumers or of socialized factories needing semi-finished goods for their own production. This would leave possibilities open to choose another supplier if one is not satisfactory.

- What does exist (and is developing in existing capitalist factories) is a great possibility of using new technologies and computers to *adapt production to direct orders*, thus reducing stocks. Many choices could be made at home, as is often done through catalogues which could be computerized with individual designs. It is also already possible to purchase through computers – but that is still purchasing.
- It is also true that computers can vastly increase the possibilities for decentralized decision-making, in ways compatible with central measurement of resources and constraints. But that still does not tell us how to measure production (in direct labour time?).

Mandel's standpoint clearly flows from his radical rejection of alienation through commodity relationships in the capitalist market. But does criticism of the capitalist market and alienation necessarily mean rejecting money and prices, or rather rejecting the social relations behind them? And are those oppressive social relations linked to the existence of a market or rather with its dictatorship, including a labour market and a capital market? In other words, are they linked to specific class criteria for measuring costs and needs?

Elson, criticizing Mandel's definition of socialism 'in terms of the absence of commodity production', stresses:

> The commodity in Marx's writings is not fundamentally a good which is bought and sold for money . . . The structure of Marx's texts as a whole suggests something less banal. The problematic status of commodities derives not from the mere fact of sale and purchase, but from the fact of sale and purchase under conditions which enable them to take an independent life of their own. It is this independence of commodities which enables a social relation between men to assume a fantastic form of a relation between things: 'The persons exist for one another merely as representatives and hence owners of commodities.'[35]

What is at stake: 'This interpretation leaves open the possibility of creating a society in which goods are exchanged for money but do not have an independent life of their own; and in which persons do not exist for one another merely as representatives of commodities.' Elson analyzes this possibility, 'which requires not the abolition but the socialization of buying and selling', in her stimulating essay.[36]

In a parallel discussion of that very topic in *Plan, Market and Democracy*, I quoted Bettelheim, who rightly stressed in *Economic Calculation and Forms of Property* that transitional societies had not yet developed 'adequate concepts for measuring social labour, which is never summed up in the dimension of physical labour'.[37] The socialist 'equivalent of "socially necessary labour" related to "useful social effect" has not yet been found', he said. In contrast with the 'law of value', I stressed the fact that prices in a transitional society will define both the way needs and costs are measured and social relationships. In the capitalist world 'abstract labour' dominates because it is the substance of value which takes the form of money, and because *there is no capitalism if money cannot make more money*. Therefore 'concrete labour' and use-value are subordinate categories. The opposite should be the rule in transitional societies; but the space and time for rational judgement should also be enlarged, making possible adequate planning and *social control*. I therefore suggested the following guideline for further elaboration:

> In the same way as the commodity . . . incorporates a threefold judgement on costs, needs and social relations, social control must extend its way over these three fields: but the techniques for recording costs and inventorying needs must be subordinated to overall social choices.[38]

There can be no socialist project:
- Without rejecting the rule of capital markets – and rejecting the absurdity of financial markets 'reacting negatively' when unemployment goes down.
- Without refusing to consider the work-force as a 'thing', a commodity with a cost to be weighed against other costs (those of machines). The right to have a job must be a point of departure, not the uncertain result of the way economy is regulated.
- Without the radical aim of human control (by men and women, workers and consumers, parents and children, individuals and communities of all kinds) over daily life and the future. This means a complete reorganization of life, a transformation of the 'necessary' labour time, of education, leisure and domestic tasks, of the material and cultural conditions of life, of human relationships in all aspects of life, and of our relationship with the environment.
- Without alternative choices: in the rhythm of work and its organization; in the priorities of needs to be satisfied for all; in the system of incentives; in technologies; in forms of solidarity.
- Without solidarity with the weakest and rejection of the struggle of any against all.

If Marxism means anything it is a radical criticism:

- First, of the law of value in the capitalist system presenting itself as an 'objective law', with prices that conceal social relationships and choices based on *class criteria for measuring costs and needs*. This also means taking only those needs and costs into account that can be expressed through prices.

- Second, of any form of 'normative' choice imposed on human beings on behalf of a so-called universal economic (or class) rationality, whether imposed by a market or by a plan.

This means that the 'law of value' cannot be the regulator of a socialist society. It also implies a radical criticism of any 'model', called 'socialist' or not, that hides social relationships behind prices and commodity relationships. In fact, it rejects any static model that aims to 'define' an optimum through calculation.

This means then that the regulator of the economy cannot be a 'tool', either market or plan as such. Calculation and market indications must be subordinated to human judgement, because this is the only 'regulator' that corresponds rationally to socialist aims. But who makes the 'final judgement', and how: human beings, as workers and consumers, men and women, individuals and communities. Socialist democracy is much more complex than previously foreseen. Self-management requires experts and counter-experts using calculations, as well as market indicators. But it also requires political debates through parties and mass organizations defending specific interests, in order not to leave the last word to experts. All of this is needed in order to broaden the horizon of the final choices.

There must therefore be as much clarity as possible about what is considered as a cost or as a right for human beings:

- Full employment is a *cost* for a capitalist society, a *right* and a source of better efficiency for a socialist one.
- Economic democracy, education and job security are *costs* to be minimized for the bourgeoisie; they are *rights* and a source of productivity in a socialist logic.
- Equality must cover up and maintain real class and property inequalities in a bourgeois legal system; it is a right that demands effort and expense to be genuinely upheld in a socialist society.

There must also be an *expression of needs* not limited to measurements in money or prices, even if we know today how to 'internalize' many 'externalities' in prices (for instance in the field of environment policies).

Mandel's argument was not convincing when it tended to present workers' democracy as simple and able to solve all problems without tools and institutions, including a 'socialized market'. In substance what Mandel wanted to stress is that the final judgement must be made by workers (let us say human beings as workers and consumers). In that respect he was convincing.

Evolution of the debate

In 1986, Mandel stressed in the debate with Nove:

> The real stake of current debates is not the *short term* issue of how far reliance on commodity exchange is necessary in the immediate aftermath of an anticapitalist revolution, but whether the long-term goal of socialism itself – as a classless society . . . is worthwhile realizing at all.[39]

As we saw before, he identified the process of withering away of classes and that of the withering away of commodities (which according to his model existed only in exchanges with the private or co-operative sector). But in an article written in November 1990 and published in *Critique communiste* under the title 'Plan ou marché, la troisième voie', Mandel shifted the axis of the debate completely and gave another presentation of his position:

> The debate is not over whether or not *during the long transitional period* between capitalism and socialism one can still use market mechanisms . . . The debate is around the following question: *should the fundamental choices about the distribution of scarce resources be taken by the market or not?*[40]

Here the transitional period – which will last a long time – is the real horizon of the debate. In transitional societies, Mandel was always in favour of using some market criteria, and argued that the existence and use of commodity categories does not prove that the market and capitalist relations predominate. That is clearly the more sophisticated question on which Elson developed her approach. The question is what the dynamics will be of the use of money *according to its different functions*.

'What is at stake', according to Mandel's new formulation, is: *should the market determine the main choices?* The answer is obviously 'no'. Priorities must be 'decided democratically by workers/consumers/ citizens together, choosing among several consistent alternatives.'[41] But then the debate is no longer the same. Mandel lays out in a more convincing way a differentiated approach:

> There is no reason to restrict *free choice by the consumer*. All this should be *extended and not restricted* . . . There is also no reason to suppose that in the transitional period from capitalism to socialism the use of money

(which requires a stable currency) and of market mechanisms, essentially to ensure more consumer satisfaction, should be put aside or even reduced. *The only condition is that it should not produce a determination by the market of priorities in social and economic choices* . . .

The use of money as a unit of *account* is to be distinguished from its function as an instrument of *exchange*, and even more from its use as a *means of accumulating wealth and making choices and investment decisions*.

The first use *will last and be generalized in socialist planning*. The second has *already begun to decline* under capitalism and will continue to decline during the transitional period, with exceptions for certain goods and services. There will probably be an increase of 'free goods and services'. The third use of money should be *severely restricted and progressively eliminated*.[42]

Further debates are evidently still needed on this subject, especially on the form of planning, not only in the consumer goods sector but in factories producing means of production. Mandel was always very hostile to the 'autonomy' of units of production and any notion of enterprise self-financing. In this area too, different kinds of 'market socialism' have very different logics: competition between independent units (with greater or lesser degrees of workers' self-management) and banks on the basis of profitability, on the one hand, and on the other hand the 'socialized market' and planning that Elson proposes, without capital markets, whose logic is to encourage systematic association and not 'predatory competition'.

Yugoslavia experienced very different combinations of plan, market and self-management, within the political limits of the system. Both the conflicts between self-management and a bureaucratic or techno-cratic form of planning (in the initial period) and those between self-management and the logic of the market (later on) are worth studying. I have studied these contradictions[43] because I share with Nove the conviction that we can learn more from the concrete analysis of the so-called 'socialist' countries than from Marx, if what you are looking for in Marx is a concrete model of socialism. But in order to judge from experience, you need criteria. Nove's very interesting bal-ance sheets of the Soviet Union and of the reformed system in Yugo-slavia are based on a rejection of Marxist criteria. Self-organization and disalienation of workers play no role in his model. I also tried to make a balance sheet and draw lessons from the Yugoslav accumula-tion of 'models' (four different models in four decades). But I did it with different 'spectacles' from Nove's. I tried to lay bare the ration-ality of workers' self-management, to draw a balance sheet using the criteria of the emancipation of workers and citizens, using Marx's guidelines. This led me more towards Elson's views (and Mandel's convictions) than to Nove's model.

Using the market should not mean giving up the Marxist approach to what is going on behind it, or having a naive view of the market as a neutral tool. Such a naive view leads to acceptance of its dictatorship. This is even more true in the context of a capitalist environment and a transitional society where private capitalist ownership still exist. Through markets and prices, *different criteria of efficiency conflict*. This is an issue behind world market prices determined by the law of value in the present 'globalized capitalism'. It is a proven fact that the most regressive social relationships are easily the 'most competitive': they will exercise their pressure on any society aiming to begin a socialist transformation. Here again transparency is needed in order to evaluate the optimal degree and forms of 'progressive protectionism', so as to manage the necessary but conflictual relationship with capitalism as long as it exists.

Let us finally stress Mandel's conclusion. At the end of the article written in 1990 (cited above), Mandel disposes of a certain way of reading Marx.

> In reality, the most efficient and human way to build a classless society is through experiment, and it must be improved through successive approximations. There is no good 'cookbook' with which to do this – neither that of 'total planning' nor that of 'market socialism'.[44]

He then argues that we have to use all three elements specified by Trotsky (plan, market and democracy), adding a fourth one: the radical reduction of labour time, an essential measure for workers to simply have time for direct democracy.

If we recall the introductory remarks I quoted from Mandel on the limits of Marxist thinking about the transition to socialism, this final text reads as a sort of testament – and amendment. From the first text to this final one, Mandel seemed to be sure of what socialism was not: a society using commodities. In the end he left that debate open – even if he did not recognize explicitly that he had changed his mind. To be sure, this was not the best way of debating. But it was better than not being able to change his position at all.

It was also better than changing his position on the fundamental principled issues: the necessity and possibility of a struggle for emancipation based on the self-organization, disalienation, and responsibility of human beings in all dimensions of their lives and on a world scale. These were Mandel's convictions, and the basis of his well-known optimism and activist commitment.

Notes

1. Ernest Mandel, 'What is the Bureaucracy?', in Tariq Ali, ed., *The Stalinist Legacy: Its Impact on 20th-Century World Politics*, Harmondsworth 1984, p. 78.

2. Mandel, 'In Defense of Socialist Planning', *New Left Review* 159, September/ October 1986, p. 5.

3. See for instance Mandel's debate with Hillel Ticktin, 'Once Again on the Trotskyist Definition of the Social Nature of the Soviet Union', *Critique* 12, Autumn–Winter 1979–1980, pp. 117–26.

4. See e.g. on the Cuban debate, Mandel, 'The Law of Value in Relation to Self-Management and Investments in the Economy of the Workers States: Some Remarks on the Discussion in Cuba', *World Outlook*, 1963.

5. See Mandel, 'Mercantile Categories in the Period of Transition', in *Man and Socialism in Cuba: The Great Debate*, ed. by Bertram Silverman, New York 1971; and Mandel, 'The Economy of the Transition Period', chapter 16 of *Marxist Economic Theory*, London 1968, vol. 2, pp. 605–53.

6. Mandel, 'The Transitional Regimes in the East', in *Revolutionary Marxism Today*, London 1979, pp. 151–2.

7. Ibid., pp. 142–3.

8. Ibid., pp. 138–9.

9. Ibid., pp. 145–7.

10. Ibid., p. 148.

11. Ibid., p. 150.

12. See Henri Wilno, 'Europe de l'Est: le capitalisme difficile', *Critique communiste* 112–113, November 1991. I contributed to this necessary analysis in Samary, 'Eastern Europe and the Former USSR Five Years on: Economic Reform in the East', *International Viewpoint* 264, March 1995, which is a shortened version of the French article 'La "transition" dans tous ses états', *Inprecor* 388, February 1995.

13. See Mandel and Chris Harman, *Fallacies of State Capitalism*.

14. See Catherine Samary, 'Social Relations under Bureaucratically Centralized Planning' in *Plan, Market and Democracy: The Experience of the So-Called Socialist Countries*, IIRE Notebook for Study and Research no. 7/8, Amsterdam 1988.

15. Saying that such a system was anything but capitalist does not mean that it was good. Charles Bettelheim, *Economic Calculation and Forms of Property*, New York 1975, raises key questions about the necessity and difficulties of calculation in a society in transition towards socialism.

16. See Jacques Sapir's contributions in *Monnaie et finances dans la transition en Russie*, Victor Santer and Jacques Sapir, eds., Paris 1995, pp. 72–3.

17. Ibid., pp. 257–8.

18. Ibid., pp. 263–4.

19. *Conjoncture* 5, May 1996, p. 10.

20. See Samary, *Plan, Market and Democracy*.

21. See the interesting remarks and conceptual proposals on this point in Gérard Roland, *Economie politique du système soviétique*, Paris 1989.

22. Some years ago I wrote a polemical piece under the provocative title 'The

Anti-Worker Workers' State'. It was not only a provocation. I will come back to that debate in section 1.4 below.

23. See Maxime Durand's contribution to those debates: 'Planification: 21 thèses pour ouvrir le débat', *Critique communiste* 106–107, April–May 1991.

24. Alec Nove, *The Economics of Feasible Socialism*, London 1983.

25. See for instance Mandel, 'Mercantile Categories in the Period of Transition'.

26. Mandel, 'Du "nouveau" sur la question de la nature de l'URSS', *Quatrième Internationale* 45, September 1970.

27. Engels to C. Schmidt, 5 August 1890, in Karl Marx and Frederick Engels, *Selected Works in Three Volumes*, Moscow 1970, vol. 3, p. 484; cited in Roman Rosdolsky, 'La limite historique de la loi de la valeur: l'ordre social socialiste dans l'oeuvre de Marx', *Critiques de l'économie politique* 6, January–March 1972.

28. Samary, *Plan, Market and Democracy*, p. 56.

29. Mandel, 'In Defence of Socialist Planning', NLR 159, September/October 1986; Alec Nove, 'Markets and Socialism', NLR 161, January/February 1987; Mandel, 'The Myth of Market Socialism', NLR 169, May/June 1988.

30. Trotsky, 'The Soviet Economy in Danger' (22 October 1932), in *Writings of Leon Trotsky (1932)*, New York 1972, p. 274.

31. In *Problèmes théoriques et pratiques de la planification*, Paris 1949, as well as in later books such as *Economic Calculation and Forms of Property*, Charles Bettelheim argued that the need for economic calculation meant that prices could not be suppressed in socialist planning. Such questions require specific debates.

32. Trotsky, 'The Soviet Economy in Danger', pp. 274–5.

33. Mandel, 'In Defence of Socialist Planning', pp. 27–8.

34. Ibid., p. 32.

35. Diane Elson, 'Market Socialism or Socialization of the Market?', NLR 172, November/December 1988, p. 4.

36. Ibid.

37. Bettelheim, *Economic Calculation*, p. 11, cited in Samary, *Plan, Market and Democracy*, p. 56 (I have corrected here the English translation).

38. Samary, ibid., p. 57 (emphasis in original).

39. Mandel, 'In Defence of Socialist Planning', p. 9 (my emphasis).

40. Mandel, 'Plan ou marché, la troisième voie', *Critique communiste*, 106–107, April–May 1991, p. 15 (my emphasis). Several debates were also published in *Critique communiste* about the model proposed by Tony Andreani, 'Pour un socialisme associatif', in issue no. 116–117, February–March 1992. See also J. Vanek, *The Labor-Managed Economy: Essay*, Ithaca 1977.

41. Mandel, 'Plan ou marché', p. 16.

42. Ibid., pp. 20–21 (my emphasis).

43. Samary, *Le Marché contre l'autogestion: l'expérience yougoslave*, Paris 1988.

44. Mandel, 'Plan ou marché', p. 21 (my emphasis).

9

Marxists before the Holocaust: Trotsky, Deutscher, Mandel

Norman Geras

I shall begin here from an astonishing fact. In December 1938, in an appeal to American Jews, Leon Trotsky in a certain manner predicted the impending Jewish catastrophe. Here is what he wrote:

> It is possible to imagine without difficulty what awaits the Jews at the mere outbreak of the future world war. But even without war the next development of world reaction signifies with certainty the *physical extermination of the Jews.*[1]

This was just a few weeks after Kristallnacht and it was one month before Hitler's famous Reichstag speech of 30 January 1939 in which he 'prophesied' the annihilation of European Jewry in the event of a world war.

I call Trotsky's prediction an astonishing fact. For it is a common and well-grounded theme in the literature of the Holocaust that the disaster was not really predictable. It was outside the range of normal experience and of sober political projection or indeed imagination. Even once the tragedy began to unfold, many people found the information on what was being done to the Jews hard to absorb, hard to connect up into a unified picture of comprehensive genocide, hard to believe; and this applied to wide sections of the Jewish population itself. Then, after the event, its enormity has seemed to many difficult to grasp. It has seemed to be in some measure beyond understanding and explanation. We have the evidence of such a reaction from none other than Trotsky's great biographer. Referring to 'the absolute uniqueness of the catastrophe', Isaac Deutscher would later write:

The fury of Nazism, which was bent on the unconditional extermination of every Jewish man, woman, and child within its reach, passes the comprehension of a historian, who tries to uncover the motives of human behaviour and to discern the interests behind the motives. Who can analyse the motives and the interests behind the enormities of Auschwitz? ... [W]e are confronted here by a huge and ominous mystery of the degeneration of the human character that will forever baffle and terrify mankind.[2]

How are we to account for Trotsky's prescience in this matter? Was it perhaps just some sort of stray, dark intuition? Or was it rather a hypothesis founded on the forms of knowledge which he brought to trying to understand the realities of his time? I shall in due course propose as an answer that it was something in between. But I will come to this answer by way of a critical review of Ernest Mandel's thinking on the same subject. This is the main purpose of what I want to present here, though my aim will be as well, through it, to offer some more general reflections on Marxism as a body of theory in relation to the Nazi genocide against the Jews.

I say a critical review of Mandel's thinking on the subject and critical is what it will be; although it will be somewhat less so in relation to his later views as compared with the earlier ones, since there was an internal development and enlargement of these. Still, overall, it will be critical. And I am bound to observe, therefore, that so critical a review may seem out of place on the occasion, devoted as it is to registering and honouring Mandel's achievement. Let me just say three things about this. First, like other participants here I held, and I hold, Mandel's life's work in the highest regard, and nothing in what follows affects that. Second, in the proper place I have recorded my own debts to him. In particular, his work helped me to an understanding of something centrally important in the thinking of Rosa Luxemburg, as also in any rounded conception of emancipatory socialist struggle.[3] (I refer by this not only to what he wrote specifically about Rosa Luxemburg but also to his political writings more generally.) Third, Mandel himself, I believe, would not have been happy with anything less: anything less than the frankest appraisal on whatever question, and if frankly critical, then so be it.

An early effort by him to take the measure of the Jewish tragedy is an article of 1946, 'La question juive au lendemain de la deuxième guerre mondiale'. Please keep in mind that it was written by Mandel at the age of 22 or 23, and also (in light of that date, 1946) how much difficulty in general people have had, over several decades, in facing up to the implications of this catastrophe. Mandel begins by evoking

the horrors of it, and he then gestures towards the sort of uncompre-
hending response I have already illustrated with the words of Isaac
Deutscher. The human imagination has trouble grasping the significance of the experience, Mandel writes; the misfortune of the Jews
seems 'absurd'. The mind 'refuses to admit that material interests
could have determined, in cold logic, the extermination of these
innumerable defenceless beings'.[4]

This is not, however, the response that Mandel for his part wants to
recommend. The fate of the European Jews he firmly situates, as being
explicable by it, in the broader context of the mortal crisis of capitalism;
and in the context, a product of this crisis, of the other horrors of the
Second World War. It is 'capitalism [that is] responsible for their [the
Jews'] tragic fate and for the impasse in which the whole of humanity
finds itself'.[5] The Nazi genocide against the Jews is also 'contextualized'
by the young Mandel by reference to certain actions and attitudes of
the Allied powers: the deportation of ethnic Germans from parts of
east and central Europe at the end of the war; the callousness of the
British towards mass suffering in India, or of the Americans in connection with the use of the atomic bomb at Hiroshima; the responsibility
borne by the whole capitalist order, by 'all the governments of the
world', in not coming to the aid of the Jewish people. And next to 5
million murdered Jews (the figure Mandel gives), 'one finds the 60
million victims of the imperialist war'. The general spirit of this
assessment is captured by formulations like the following:

> The barbarous treatment of the Jews by Hitlerite imperialism has only
> pushed to paroxysm the barbarism of the habitual methods of imperial-
> ism in our epoch.
>
> Far from being isolated from, or opposed to, the destiny of humanity, the
> Jewish tragedy only announces to other peoples their future fate if the
> decline of capitalism continues at its present rate.[6]

This early attempt by Mandel to assess the significance of the Shoah
is marked, in my opinion, by a triple weakness. It can be described in
terms of the three polar oppositions set out below. The destruction of
the Jews of Europe:

is comparable to other crimes / is singular or unique;

is rationally explicable / is beyond comprehension;

is the product of capitalism and imperialism / is due to some other
combination of factors.

Now, I do not believe any adequate assessment can be made by just
embracing either one pole or the other of these three oppositions. A

certain (particular) intermediate standpoint is called for in relation to each. The weakness of this initial article by Mandel is that he pretty well does embrace the first pole of each opposition. According to him, the destruction of the Jews of Europe is *rationally explicable* as the *product of imperialist capitalism*, and as such it is manifestly *comparable* to the other barbarisms which this socio-economic formation throws up. That both the specificity of the event and a certain 'elusiveness', such as very many people have felt and expressed about it, are thereby levelled or lost, is perhaps best brought out by this hypothesis towards the end of the essay:

> [I]t is not just possible but probable that an American fascist movement will go beyond, in its technical 'perfection', the brutalities of Nazi anti-semitism. If the next decade is not witness to the proletarian revolution in the United States, it will prepare for American Jewry hecatombs that will surpass Auschwitz and Maidanek in horror.[7]

The Holocaust is here turned into a more or less regular type of occurrence of our epoch. Terrible as it may have been, it only antici-pates much worse, and this within a decade or two should capitalism survive.

I may as well indicate before proceeding any further that I do not think Ernest Mandel ever made good the three weaknesses I have identified from this early article (and will shortly come back to enlarge upon). Although in the last decade of his life, returning to the same subject, he would elaborate a view of it more qualified and enriched, the same weaknesses in one way or another were to remain.

That they continued at least into the 1960s and 1970s can be marked by drawing attention to a certain absence. In his Introduction of 1969 to the collection of Trotsky's texts *The Struggle Against Fascism in Germany*, Mandel does not even directly mention the Holocaust. The same thing in the relevant chapter (chapter 8) of his *Trotsky*, published in 1979. There are some generic references to 'an advancing barbar-ism', and to threats to the survival of 'broad human groups' or to 'human civilization' itself. But this is as close as he gets.[8] To be sure, the writings of Trotsky that Mandel here introduces themselves predate the 'Final Solution', so one would not expect the topic to loom enormously large in what he says about them. Even so, Trotsky *before* the event, in some well-known passages to which I shall later return, seems to anticipate the extremes of barbarism that a triumphant National Socialism would portend. Is it not remarkable that twenty-five, and thirty-five, years *after* the event, in full awareness of what one of these extremes turned out to be, Mandel finds no place to mention it directly, much less to discuss it, in presenting Trotsky's ideas about the rise and the victory of Nazism?

What he does present is a general theory of *fascism*: a theory of it centred on the crushing of the workers' movement, and articulated through Marxist concepts of class, capitalist economic crisis, the different political forms and methods of rule of the capitalist state.[9] We may note two particular claims made by Mandel in presenting this theory. First, fascism, he insists, is 'a universal phenomenon that knows no geographical boundaries [and which] struck roots in *all* imperialist lands'; 'attempts at explanation that chiefly emphasize this or that national peculiarity are wholly inadequate'.[10] While I have, on one level, no quarrel with this, it is nevertheless an optic likely to discourage attention towards a certain specificity of German National Socialism and of one of its policies. Second, the superiority of the Marxist method of social analysis, Mandel contends, lies in its total character. It seeks 'to comprehend all aspects of social activity as connected with and structurally coordinated to one another.' This is a thesis put forward also at other places in his writings. But it is not tested here against the difficulties of explaining the 'Final Solution'.[11]

In 1986, coming back to the subject forty years after his first youthful assessment, Mandel tried to meet this test – in his book on the Second World War. Even here the first signs are not propitious. Only three pages are devoted by him to the Holocaust, and the context plainly renders it a subordinate issue. For his discussion of it occurs in a country-by-country survey of *ideology* within the major arenas of the war. The fate of European Jewry figures only as part of this survey. The discussion nevertheless marks a definite development of Mandel's viewpoint as compared with his essay of 1946. No longer is it only 'material interests', capitalist economy and crisis, that are at work. His explanation of the Holocaust now combines a particular form of ideology on the one hand, with features of capitalist modernity on the other. The ideology is racism. This, Mandel argues, is 'congenitally linked to institutionalized colonialism and imperialism', owing to the need with these political and economic formations to dehumanize whole groups of people in order to rationalize and justify oppressing them in extreme ways. It is then a short step from there, from dehumanizing them, to denying such groups the right to life itself. When racist ideology combines with the global irrationality of capitalism and '[its] "perfect" local rationality' – what Mandel calls also 'the deadly partial rationality of the modern industrial system' – that step, according to him, 'is frequently taken'.

Further, a number of additional factors, political and psychological, are brought in by Mandel to account for the particular result that was the Nazi genocide. Amongst these factors are: a desperado elite holding political power; the *va banque* aggression unleashed by it in conjunction with sectors of big business; a policy of state terrorism with 'an implacable logic of its own'; the passive complicity of thousands of people, civil servants and other executive agents; and 'a fetid substratum of unconscious guilt and shame'.[12] I shall come back to the significance of these other factors. But clearly there has been an inner differentiation and some filling out of Mandel's thinking on this question, as one would expect from a writer of now greater maturity. I find, all the same, that the key problems are unresolved.

First, Mandel offers precious little sense, and certainly no attempt at an elaboration, of the singularity or specificity of the Shoah. On the contrary, the overwhelming weight of his emphasis is, once again, on contextualizing it – on its comparability with other historical phenomena. We are referred by him to 'the mass enslavement and killing of Blacks via the slave trade' and to the extermination of Indians by the *conquistadors*; to the fact that gypsies and 'sections of the Slav people' also figured on the list of the Nazis' victims, as did tens of thousands of ethnic Germans murdered in the T4 (so-called 'euthanasia') programme; to the Japanese atrocities in 'Unit 731' in Manchuria, 'only one rung below Auschwitz'; to the bombing of Hiroshima and Nagasaki, reflecting a contempt for human beings 'not far removed from extreme racism'; and to the fact that anti-semitism and other Nazi attitudes were and are widespread beyond Germany.

True, Mandel also writes this: 'the Holocaust – the deliberate and systematic killing of six million men, women and children simply because of their ethnic origin – stands as a unique crime in mankind's sad criminal history'. But that is all he writes. And it is not now clear in what the Holocaust *is* unique, if it is.

I do not want to be misunderstood. I am not suggesting that the Jewish tragedy is not at all, not in any way, comparable to other great horrors and crimes. Of course it is. But these are the respective weights Mandel gives to the two sides of the question: several paragraphs on the comparability of the tragedy; a single, unexplicated sentence on its specificity or uniqueness. This is a much debated and difficult question within a now very extensive literature (though, like many of the other difficult questions there, it is not one much reflected on by Marxists). The historian Yehuda Bauer has proposed in connection with it the metaphor of a huge volcano rising out of a dark, forbidding landscape: the volcano is part of the landscape; but it also stands out against it.[13] Mandel says much about the landscape ('mankind's sad criminal history') and about the Holocaust's being part of this. He says nearly nothing about the Holocaust standing out. Or he says only *that* it stands out, but not how.

Second, Mandel is extremely confident of the power of social and political explanation here. Referring to 'those who have treated Hitler's fanatic anti-semitism leading to the Holocaust as beyond rational explanation', he writes that 'such drastic historical exceptionalism' cannot be sustained – then going on to proffer the explanation I have summarized. Now, again, in order to avoid being misunderstood, let me say that I do not support any radical incomprehensibility thesis. The attempt to destroy the Jews was an event in history, and its preconditions, causes, processes, can and must be investigated with a view to trying to understand them. In this matter more perhaps than any other we need to understand as much as we can, so as to be able to resist as well as we can all further projects of mass murder and appalling cruelty. However, the sort of opinion I have quoted from Isaac Deutscher (and which is shared by many others) expresses the sense, even if sometimes exaggerated, that there is a residue within this historical experience beyond the regular forms of social, political or ideological explanation: a residue which is called by Deutscher baffling, and 'degeneration of the human character', and called by other people other things. Mandel seems to give it no legitimate place. This will become clearer in light of my last critical point.

Which is that, third, for all the greater complexity of his analysis at this later date, the Holocaust is still presented by him as being an effect of *capitalism*; as the product of its global irrationality, its partial (functional) rationality, and the racist ideology generated by its imperialist forms. But this explanation does not suffice to its object, no more than do explanations of the catastrophe as a product of modernity. Faced with either one or the other we may legitimately ask why, in view of the generality of the social condition invoked as primary to the event, *this* has happened so far only once. (The question should not be taken to imply that the structures of capitalism or of modernity do not have any important part in an overall explanation.) In truth, Mandel is obliged for greater completeness to bring in as factors of his own explanation less class-specific and capitalism-specific causes, both motivational and political: such as the servile complicity and lack of critical judgement of tens of thousands of people; unconscious guilt and shame; extreme policy choices with a dynamic of their own; and indeed dehumanization itself, now become a central category and for its part a rather widespread and familiar human disposition. But none of this is recognized by Mandel as having broadened the scope of the analysis to encompass more general, less historically specific themes – perhaps even to the point where a residue of sheer, ungrounded excess may remain.

This failure to recognize the now broader nature of his analysis is highlighted by one startling and cavalier judgement which he allows himself. Having got to the end of his multi-factor exposition of what led to the Jewish catastrophe – not only extreme racism and the irrationality of capitalism, coupled with its functional, industrial rationality, but also widespread complicity, a desperado political elite, its *va banque* policy of aggression, a state terrorism with its own logic, and then an unconscious layer of guilt and shame as well – Mandel comments: 'The Holocaust only comes at the end of this long causal chain. But it can and must be explained through it. Indeed, *those who understood the chain were able to foresee it.*' (Emphasis added)

The reference here is to Trotsky's prediction from which we began, and to me this is a *reductio ad absurdum* of the totalizing ambition of Mandel's approach: attempting to 'recover' the heterogeneity in the explanation by treating everything in it as part of one unified chain, and then imagining that Trotsky's 1938 prediction might really have been based on being able to foresee all the individual links in it *and* their connection. I cannot take the suggestion seriously. Especially not, remembering the context of general unpreparedness and incredulity vis-à-vis the Jewish calamity as it first loomed and then became a reality. Trotsky would have needed to be superhuman to have had this much understanding in advance. I think we have to look, rather, towards a looser kind of foresight on his part, although coming together this, needless to say, with his Marxist knowledge of the grave dangers of capitalist crisis and of the typical conflicts it throws up and the ugly new forms it can breed.

Intimations of what I am getting at in speaking of this looser kind of foresight are to be found in observations Ernest Mandel himself made about Trotsky, both earlier and later. Earlier, in his study of him already referred to, Mandel writes that Trotsky understood 'the fact that irrational ideas, moods and yearnings of great force had survived from pre-capitalist times in large parts of bourgeois society'; and that though racism is a typical ideology of the colonial-imperialist epoch it is combined with 'remnants of pre-bourgeois ideology'.[14] Later, in *Trotsky As Alternative* (first published in German in 1992), he repeats this latter point. And he says also that Trotsky saw fascist ideology and rule as involving, at one and the same time, a 'relapse into pre-capitalist reaction and obscurantism' and a late, catching-up form of modernization.[15]

Many of you will be familiar with the better known passages on which Mandel here draws; passages, in particular, from the article of 1933, 'What is National Socialism?'. In this, Trotsky characterizes Nazi ideology as a reaction against the rationalism and materialism of the last two centuries, and as integrating a pogromist anti-semitism into the defence of capitalism against the threat represented by the working class. He goes on to talk of 'the depths of society' having been opened up; of 'inexhaustible reserves . . . of darkness, ignorance, and savagery'. And he says that what should have been eliminated as excrement from the national organism with 'the normal development' of society 'has now come gushing out from the throat; capitalist society is puking up the undigested barbarism. Such is the physiology of National Socialism'.[16] It is a repugnant image but in its own way also a prophetic one. Undigested barbarism. Its final consequences of a darkness inexhaustible indeed. Trotsky would later, in a manifesto of the Fourth International on the war, describe fascism 'as a chemically pure distillation of the culture of imperialism', with anti-semitism a stable element within the racial themes of Nazi propaganda and belief.[17]

Now, in an illuminating analysis of the development of Trotsky's thinking on the Jewish question, Enzo Traverso has presented us with an evolution broadly as follows: from anti-semitism being seen by him initially as a feudal survival in the process of dying out, to a later appreciation of its significance as a symptom of capitalist crisis and modernist barbarism. Anti-semitism within Nazi ideology, Traverso proposes likewise, was at first viewed by Trotsky as part of an obscurantist reaction to modernity, then later understood as an authentic expression of contemporary capitalism and imperialism.[18] While there is a clear textual basis for this interpretation,[19] nevertheless I think, myself, that in his emphasis on the change in Trotsky's thinking Traverso bypasses the importance of the *combination* (of new and old ideological forms) that some of Mandel's quoted formulas bring out. The continuity – and so susceptibility to such combination – between pre-modern and modern forms may be highlighted in two ways.

Consider, first, the category of dehumanization, become pivotal to Mandel's account. Undoubtedly a development occurs between older forms of Christian anti-semitism and the Nazi, racial, variant of it. However, whether the Jews are seen as refusing the truth they themselves had anticipated, as God-killers and in some sort a demonic influence, or are seen rather as beings of a biologically inferior type, they are placed at the margins of, or actually excluded from, the sphere of the fully human and from the reciprocal moral consideration associated with it. Nazi popular attitudes were certainly hybrid here, drawing on long-standing Christian prejudices and linking these with a pseudo-scientific racial theory. More generally, it is hard to believe that just *any* people could have been as murderously dealt with over a whole continent, or as readily abandoned to its torment, rather than this particular people, hated and vilified there for going-on two millennia. The psychological distancing effected by fixing others as in one way or another menacingly alien is at any rate an age-old symbolic mechanism. It has a transhistorical dimension.

Similarly, the content of the category of barbarism as used by Mandel and other Marxists (whether wittingly or not) is of a highly generic kind, and is, I would suggest, essentially anthropological. The category is used to refer loosely to such phenomena as obsessive, unreasoning hatreds, extreme or endemic violence, the enjoyment of cruelty, indifference to great suffering and so forth. None of this is specific to capitalism.

The centrality of such categories to Mandel's understanding of the Holocaust indicates why it is not genuinely containable by an explanation in terms of the socio-economic and ideological forms of capitalism. I shall come to an elaboration of this point by way of examining his last and most developed attempt to grapple with the issue. I mean the article of 1990, 'Material, social and ideological preconditions for the Nazi genocide'. (In discussing it I shall make supplementary reference also to an appendix Mandel wrote for the German edition of his book on the Second World War, published just one year later than this article. What is relevant in the appendix for the most part reproduces the theses of the article. So far as it differs from it in one interesting respect, I shall speak of the difference later, in concluding.) The central strands and weaknesses of Mandel's approach in this article remain basically unchanged. But it represents, all the same, a further development of his thinking, because the residual factors in the explanation have been reinforced. I shall take these two sets of features of the article in turn.

We still find here just a couple of brief phrases on the singularity of the Holocaust. Mandel writes of it as 'a unique event in history so far', and as involving 'the worst crimes in history'. His reasons for the judgement remain to be clearly spelled out.[20] The 'contextualizing' material, on the other hand, is rather fuller. We are reminded with a multiplicity of references – to slavery in the ancient world, the persecution of witches, the fate of the American Indians, black slavery; and to the murder of gypsies, Poles and Russians during the Second World War – that, whether as victims *tout court* or as victims of the Nazis, the Jews belong to a very much larger company.[21] Who amongst serious people is in need of this reminder?

Then, too, Mandel continues to reject as (without qualification) 'obscurantist' the view that the Holocaust is incomprehensible. I return shortly to a claim he makes in that connection.[22] And the key to his own explanation remains what it was before. The Holocaust is to be understood as 'the ultimate expression so far of the destructive tendencies existing in bourgeois society'.[23] It is the product of a biological racism itself arising from socio-economic practices that require the systematic dehumanization of other peoples; linked, this, to that 'typical combination of perfected partial rationality and global irrationality ... characteristic of bourgeois society'; in conditions, generally, of the crisis of imperialism; and conditions, specifically, of a profound social and political crisis in the given (that is, German) national arena.[24]

That all this is to the point is one thing. That it fully captures its intended object is another. It does not. We begin to see why by looking at what Mandel throws in here, sometimes just by the way, as additional factors: factors of a psychological, ethical and experiential nature.

Thus, first, in connection with dehumanizing racist ideologies that rationalize the mistreatment of other human beings, he speaks of a need, consequent upon such mistreatment, 'for a "neutralization" of the perpetrators' guilty consciences and feelings of individual guilt' – but without any further enlargement.[25] Second, in connection with the Nazi policy of extermination having 'begun with the Jews', Mandel gives as a partial cause of this 'the demented faith of Hitler and some of his lieutenants in the "world Jewish conspiracy".'[26] Third, there is a passing reference to the First World War as an event without which Nazism as a mass phenomenon would have been unthinkable. In the aforementioned appendix to the German edition of his book on the Second World War, Mandel deals with the same point at greater length and says that 'the chauvinist enthusiasm [of 1914] ... the acceptance of senseless mass killings and boundless destruction constitute the great break in contemporary history. This was the first decisive step towards barbarism ...'[27] Is there not an important insight here? The suggestion may be speculative, but could not this trauma of mass death, this prolonged, unprecedentedly large and useless slaughter, with its scarring effects on the consciousness of a generation, have had some part in preparing the 'moral' ground for the genocide to follow?

However that may be, Mandel addresses himself also, fourth, and perhaps most crucially in this context, to reasons for the Jewish tragedy 'of an ethical order': to do with the complicity and obedience – and whether on account of routine, self-interested calculation or cowardice – of millions of Europeans, ordinary people accepting the authority of the State rather than 'the fundamental rules of ethics'. He concludes in this regard: 'In the face of massive injustice, resistance and revolt – including individual resistance, but above all collective resistance and revolt – are not only a right but a duty . . . This is the main lesson of the Holocaust.'[28]

In touching on such matters Ernest Mandel connects to a wider historiographical, socio-psychological and other literature on the Holocaust, adding to it, to be sure, what Marxism is best-placed to add. He connects there also to another layer of human understandings *as well as* difficulties of understanding. It is doubtful these can be easily recuperated within a crisis-of-capitalism type of explanation as it is Mandel's constant tendency to try to recuperate everything.

For think of it now: bad conscience and guilt. Think, even in terms of quite ordinary experience, of some of the behaviours this can produce. Think of *demented* beliefs and what they can produce. Think of mass death and those who take part in the experience of it, and of those who have to cope emotionally with its enduring effects. Think of moral cowardice or merely moral 'slippage', of failure to act against known wrongs and of the many different ways there are of living comfortably with that. We begin to reach into the sub-soil, so to say, of the human psyche. And we are not so far, surely, from Deutscher's 'degeneration of the human character'. But for Deutscher something here was still baffling where for Mandel, seemingly, everything is clear. The former view for many people has appeared to be more persuasive: that, in the excess, the passage to the limit of what the 'Final Solution of the Jewish Question' envisaged, indeed the passage in the execution of it beyond every familiar limit, there was something which eludes historical understanding and social scientific explanation. You can spell out all the conditions, factors, contributory causes; still, these were not bound to produce exactly *that*. By themselves, therefore, they do not altogether explain it.

One especially influential voice has argued to this effect. I refer to Primo Levi. Levi wrote that the commonly accepted explanations did not satisfy him. 'They are reductive; not commensurate with, nor proportionate to, the facts that need explaining . . . I cannot avoid the impression of a general atmosphere of uncontrolled madness that seems to me to be unique in history.' For Levi, multi-factor explanations were necessary but they also fell short. He preferred, he said, the humility of those historians who 'confess to *not understanding*', to not understanding *such* a furious hatred. It was, Levi wrote, 'a poison fruit sprung from the deadly trunk of Fascism, but outside of and beyond Fascism itself'.[29]

In his essay on the 'Material, social and ideological preconditions for the Nazi genocide', Mandel seeks to fend off views of this kind with the argument that they generalize responsibility for evil to humanity at large, in effect accusing everybody and consequently nobody in particular, not Hitler, nor the Nazis, nor their supporters.[30] But to me this is an obvious *non sequitur*, not worth lingering over. That we may not be able to comprehend everything about the calamity visited on the Jews in no way entails that we are then unable to see any difference between the innocent and the guilty.

I come back now to Trotsky's remarkable prediction of 1938 and I ask again: what was its basis? Doubtless his Marxist understanding of the dangers of fascism in general and of German National Socialism in particular had something to do with it. But this on its own could not have sufficed to yield the extremity within the prediction he made. I want to suggest that there was an element of plain intuition here, spun from Trotsky's broader human sensibility in which something was already known about 'uncontrolled madness', deadly hatred and the passing of all limits. Of this broader sensibility one could cite much evidence. It is what made Trotsky the powerful and creative Marxist intellect he was, his many calumniators notwithstanding. But I shall cite only a single relevant piece which I have had occasion to draw attention to once before.[31]

It is an account of a pogrom from his book *1905*, an episode narrated there of the failed Russian revolution of that year. Describing the build-up to the pogrom, Trotsky – Marxist – sketches both its political background and something of the social composition of the mob. Then he writes this: 'the gang rushes through the town, drunk on vodka and the smell of blood.' Drunk *on the smell of blood.* What specifically Marxist category is there for that? Trotsky relates:

> Everything is allowed to him [the member of the gang], he is capable of anything, he is the master of property and honour, of life and death . . . If he wants to, he can throw an old woman out of a third-floor window together with a grand piano, he can smash a chair against a baby's head, rape a little girl while the entire crowd looks on, hammer a nail into a living human body . . . He exterminates whole families, he pours petrol over a house, transforms it into a mass of flames, and if anyone attempts to escape, he finishes him off with a cudgel . . . There exist no tortures, figments of a feverish brain maddened by alcohol and fury, at which he need ever stop. He is capable of anything, he dares everything . . .

And Trotsky goes on:

> The victims, bloodstained, charred, driven frantic, still search for salvation within the nightmare. Some put on the bloodstained clothes of people

> already dead, lie down in a pile of corpses . . . Others fall on their knees
> before the officers, the policemen, the raider, they stretch out their arms,
> crawl in the dust, kiss the soldiers' boots, beg for mercy. In reply they
> hear only drunken laughter. 'You wanted freedom? Here, look, this is it.'

In these last mocking words, Trotsky says, 'is contained the whole
infernal morality of the pogrom policy'; and he repeats once again,
'capable of everything'.[32]

Already long before 1938 Trotsky had seen into the depths. He had
seen the spirit of limitless excess, the exaltation people can feel in
exercising a merciless power over others and the 'total-ness' there can
be in a humiliation – both the horror and the joy that is taken in
inflicting it, lethal couple in what is already an annihilation. He had
seen also one of the more terrifying faces of human freedom, self-
consciously turned against its other, better faces. In all of this he had
seen part of what there would subsequently be in the Shoah, including
the element of an irreducible choice. The preconditions and the
surrounding context of this kind of choice can and always must be
explored and described. But it remains in the end what it is: underde-
termined, a choice.

Whether or not there was in Trotsky's mental processes any direct
route running from the memory of his earlier description of a pogrom
to predicting in 1938 the physical extermination of the Jews cannot, of
course, be known. I simply offer as a hypothesis that it was out of the
kind of understanding which that narrative of his betokens, as much as
it was out of his Marxist theorizing about capitalism or fascism, that his
anticipation of Nazism's ultimate barbarity may have come. What he
wrote there in any case foreshadows themes that were to be proposed
later by others in thinking about the Shoah itself. I want to mention
two of these others.

Saul Friedlander has written of a feeling evident alike within the
Nazi leadership and amongst some of its followers, 'of accomplishing
something truly, historically, meta-historically, exceptional'; a feeling
manifested, for example, in 'the insistence of some of the commanders
of the *Einsatzgruppen* [engaged in the mass murder of Jews by shooting]
to stay on duty'.[33] Developing the point he has argued that, beyond the
undeniable explanatory importance of anti-semitic ideology and the
dynamics of bureaucracy, there is also 'an independent psychological
residue [that] seems to defy the historian'. It concerns, Friedlander
says, 'a compelling lust for killing on an immense scale, driven by some
kind of extraordinary elation . . .' And it is just here, with this elation,
that 'our understanding remains blocked on the level of self-awareness':

'The historian can analyse the phenomenon from the "outside", but . . . his unease stems from the noncongruence between intellectual probing and the blocking of intuitive comprehension . . .'[34]

Friedlander reads such a feeling of elation in a notorious speech of Himmler's before a gathering of SS officers, at which the Nazi leader praised the magnitude of their accomplishment in the destruction of the Jews. The same thing can be read, repeatedly, in testimonies from those present at the sites of mass murder.

The elation and the lust for killing. A battalion of German reserve policemen on duty in Poland and drafted into rounding up and shooting Jews is enjoying a visit from an entertainment unit from Berlin. 'The members of this unit had . . . heard of the pending shooting of the Jews. They asked, indeed even emphatically begged, to be allowed to participate in the execution of the Jews.'[35] Again: 'Members of the Grenzpolizeikommissariat were, with a few exceptions, quite happy to take part in shootings of Jews. They had a ball! . . . Nobody failed to turn up' . . . 'As usual a few of the new officers became megalomaniacs, they really enter into the role wholeheartedly' '. . . after a while we saw numerous soldiers and civilians pouring on to an embankment in front of us, behind which . . . executions were being carried out at regular intervals.' '. . . some marines from the naval unit came past . . . they had heard that Jews were always being shot in the town and . . . they wanted to see this for themselves . . . The execution area was visited by scores of German spectators from the Navy and the Reichsbahn (railway).' 'I saw SD personnel weeping because they could not cope mentally with what was going on. Then again I encountered others who kept a score-sheet of how many people they had sent to their death.'[36] Or here, a Norwegian imprisoned at Sachsenhausen describes a group of young Germans let loose with truncheons on hundreds of starving Jews: '[T]he act of striking intoxicated them and drove them wild . . . they were living devils, possessed, transported with ecstasy . . . they went on striking at them as they lay, trod upon them, kicked them, while the blood was streaming from mouths, ears, and wounds. Every time they needed a rest, they turned exultantly to their laughing and smiling comrades, laughed back, and gave the truncheon a limber, playful swing round their heads. Then they flew at it again.'[37]

The critic George Steiner, like Friedlander acknowledging the importance of what has been explained of this historical experience by the various disciplines of empirical enquiry, suggests that these have been unable nonetheless to fathom the intensity of the hatreds that were unleashed, or to account for the extreme lengths to which the Nazis were willing to go in pursuit of their murderous objective. In a thesis he concedes to be unprovable, Steiner argues that it might have been as the inventors of monotheism, of 'an infinite ... ethically imperative God', that the Jews drew upon themselves all the furies released in the course of the Nazi-led assault against them. Representing what he calls the 'blackmail of perfection', they perhaps incurred a hatred the more intense because of a recognition at some level by their tormentors of the desirability of the ethical demands embodied in the Jewish tradition.[38] The thesis is of a guilt turned outwards, of resentment focused on a people which had thought to make itself the bearer of hope for a better world. It recalls hints we have encountered in Mandel and Trotsky: the former's allusion to bad conscience; the scene narrated by the latter of a freedom not liberating, but cruelly, wilfully, destructive. Unprovable as Steiner's thesis may be and in manifest tension even with other more familiar, dehumanizing and demonizing tropes, it is hard, I believe, to refuse it any weight once one has absorbed from the vast chronicle of this catastrophe the sense that is so pervasively present in it of a determination by the perpetrators, a glee almost, in taking advantage of the innocence, vulnerability, persistent hope and propensity to think in terms of what was reasonable, of their targeted victims.

Whatever the sources of the anti-Jewish fury, and they are probably multiple, no one reading at all widely in the testimony and historiography of the Holocaust could fail to notice what both Friedlander and Steiner speak of in their different ways, neither the cruel desires and sense of an unusual elation, nor the emotional charge produced – and maybe required – by the assault upon the innocent. Such features are obscured, however, in a certain body of the theoretical literature by alternative discourses there. One of these is the 'banality of evil' argument, due originally to Hannah Arendt but disseminated very widely since. The other, frequently related to it, is a broader argument about modernity to be found in the work of many different writers.

Both of these arguments register things that are important to understanding the Nazi genocide. In a nutshell, the first draws attention to the general normality of the perpetrators from a psychological point of view: to their kinship with the rest of humankind as, mostly, ordinary people, not monsters and, especially, not animals. The second argument draws attention to the characteristically modern structures and resources, social, organizational and technical, without which an enterprise of this type and scale – gathering and transporting six million people from across the countries of Europe in order to kill them all, and this within a period of less than four years and under a blanket of attempted secrecy – would have been much more difficult, if not actually impossible. But despite the pertinence of these arguments, they can come, when given a too unilateral emphasis, to present a picture of rule-governed, bureaucratic murder in which some of the other aspects we have been concerned with, symbolic, emotional and to do with the unfettered 'play' of destructive human capacity and imagination, are all but marginalized. There is something here that is not about modernity; something that is not about capitalism either. It is about humanity.

It is something that Marxists have often been reluctant to face up to but with which – returning now to him – Ernest Mandel ought to have had no trouble. In an essay of 1980 entitled 'Man is the supreme being for man', he wrote of there being anthropological constants. One such constant was expressed in a yearning for freedom and in 'the inextinguishable spark of revolt' against injustice and oppression. But there were also, Mandel recognized, 'deeply embedded in human beings', impulses towards tribalism and destructiveness.[39]

Confronted with the enormities produced by these latter kind of impulses, the better side of human nature that is represented by impulses of the former kind can find itself, it seems, at a loss – as to how to understand. This is what Deutscher and Levi and Friedlander all tell us, each in his own particular accents. It is good that human beings experience the difficulty as widely as they do. Should we ever entirely cease to, we would be entirely lost. This, for its part, is the meaning – an ethical rather than psychological meaning – of the discourse of the *monstrosity* of radical evil.

I want, finally, to note a respect in which, in the pages he appended to the German edition of his book on the Second World War, Mandel found it necessary to express himself more fully than he had ever done before. It was on the issue of the uniqueness of the Jewish calamity. I conclude with some observations arising from a certain change of emphasis about this.

Hitherto, at least after the initial article of 1946, although Mandel characterizes the Holocaust as unique (and not in any trivially individuating sense but in the sense, as we have seen, of uniquely criminal, worst), he does so without spelling out the reasons for his view. The texts we have so far considered oblige us to rely on the briefest of indications to gather what those reasons might be. Thus, in both *The Meaning of the Second World War* and in his 'Preconditions' essay, he refers to the systematic nature of the killing. Other comments made by him suggest that 'systematic' might unpack into two features commonly cited in debates on this question, features which we may label, for short, *modernity* and *comprehensiveness of intent*. Mandel writes that the perpetrators of earlier massacres were not more humane than the perpetrators of this one; it is just that 'their resources as well as their socio-economic and political plans were more limited'. And he writes of the Jews being killed 'simply' on account of their ethnic origin.[40] Is it, then, because of the modern methods applied to their murder and because the intention of the Nazis was a total one, to kill them all, that the crime against the European Jews is to be seen as a *novum* morally speaking?

It turns out to be so. Such is what Mandel now puts forward in a more explicit and elaborated way in this German appendix. He begins with a description of the crime as the 'systematic, carefully planned and rapidly industrialized' murder of six million people for the 'single reason [of] their supposed descent', and he goes on to present a version of the modernity thesis, a version of it of strong Marxist coloration. This emphasizes, on the one hand, the technical, administrative and division of labour aspects of the genocide, and its dependence on the railways and the chemical and building industries. And it insists on the part played, on the other hand, by 'the "basic moral values" of the ruling class': a pervasive mentality of obedience to the state, patriotism, nationalism and conformity. It was such organizational structures and such attitudes making for passive complicity that were, according to Mandel, decisive; as much as it was fanatical anti-semitism and much more than it was any 'moral nihilism'.[41]

Now, there are some difficult and unpleasant questions here about why these features, whether separately or jointly, should distinguish the Holocaust as uniquely bad – questions about the normative comparison of evils that I will have to leave to one side. I intend to address them on another occasion.[42] It is interesting, however, to consider why it should have been just at this juncture, in this particular text, that Mandel endeavoured at last to lay out more fully the view that the Holocaust was unique, where before the weight of his emphasis had been much more upon its comparability with other historical experiences. Naturally, it is hard to be sure about the answer, but I would venture that the literary context is significant: an afterword for a German audience, in the wake of the recent 'Historikerstreit' (the historians' controversy), and dealing with the views of Ernst Nolte and their manifest tendency to apologia.

What follows should only be said bluntly. Within this apologia there is a standpoint bearing a formal resemblance to something I have criticized in Mandel. I mean the energetic contextualization of Nazi crimes by Nolte, even while briefly conceding their singular and unprecedented character: his insistence that they belong to the same history of modern times as the American war in Vietnam, the Vietnamese invasion of Cambodia, the exodus from Vietnam of the boat people – a 'holocaust on the water' – the Cambodian genocide, the repression following on the Iranian revolution, the Soviet invasion of Afghanistan and, above all, the liquidation of the kulaks, and the Gulag. Against that backdrop, Nolte urged that the Third Reich 'should be removed from the isolation in which it still finds itself.'[43] This is what came, in the debate in question, to be called 'relativization' of the Holocaust; and it is what Mandel himself calls it in taking issue with Nolte's views.[44] He (Mandel) continues even now to assert that the Holocaust was an extreme product of tendencies which are historically more general.[45] But he perceives a need, evidently, to balance the assertion with a greater emphasis on the singularity of the fate of the Jews.

On this matter especially, let there be no misunderstanding. I speak of a formal resemblance. But the same moral significance is not to be attached to the two standpoints formally alike: that of a German conservative historian and that of a Jewish Marxist revolutionary. For what motivated their respective emphases was not the same. A national particularism concerned with 'normalizing' Germany's modern historical identity was plainly at work in the first case. And the very opposite was probably at the root of the second, a socialist and in its way Jewish universalism that would not risk belittling the sufferings of others by dwelling too emphatically on the tragedy of the Jews.

It is an old story of socialism, going a long way back. It was represented by a figure of great importance for Mandel, of great importance for him in many respects, but one of these in having voiced the clearest of warnings about capitalist barbarism. From prison during the First World War, Rosa Luxemburg wrote to her friend Mathilde Wurm:

> What do you want with this particular suffering of the Jews? The poor victims on the rubber plantations in Putumayo, the Negroes in Africa with whose bodies the Europeans play a game of catch, are just as near to me. Do you remember the words written on the work of the Great General Staff about Trotha's campaign in the Kalahari desert? 'And the death-rattles, the mad cries of those dying of thirst, faded away into the sublime silence of eternity.' Oh, this 'sublime silence of eternity' in which so many screams have faded away unheard. It rings within me so strongly that I have no special corner of my heart reserved for the ghetto: I am at home wherever in the world there are clouds, birds and human tears.[46]

An old story of socialism and an old story of Jews on the Left, and these words of Rosa Luxemburg are excellent ones, not to be forgotten or

renounced, especially not today. Still, in the second half of the twentieth century, they are also less than adequate. A Jewish socialist ought
to be able to find some special corner of his or her heart for the
tragedy of the Jewish people. A universalist ethic shorn of any special
concern for the sufferings of one's own would be the less persuasive
for such carelessness. Whatever one may think about that, a balance is
at any rate called for in estimating the place – comparable *and* unique
– of the Shoah.

I take one last precaution to avoid the risk of an imbalance here
myself. Writing about the Jewish question, both Mandel and Trotsky
argued that there could be no satisfactory resolution of it except
through the achievement of socialism.[47] All of the foregoing indicates,
I hope, the shortcomings I see in that formula. Nevertheless, it secretes
a certain truth as well. If we generalize from the so-called Jewish
question to other cases of extreme persecution and oppression, the
link which has so often been made by the political tradition of Mandel,
Trotsky and Luxemburg, the link between capitalism and barbarism, is
not to be lightly shrugged aside. Capitalism is a social and economic
order systematically producing for millions of people – and all confident contemporary liberalisms notwithstanding – conditions of extreme
want and oppression, in which hatreds are the more likely to accumulate, fester, erupt. It encourages moral attitudes, moreover, that may be
described as underwriting a 'contract of mutual indifference': under
which people in acute danger or trouble may be simply left there, so
far as their situation is considered to be the business of anyone else.
Not responsible for all evil, capitalist social relations and values contribute their massive share to it. Socialism represents the hope of another
moral universe, one in which, to advert again to Mandel's 'principal
lesson of the Holocaust', there might come to be enough people no
longer willing to tolerate the morally intolerable that the instances of
this could be at last radically reduced. It is to that vision that, balanced
or not on any particular question, Mandel devoted his life.

Notes

1. Leon Trotsky, *On the Jewish Question*, New York 1970, p. 29 (emphasis in the
   original).
2. Isaac Deutscher, 'The Jewish Tragedy and the Historian', in his *The Non-
   Jewish Jew and other essays*, London 1968, pp. 163–4. For discussion of the
   unpredictability of the Holocaust and the initial difficulties of belief, see:
   Yehuda Bauer, *The Holocaust in Historical Perspective*, Seattle 1978, pp. 7,
   16–22, 81; Jacob Katz, 'Was the Holocaust Predictable?', in Y. Bauer and N.

Rotenstreich, eds., *The Holocaust as Historical Experience*, New York 1981, pp. 23–41; Walter Laqueur, *The Terrible Secret*, London 1980, pp. 1–10; and Michael Marrus, *The Holocaust in History*, London 1987, pp. 156–64. Yehuda Bauer goes so far as to say that nobody predicted the Holocaust, whatever may have been claimed to the contrary; that the most that anyone could have envisaged was 'pogroms, economic destruction, hunger, or forced emigration', not 'the mass murder of millions of human beings'. I have no way of knowing whether Bauer is familiar with Trotsky's quoted remarks but, however things may be in general on this score, I do not see how those remarks can be taken in the way Bauer suggests. It is not only that Trotsky puts it so, and emphasizes: the *physical extermination* of the Jews; repeating the point, indeed, a few lines on with the claim that 'not only their political but also their physical fate' is tied to the struggle of the international proletariat. It is also that immediately before making this prediction he speaks of an ever-diminishing space for the Jews on the planet, with the number of countries that expel them ceaselessly growing, the number willing to accept them always decreasing. In *this* context 'physical extermination of the Jews' is what he sees as logically coming next and what he actually says; and physical extermination of the Jews is what Hitler and his accomplices undertook. Naturally, this is not to say that Trotsky foresaw the specific form of what was to happen.

3. See my *The Legacy of Rosa Luxemburg*, London 1976, p. 119.
4. E. Germain [Mandel], 'La question juive au lendemain de la Deuxième Guerre mondiale', afterword to A. Léon, *La Conception matérialiste de la question juive*, Brussels 1946, p. I.
5. Ibid., p. VI.
6. Ibid., pp. I–III.
7. Ibid., p. XI.
8. See the Introduction to Leon Trotsky, *The Struggle Against Fascism in Germany*, New York 1971, pp. 9, 39; and Ernest Mandel, *Trotsky: A Study in the Dynamic of his Thought*, London 1979, p. 88.
9. In this connection, see particularly *The Struggle Against Fascism in Germany*, pp. 17–21.
10. Ibid., p. 15.
11. Ibid., pp. 12, 17. And cf. Ernest Mandel 'Der Mensch ist das Höchste Wesen für den Menschen', in F. J. Raddatz, ed., *Warum Ich Marxist Bin*, Munich 1978: 'The greatest intellectual attraction of Marxism lies in its (up till now unique) ability to achieve a rational, all-inclusive and coherent integration of all social sciences'; it is 'in the final analysis the science of mankind *tout court*'. Quoted from the English translation published for the first time in this volume.
12. See Ernest Mandel, *The Meaning of the Second World War*, London 1986, pp. 90–92. Reference to Mandel's views in the paragraphs following is to these pages until otherwise indicated.
13. *The Holocaust in Historical Perspective*, pp. 37–8.
14. *Trotsky: A Study . . .* , pp. 89–90.
15. Ernest Mandel, *Trotsky As Alternative*, London 1995, p. 108.

16. *The Struggle Against Fascism in Germany*, pp. 403–5.

17. *On the Jewish Question*, pp. 30–31 – and cf. p. 20.

18. Enzo Traverso, 'Trotsky et la question juive', *Quatrième Internationale* 36, 1990, pp. 76–8; and his *The Marxists and the Jewish Question: The History of a Debate 1843–1943*, translated by B. Gibbons, Atlantic Highlands 1994, pp. 138–40, 201–5.

19. See the references given in note 17 above.

20. Ernest Mandel, 'Prémisses matérielles, sociales et idéologiques du génocide nazi', in Y. Thanassekos and H. Wismann, eds., *Révision de l'histoire*, Paris 1990 (pp. 169–74); English translation: 'Material, Social and Ideological Preconditions for the Nazi Genocide', published for the first time in this volume, sections 1 and 11. All references to this text will be given so, by section number.

21. Ibid., sections 2, 3.

22. Ibid., section 11.

23. Ibid., section 10.

24. See in turn, Ibid., sections 1, 6, 5, and 8; and also, on the rationality/ irrationality combination, Mandel's appendix ('Zum Historikerstreit') to his *Der Zweite Weltkrieg*, Frankfurt 1991, pp. 224–5.

25. 'Material, Social . . .', section 1. And cf. 'Zum Historikerstreit', p. 220: 'An investigation of this sort . . . should by no means rule out consideration of ideological, and mass-psychological as well as individual-psychological, factors in the chain of causation'.

26. 'Material, Social . . .', section 3.

27. Ibid., section 5; and 'Zum Historikerstreit', pp. 229–30.

28. 'Material, Social . . .', section 7; and cf. 'Zum Historikerstreit', p. 232.

29. Primo Levi, Afterword to *If This is a Man and The Truce*, London 1987, pp. 394–6.

30. Section 11.

31. See Norman Geras, 'Literature of Revolution', *New Left Review* 113–114, January/April 1979, pp. 25–9; reprinted in my collection, *Literature of Revolution*, London 1986, at pp. 247–50.

32. Leon Trotsky, *1905*, London 1972, pp. 131–5.

33. See Martin Broszat/Saul Friedlander, 'A Controversy about the Historicization of National Socialism', *Yad Vashem Studies* 19, 1988, pp. 28–9.

34. Saul Friedlander, 'The "Final Solution": On the Unease in Historical Interpretation', in Peter Hayes, ed., *Lessons and Legacies: The Meaning of the Holocaust in a Changing World*, Evanston 1991, pp. 23–35, at pp. 25, 30–31. The essay is reprinted, slightly modified, in Friedlander's *Memory, History, and the Extermination of the Jews of Europe*, Bloomington 1993, pp. 102–16.

35. Christopher R. Browning, *Ordinary Men: Reserve Police Battalion 101 and the Final Solution in Poland*, New York 1993, p. 112.

36. Ernst Klee, Willi Dressen and Volker Riess, eds., *'Those were the Days':The Holocaust through the Eyes of the Perpetrators and Bystanders*, London 1991, pp. 76, 89, 118, 127, 129.

37. Odd Nansen, *From Day to Day*, New York 1949, p. 438.

38. George Steiner, 'The Long Life of Metaphor: An Approach to the

"Shoah"', in Berei Lang, ed., *Writing and the Holocaust*, New York 1988, pp. 154–71, at pp. 161–6. The article is reprinted from *Encounter* 68, February 1987, pp. 55–61.

39. See the reference given in footnote 11 above.

40. *The Meaning of the Second World War*, p. 92; 'Material, Social. . .', section 2. And see also, with respect to comprehensiveness of intent, *Trotsky As Alternative*, p. 155, note 25.

41. 'Zum Historikerstreit', pp. 209, 222–3.

42. There is also the explanatory question already once mooted. Mandel is unable to account even for the unique features of the event as he identifies these, since neither the structures nor the mentalities he focuses on seem to suffice, given their pervasiveness in the modern world, to the extremity of what occurred. He is aware of the problem, for he sets himself to trying to respond to it: to explaining what it was that produced the specific outcome from these more general tendencies. (See Ibid., pp. 240–43.) But his response – in terms of the failure of the German bourgeois revolution, the rapid growth of German industry and the ambitions of German imperialism for a redivision of existing spheres of influence – seems to me to fall far short of the thing it purports to address. None of these causes speaks directly to the aim of *wiping out a people*.

43. Ernst Nolte, 'Between Historical Myth and Revisionism?' and 'A Past That Will Not Pass Away', *Yad Vashem Studies* 19, 1988, pp. 49–63 and 65–73. Also in J. Knowlton and T. Cates (translators), *Forever in the Shadow of Hitler?*, Atlantic Highlands 1993, pp. 1–15 and 18–23.

44. 'Zum Historikerstreit', p. 209.

45. Ibid., pp. 239, 242, 245.

46. Stephen Eric Bronner, ed., *The Letters of Rosa Luxemburg*, Boulder 1978, pp. 179–80.

47. See Trotsky, *On the Jewish Question*, pp. 18–22, 28–9; Germain [Mandel], 'La question juive au lendemain de la Deuxieme Guerre mondiale', p. XII; and Ernest Germain, 'A Biographical Sketch of Abram Leon', in Abram Leon, *The Jewish Question: A Marxist Interpretation*, New York 1970, p. 17.

Part II

An Interview and Two Previously Unpublished Articles by Ernest Mandel

The Luck of a Crazy Youth

Ernest Mandel interviewed by Tariq Ali

Ernest, you were ten years old when Hitler seized power in Germany and sixteen when World War Two broke out. It was surely an awful time to be young, especially for someone like you, from a Jewish background. What are your first memories of that period?

Well, strangely enough – but this is probably part of a special mentality, not very close to the average – I have no bad memories at all of that period. On the contrary. I have rather a memory of tension, yes, excitement, yes, nervousness, but not at all of despair. Absolutely not. This has something to do with the fact that we were a highly politicized family.

Your father was an activist?

At that time my father was not an activist. He had been an activist at the time of the German revolution. He had fled from Belgium to Holland in the First World War because he didn't want to do his military service. He was already a very left-wing socialist and he had met Willem Pieck – who was later President of the German Democratic Republic – in Holland. When the German revolution broke out they went to Berlin together. He worked for some months in the first press agency of Soviet Russia in Berlin. He knew Radek personally and met a lot of other people. And so I found on our bookshelves a fantastic collection of old publications – books by Marx, books by Lenin, books by Trotsky, the International Bulletin *Inprekorr* of that time, Russian literature, and so on. He dropped out of politics around 1923. His life was very much attuned to the general ups and downs of world revolution. When Hitler came to power he got a shock. He was very conscious of what that would mean for the world. I remember – it's perhaps my first political memory, I was nine years old in 1932 – at the time of the so-called Papen putsch when the Social-Democratic government of Prussia was eliminated, and Severing the Minister of the Interior, together with the chief of the police, made this famous or infamous statement, *Ich weiche vor dem Gewalt* – 'I yield before violence'. A lieutenant and two soldiers had entered his office and he dropped all the power which they had accumulated in the fourteen years since 1918. He dropped it in just five minutes. This news appeared in the social-democratic daily paper of Antwerp, our home town. My father made very sharp comments. He said it will end very badly: this is the beginning of the end. I remember that very well. And then when Hitler came to power we had some of the first refugees come to our home, also some members of our family and some friends. The years 1933 to 1935 were very terrible years in Belgium; it was the depth of the crisis and people were very hungry. Of course it was much worse than today, much worse. The Queen of Belgium became popular simply because she distributed bread and margarine to the unemployed. One of the refugees who came to our home told us, as if it was normal, that they had sold their bed in order to buy bread in Berlin. They were sleeping on the ground because they had to buy bread. These were terrible times. My father also went through some bad periods, but we never were so badly off as that. We never went hungry but we saw our standard of living drop dramatically in that period. These years 1933, 1934, 1935 were a bit less political.

Your political engagement began when the war broke out?

Much earlier than that, 1936 was a turning point for me, and for my father. Two things came together, the Spanish Civil War and the Moscow trials. These events had a major impact on us. The working-class movement in Antwerp and in Belgium played an important role. The Spanish Civil War evoked a tremendous wave of solidarity. I remember well the demonstration of May 1st, 1937. There were perhaps a hundred thousand people in the streets, and the people coming back from the International Brigades in Spain and people collecting money. They were received by an ovation which I will never forget. Prior to the Vietnam Solidarity Campaign, it was the biggest international event which we had ever had in Belgium. Then there were the Moscow trials, which were a tremendous shock for my father. He had personally known several of the defendants of the first trial who were functionaries of the Comintern. Radek was one of the main defendants of the second trial. My father got angry beyond description, beyond description – and on the spot he organized a committee of solidarity with the Moscow trial defendants. He got in contact with a small Trotskyist group in Antwerp. They met at our place and I became, at the age of thirteen, a Trotskyist sympathizer – not a member because the organization was not so stupid that it would let a child of thirteen into its ranks. But I was present at meetings, listening, and was considered a bright youngster so they didn't oppose my listening. I was fifteen years old when I was formally admitted. And it was an interesting moment because this was a little after the founding conference of the Fourth International.

When was that?

1938. The Young People's Socialist League of the United States, the youth organization of the SWP, sent a man called Nattie Gould to speak to us about the founding conference. I still see him before my eyes. He toured several western European countries to give a report on the founding conference and explain the work of the SWP. He came to Antwerp and to our place where the Antwerp cell of the organization met. I think that it was after that meeting that I was formally admitted as a candidate member. Then there was a certain vacuum, the most difficult period probably in our country. In 1939 everybody was sure the war would break out. We were very isolated. We distributed a leaflet on the main streets of Antwerp – it was not such an intelligent way to act, because of the climate.

What did the leaflet say?

It was against the war. It said the war is coming, but this is not our war and so on and so forth. It was not received very well and was written in a very abstract and propagandist way. I didn't write it and don't take any responsibility for it!

But did you distribute it?

I distributed it, obviously.

You were fifteen when you distributed your first leaflet?

I was nearer to sixteen. That was a very difficult time, probably the most difficult time we have had. Our organization comprised two sectors in Belgium. One was a little mass base we had in one of the coal-mining districts where there were around six hundred members who had come to us from social democracy. We had the absolute majority in one mining town and the response of the employers was to immediately close down the pit in that town and it never opened subsequently. All those miners who voted for the extreme Left were victimized for their political engagement. Before the war, during the war, after the war, they were never employed again. Comrade Scargill will recognize this. There's nothing new under the sun.

When did you join the resistance?

Well, the group that I have been talking about dropped out as soon as the organization had to go underground. Their leader was killed by the Stalinists with the slanderous accusation of collaboration with the Nazis. This was just a lie. After the war these comrades – I have to call them that, though they were not Trotskyists any more, but oppositional socialists, left socialists – they ran for the municipality and again got the absolute majority. So that is an indication that they were not collaborators with the Nazis: this was a ridiculous slander. With the loss of these people we reached a low point of the organization. We had perhaps a dozen or two dozen members in the winter 1939–40, just before the German invasion. The organization was underground. The atmosphere in the country was terrible. The German army invaded on the 10th May, and military operations were concluded with the capitulation on the 28th May. The country was occupied and the first weeks produced total disorientation. Henri de Man, the leader of the Socialist Party, remained as assistant prime minister. He capitulated before the Nazis. He made a public appeal to collaborate with the occupation. Part of the trade-union apparatus supported him. As for the Communist Party, it published a legal newspaper. Because of the Stalin–Hitler pact they were prepared to submit to the Nazi censorship. All these events were a shock to us. We were very weak and very small. Then we heard of the murder of the Old Man, the murder of Trotsky. The Belgian papers published the information around the 21st August. Immediately one of the legendary figures of Belgian Communism, a comrade Polk who had been a founding member of the party, a member of the central committee in the twenties and who had become a Trotskyist, a left oppositionist, came to my father's house. He was crying. He had known the Old Man personally. Others came too. There were seven or eight people who all said the same thing. The only way to answer this assassination was immediately to restart the organization, to show this dirty murderer that he just can't suppress ideas and he can't suppress a current of resistance. We decided to rebuild the organization and sent people to other parts of the country.

Was this done clandestinely?

It was totally clandestine. We found out that the comrades in Brussels were thinking along exactly the same lines. Within a couple of weeks we set up the skeleton of an organization. We started to publish our first illegal newspaper before the end of the year, 1940. We set up a little illegal print shop, and all that started to function, I must say, rather well under the circumstances. There was a small illegal organization and we had a good response in some workers' quarters because, in a certain sense, we had a monopoly. The Communist Party was not at all identified with resistance. The Social-Democrats were identified, rather, with collaboration. I must add immediately that resistance was not so popular. Most people still thought the Germans would win the war. They were in the best of cases abstentionist and passive. In the worst of cases they wanted to get on the side of the victors.

You were still isolated?

After the winter things changed. The defeat of the Germans in the Battle of Britain had something to do with that. The experience of the winter was very bitter, very hard. Food rations were very low, so there was much discontent among the workers. The first strikes broke out in March. Then the Communist Party started to change. It's not true that they waited until the attack on the Soviet Union. As soon as they saw some movement, a massive movement, they acted cautiously in order not to be cut off completely from events. They did not wish to give us and other new resistance groups a monopoly, because that would have been the price for doing nothing. And of course when the attack on the Soviet Union took place, then they were bolder. Then it became more difficult for us but at the same time the general scope of the mass resistance enlarged. I must say that I never doubted for a single day that the Nazis would lose. I can say that with a certain self-satisfaction when I look back. I was a young man, not very mature – very foolish from many points of view – but I must say that I never doubted that one day the Nazis would be defeated. Of that I was absolutely convinced. This led me into some crazy actions.

You distributed leaflets to German soldiers?

Yes, but that was not the most crazy thing to do. That was rather correct. When I was arrested for the first time, I managed to escape prison. I was caught a second time, and escaped from the camp. The third time I was caught I was brought to Germany. I was very happy. I didn't understand at all that there was 99.9 per cent chance that I would be killed. A Jew, a Marxist, a Communist and a Trotskyist. There were four reasons to be killed by different groups of people, if you can put it like that. I was happy to be deported to Germany because I would be in the centre of the German revolution. I was just saying,

'Wonderful, I'm just where I want to be.' It was completely irresponsible of course.

And you did try to escape again?

Well, this also is a story of folly. The fact that I am still alive is really the exception to the rule. In a certain sense, again, I can say with satisfaction that my outlook helped – I shouldn't exaggerate because there was just luck in it too. But through political behaviour and I think a correct approach to a certain number of basic problems, I could immediately establish good relations with some of the guards. I did not behave like most of the Belgian and the French prisoners who were very anti-German. I deliberately looked for politically sympathetic warders. That was the intelligent thing to do even from the point of view of self-preservation. So I looked for Germans who were friendly, who gave evidence of some political judgement. I immediately found some former Social-Democrats, even a few old Communists.

Amongst the guards in the concentration camp?

Amongst the guards, yes. It was not a concentration camp, it was a prison camp. I was sentenced, so this was already an advantage. In a concentration camp you had the SS, the worst people. In these prison camps you had functionaries of the prison system, like in a British prison. So you had some people who had been there since the twenties or thirties; I thought some of them would be Social-Democrats because Social-Democrats had been ministers of the interior for so long. And that was exactly the case, as I found out. Also amongst the prisoners I tried to find some young Germans – many of them, more than you might think – who were leftists and were anti-war. I found them and made friends. My first friend there was a very fine person who had been condemned to life imprisonment because he had spoken against the war. He was the son of a socialist railway worker in Cologne. After seeing that he could have confidence in me, he gave me his father's address and the address of friends of his father, saying 'If ever you escape to their place, they will help you, they will put you on a train, you can go back to your country.' So I developed a plan. But the whole thing was crazy anyway, you understand. We worked in an unforgettable place – one of the largest plants in Germany, perhaps it was even the largest.

What did you produce?

Gasoline, synthetic gasoline for the war machine, for the airplanes and the tanks. That was like a microcosm of Europe. You had the Russian prisoners of war, Western prisoners of war, political prisoners and inmates of concentration camps, civilian forced labour, and civilian free labour, some German workers. There were sixty thousand people working there. It was like a microcosm of European society under the Nazis. And there was a group of Belgian workers, even some from Antwerp, from my home town. I befriended them and I asked them to give me clothes so that I could change out of my prison uniform. I looked at the electric security fences around the camp and found that they were turned off for specific reasons in the morning when they had to change the watch in the towers. I saw that and I just climbed over the wall, over that wire. I had gloves, but I was absolutely crazy, absolutely crazy.

The sort of crazy act that saved your life.

In a certain sense. It was a terrible risk that I would be caught and shot immediately. In fact unfortunately I was caught. I had three days of freedom, which were very exhilarating, very intoxicating. I obtained some fresh fruit for the first time since I had been in prison. A German woman gave me apples and pears, and that made me very happy. I knew the way to the border to Aachen. But I was caught in the woods on the third night. I was again very lucky. I started to talk to the *garde-chasse* [gamekeeper], who had arrested me. I said to him, 'Listen, have you seen the newspapers? The Allies are already in Brussels, they will be in Aachen soon. If you kill me now you'll get into big trouble very soon. Better put me in prison without too much trouble.' He understood and was rather sympathetic.

You were a convincing talker even then, Ernest?

If you want to put it like that. He even gave me a big loaf of bread. I don't want to boast; what I did was elementary. Of course, I gave a false name. I didn't give the exact name of the camp from which I had escaped, so they took me to another prison. But they eventually found out, and after two weeks I was held in very bad conditions, in irons and so on, because they knew I was an escaped prisoner. But I was much safer there despite the conditions. The commander of the camp from which I had escaped came to see me in the prison – a terrible, dark cell – and he said to me. 'You are a rare bird. Do you know that if you had been brought back you could have been immediately hanged?' I said yes. So he just looked at me in total amazement. But of course in this new prison he couldn't hang me. I was already under sentence so they kept me there in Eich from October 1944 until the beginning of

March 1945. Then I was transferred to another camp for three weeks and liberated at the end of the month.

This interview was filmed for Bandung Productions in 1989. It was first published in New Left Review *213, September/October 1995 (pp. 101–6).*

Material, Social and Ideological Preconditions for the Nazi Genocide*

Ernest Mandel

1. What made the Holocaust possible – a unique event in history so far – was first of all a biological variant of an ultraracist ideology, an extreme form of Social Darwinism. According to this doctrine there existed 'subhuman races' (*Untermenschen*), whose extermination was justified and even essential. For those who upheld this ideology, Jews were 'vermin to be wiped out', Blacks are 'apes', 'the only good Indian is a dead Indian', and so forth.

The doctrine of extreme biological racism does not fall from the sky. It has a material basis in socio-economic and political practices that treated particular human groups in such an inhuman way that the need for an ideological justification – an ideology of dehumanization – and for a 'neutralization' of the perpetrators' guilty consciences and feelings of individual guilt (see Himmler's speech of 6 October 1943) arises almost necessarily.

2. The Nazis' systematic dehumanization of the Jews is not an isolated phenomenon in history. Comparable phenomena arose in respect to slaves in Antiquity, midwives ('witches') during the fourteenth and seventeenth centuries, the American Indians, Blacks sold into slavery, and so forth. Victims of these phenomena can be counted by the millions, including women and children. If none of these

* This is the text of Ernest Mandel's contribution to a symposium on the Nazi genocide held in Brussels in 1988. It was first published in French in Yannis Thanassekos and Heinz Wismann, eds., *Révision de l'Histoire: Totalitarisme, crimes et génocides nazis*, Éditions du Cerf, Paris 1990, pp. 169–74.

massacres attained a systematic, wholesale character equal to that of the Holocaust, it is not because the killers were more 'humane' or merciful than the Nazis. It is because their resources as well as their socio-economic and political plans were more limited.

3. It is not true that the Nazis' extermination plans were meant exclusively for the Jews. A comparable proportion of the Gypsies was also exterminated. In the longer term, the Nazis wanted to exterminate a hundred million people in central and eastern Europe, above all Slavs. If the extermination began with the Jews, this was due in part to the demented faith of Hitler and some of his lieutenants in the 'world Jewish conspiracy', but also in part to a more practical reason. Before being exterminated, the slaves had to work (thus minister of 'justice' Thierack: '*Tod durch Arbeit*'). Rightly or wrongly, the Nazis believed that the Jews would be less docile, less easily reduced to the slavery of completely resigned illiterates, than the other 'inferior races'. This meant in their minds that the Jews had to be killed (including by working them to death) *inside camps,* not in still partly 'open' villages and towns (which was the fate foreseen for the Russians, Poles, Ruthenians, Ukrainians, and others, each of which was to be exterminated in turn).

4. The doctrine of Jewish racial inferiority ('subhumanity') is linked in the minds of the most fanatical contemporary anti-semites to the myth of the 'international Jewish conspiracy' to seize power on a world scale and 'suck the blood' of all peoples. The joint instruments of this conspiracy are supposedly big speculative (banking) capital, Marxist socialism (later Bolshevism), Freemasonry, and even – the Jesuits!

This myth was not of German, but rather of Russian origin (the notorious *Protocols of the Elders of Zion,* a fabrication by the Tsarist Okhrana (secret police)). At the end of the nineteenth century it was much more widespread in France, Britain, Austria, Hungary and Poland than in Germany strictly speaking. The Ukrainian chief Petliura, responsible for pogroms that killed more than 100,000 Jews in relatively little time, was devoted to this myth. There is no reason for us to doubt that he was capable of conceiving and carrying out the Holocaust if he had had the necessary material and technical means.

5. The doctrine of biological racism can be seen in a much broader context: the rise of anti-humanist, anti-progressive, anti-egalitarian, anti-emancipatory doctrines, which openly celebrated the most extreme and systematic violence against whole human groups ('the enemy') and spread widely towards the end of the nineteenth century. It seems incontestable to us that the launching of (and to a lesser extent the preparations for) the First World War was the decisive turning point in

this regard. Without the First World War, Hitler and Nazism as a mass phenomenon would have been inconceivable. Without the launching of the Second World War, Auschwitz would have been impossible.

Yet the crisis of humanism and of civilization that began with the First World War can in fact hardly be separated from the phenomenon of the crisis of imperialism, whose early manifestations under colonialism are rightly linked to the birth of biological racist doctrines among some of the colonists (remember the signs: 'Dogs and Natives Not Allowed').

6. The Holocaust did not only have ideological roots. It would have been impossible without a given set of material and technical means. This was an industrial extermination project, not a do-it-yourself one. This is all that distinguished it from traditional pogroms. It required mass production of Zyklon-B gas, gas chambers, pipes, crematoria, barracks, and massive reliance on railways, on a scale that would have been unattainable in the eighteenth century and most of the nineteenth century, not to speak of earlier epochs (unless the project was carried out over decades or even several centuries). In this sense the Holocaust was also (not only, but also) a product of modern industry that has increasingly escaped from any control by human or humanist reason, i.e. of modern capitalist industry driven onwards by more and more intense competition that has gotten out of control. It is the most extreme example to date of a typical combination of perfected partial rationality and global irrationality, pushed to its limit: a combination characteristic of bourgeois society.

7. Alongside the ideological and material/technical preconditions for the Holocaust, we must also consider its socio-political preconditions. Carrying out the Holocaust required participation, with different degrees of active or passive complicity, by several million people: in the first place undoubtedly by executioners, organizers and camp guards, but also by statesmen, bankers, industrialists, high-ranking civil servants, army officers, diplomats, lawyers, professors, doctors, along with the 'foot-soldiers': petty functionaries, 'ordinary prison' guards, railway workers, and so forth.

A careful examination of this mass of several million accomplices would divide them by nationality, with the Germans strictly speaking doubtless making up no more than 50 to 60 per cent of the total. It would also divide them according to the degree of their irrationality, with psychopaths and fanatics in the minority, though certainly a substantial minority. But the majority acted out of habits of obedience, routine or calculation (the silence of church hierarchies falls into this last category), if not out of cowardice (the risks of individual disobedience

being considered greater than the risks of complicity in inhuman
acts).

One of the factors that allowed the Holocaust to happen was of an
ethical order, or if you like has to do with the motivation of behaviour.
It took a particular turn of mind: the Holocaust was also the result, not
just of the inclination to accept, celebrate, or even worship massive
violence, but of the acceptance of the doctrine that the state has the
right to require individuals to do things from which they should recoil,
and in their hearts do recoil, from the point of view of the fundamental
rules of ethics.

According to this doctrine, it is better to submit to the state's
authority in every case than to 'undermine political authority'. The
extreme consequences of this doctrine have proven the absurdity of
the conservatives' (including Aristotle's and Goethe's) classic thesis:
that the 'disorder' brought about by rebelling against injustice would
always lead to still more injustice. There could hardly be a worse
injustice than Auschwitz. Faced with massive injustice, resistance and
revolt – including individual resistance, but above all collective resistance and revolt – are not only a right but a duty, which overrides any
raison d'Etat. This is the main lesson of the Holocaust.

8. Minorities with fanatical, extremist and inhuman views, i.e. patho-
logical minorities and individuals, have existed and still exist in virtually
all countries in the nineteenth and twentieth centuries, not to speak of
earlier centuries. But they constitute a marginal phenomenon, with
minimal political influence. They were certainly marginal in Germany
in the period from 1848 to 1914.

In order for such individuals to get a response from millions of
people, a deep social crisis is necessary (as Marxists we would say: a
deep socio-economic crisis, a deep crisis of the mode of production,
and a deep crisis of the power structures). In order for such individuals
to have a short-term chance of gaining power, still more for them
actually to take power, there must be a correlation of social forces that
makes this possible: weakening of the traditional workers' movement
(and to a lesser extent of traditional bourgeois liberalism); strengthening of the most aggressive layers of the wealthy classes; despair among
the middle classes; considerable increase in the number of declassed
people, and so on. The crisis of the Weimar Republic and the 1929–34
economic crisis evidently created these conditions in Germany in
1932–33.

9. The peculiarities of German history; the specific nature of the
'bloc in power' after the German unification of 1871; the particular
weight of the Prussian junkers and their militarist tradition within this

bloc; the relative weakness of a liberal-humanist tradition compared with other countries (due to the defeat of the 1848 revolution); the evident disproportion between Germany's flourishing industry and finance capital on the one hand and its limited share in the division of spheres of influence on a world scale on the other hand: all this made German imperialism more aggressive in the period from 1890 to 1945 than its main rivals. In the eyes of much of the German 'elite' in this epoch, the struggle for world domination would take place by way of war and militarism. The empire that Germany was to conquer – the equivalent of Britain's 'Empire of India' – lay in central and eastern Europe (later to be extended from this base to the Middle East, Africa, South America and so on). This explains why much of the German ruling classes were prepared to accept Hitler, without fully realizing where this would lead them (though as early as 30 June 1934 it was clear to anyone who wasn't blind that the man was prepared to tread underfoot the most elementary principles of morals and the rule of law, in fact that he was a ruthless murderer).

Both the liberal-humanist tendency and the conservative militarist tendency were present among each of the bourgeois classes of Europe, the US and Japan from 1885–90 on. The difference is that the latter tendency remained in a minority in France and Britain, while it became the majority tendency in Germany and Japan (in the US the two tendencies have been in equilibrium since 1940). This difference can be explained not by ethnic factors but by historical specificities.

10. If we see the Holocaust as the ultimate expression so far of the destructive tendencies existing in bourgeois society, tendencies whose roots lie deep in colonialism and imperialism, we can call attention to other tendencies going in the same direction, most notably in the development of the arms race (nuclear war, biological and chemical warfare, so-called 'conventional' weapons more powerful than the bombs dropped on Hiroshima and Nagasaki, and so forth). A nuclear war, or even a 'conventional' world war without prior dismantling of nuclear power plants, would be worse than the Holocaust. The overall irrationality of preparations for such a war is already perceptible in the language used. When they speak of 'limiting the costs' of a nuclear war, this amounts to trying to commit suicide, to destroy the whole human race, 'at the lowest possible cost'. What do 'costs' have to do with suicide?

11. This interpretation of the Holocaust is in no way meant to relativize the Nazis' crimes against humanity, which are the worst crimes in history, rich as it is in horrors. The interpretation has its specific scientific value. Those who reject it must demonstrate that it is

mistaken on the basis of the facts, their correlation and interconnec-tion. This is a debate among historians, sociologists, economists, politi-cal scientists and moral philosophers. A scientific thesis (hypothesis) can only be refuted with scientific arguments, not with extra-scientific arguments.

Nonetheless, far from being in any way a concession to the Nazis or German militarists, or even to the German 'elite', this interpretation of the Holocaust also has a subjective function. It is also useful and necessary from the point of view of the interests of the human race. It enables us to avoid the intellectual and moral risks inherent in the contrary thesis, according to which the Holocaust is beyond all rational explanation and is incomprehensible. This obscurantist standpoint is to a large extent a posthumous triumph for Nazi doctrine. For if a patch of history is irrational and totally incomprehensible, that means that humanity itself is also irrational and incomprehensible. Then the evil empire is 'in all of us'. That is a scarcely indirect if not hypocritical way of saying that the fault is not Hitler's, nor the Nazis', nor that of those who allowed them to conquer and wield power, but everybody's, which means nobody's in particular.

For our part, we prefer to observe what the historical truth was: that far from 'all being guilty', men and women everywhere, including in Germany, chose one of two camps. The criminals and their accomplices behaved differently from those who resisted. The Amsterdam workers who went on strike to protest against the first anti-Jewish decrees were not the same as the SS. The Danish resistance which saved practically all of the country's Jews was not the same as the quislings. The majority of the Italian people (a 'band of dishonest liars', as Eichmann said with a cynicism that verged on the grotesque), who made it possible to save most of the Italian Jews, was not the same as the Croatian Ustashe. The soldiers of the Red Army who liberated Auschwitz were not the same as those who created the gas chambers. Between these two camps there were, to be sure, intermediate situations and behaviours. But the two camps' existence is empirically verifiable. By explaining the causes of the Holocaust in a rational way, we explain at the same time the difference between these behaviours.

12. Our interpretation of the Holocaust also has a practical, political function. It allows us to escape from practical impotence, and from the feeling of powerlessness in face of the risks of the phenomenon's recurring. We say deliberately that the Holocaust has been the apogee of crimes against humanity *so far*. But there is no guarantee that this apogee will not be equalled or even surpassed in the future. To deny this a priori strikes us as irrational and politically irresponsible. As

Bertolt Brecht said, 'The womb from which this monster emerged is still fertile.'

In order to struggle better against neofascism and biological racism today, we have to understand the nature of fascism yesterday. Scientific knowledge is also a weapon the human race needs to fight and survive, not a purely academic exercise. Refusing to use this weapon means facilitating the arrival of new would-be mass murderers; it means allowing them to commit fresh crimes. Explaining the causes of fascism and the Holocaust means strengthening our capacity for rejection, indignation, hostility, total and unshakeable opposition, resistance and revolt, against the ever-possible re-emergence of fascism and other dehumanizing doctrines and practices. This is a basic, indispensable work of political and moral hygiene.

Why I am a Marxist*

Ernest Mandel

I

The greatest intellectual attraction of Marxism lies in its (up till now unique) ability to achieve a rational, all-inclusive and coherent integration of all social sciences. It breaks with the absurd hypothesis that the human anatomical structure bears little relation to the human being as a 'political animal' (*zoon politikon*), or that people as producers of material goods are completely different from people as artists, poets, thinkers or founders of religions. That, however, is and remains to this very day the fundamental, tacit hypothesis of all academic sciences concerned with human problems.

It is self-evident for physical anthropology that the development of human anatomy, and of the human psychological traits closely associated with it (among others, the capacity for articulate communication and for developing concepts), must be stressed. Prehistory and ethnology as well classify the primitive cultures of humanity strictly by period (frequently even too strictly, mechanically!) according to the nature of their instruments of labour and their predominant economic activity. Nevertheless academic historiography refuses to recognize in the successive modes of production the key to the development of civilization and political history, and orthodox economics holds fast to the myth of

---

* This article by Ernest Mandel first appeared in German within a collection of contributions by Marxists from various origins who were asked to give their personal answer to the title of the volume: *Warum ich Marxist bin* (Why I am a Marxist). Edited by Fritz J. Raddatz, the book was first published by Kindler Verlag, Munich 1978 (Mandel, pp. 57–94), and later in a pocket edition by Fischer Taschenbuch Verlag, Frankfurt 1980 (Mandel, pp. 52–86). Mandel's contribution held as a title a quote from the young Marx: 'Der Mensch ist das höchste Wesen für den Menschen' (For the Human Being, the Supreme Being is the Human Being).

a supposed 'acquisitive drive' rooted 'in human nature', through which – with no regard for the level of development of the productive forces and transitory forms of economic organization – private property, commodity production and competition are elevated to allegedly everlasting institutions of economic life.

Marxism allows us to transcend these obvious inconsistencies. Setting out from the anthropologically verified fact that humans, as creatures of need, can only survive as social beings,[1] it recognizes in this anatomical limitation of our species the basis of its limitless adaptability, i.e., the fact that society has become our 'second nature' and that innumerable variations of human behaviour can emerge by adaptation to different forms of social organization.

Marxism allows one to explain the historically transitory nature of these social systems – obviously not by pointing to the permanent physical and psychological properties of the species, which could change little over the last ten thousand years, but to the changing characteristics of labour as the absolute precondition for human survival. Human beings produce their material life using means of production and, in this production, enter into definite relations, which are termed relations of production. These relations of production determine in the last instance the structure of every given social order as a specific mode of production. The dialectic of the development of the productive forces (means of production and labour power, including the technical, scientific and intellectual capacities of the producers) and the development of the relations of production (in which their relative rigidity, i.e., their structural character, plays an important role) determines in the final analysis the course of human history, its progress and regressions, catastrophes and revolutions.

But for Marxism 'non-economic' social activities are in no sense of 'marginal' or even 'secondary' importance. Precisely because human beings can only survive through *social* production, social communication is anthropologically as constitutive as social labour. The two are inextricably bound up together; each is impossible without the other. By implication, humans do everything they undertake 'through the head', i.e., we generate thoughts about our own practice.[2] The production of material goods is accompanied by the production of concepts (for which the production of speech – phonemes – only supplies the raw material). Marxism tries to *explain* how non-material production (including the production of conceptual *systems*, i.e., ideologies, religions, philosophy and science) springs from the production of material life, becomes detached from it, reacts back on it, and what determines this historical movement.

In this explanation, a number of other discoveries are crucial which, just like the aforementioned, belong to the essence of Marxism. At the most general, abstract level of analysis, material production as a whole in every specific form of society (mode of production) can be divided into two main categories: the *necessary product*, which reproduces the labour power of the producers themselves and the given stock of means of production, allowing material civilization and population growth to be maintained at the same level; and the *social surplus product* that remains when the necessary social product is subtracted from the total social product. If that social surplus product is insignificant, impermanent or purely accidental, only very little growth can take place. Due to the lack of possibilities for accumulation, no significant social division of labour can develop either. Only when the social surplus product grows beyond a certain minimum level in size and permanence, can a fraction of current production be used for the sustenance of an additional population as well as for the creation of additional means of production. A real dynamic of economic growth can then set in. At the same time, an economic division of labour can unfold, and a section of society be freed from the compulsion to produce means of subsistence; handicrafts, trades, fine arts, commerce, writing, ideological and scientific production, managerial and military activity can develop as separate full-time occupations independent from this production for subsistence. This, in turn, facilitates the accumulation and the transmission of experience, knowledge and accumulated economic resources, leading in due course to a further improvement of the productive power of human labour and further growth of the social surplus product.

At a definite stage of development, this economic division of labour leads also to a social one; that is to say, the former intertwines itself with the latter. One section of society makes use of the functional division of labour (among others the functions of managing reserve stocks, military campaigns, the command over prisoners of war, and so forth) to gain control over the social surplus product and force a section (or all) of the direct producers to leave this surplus product to them. Thus society splits into *antagonistic social classes*, between whom there rages a sometimes obscured or peaceable, at other times open and violent *permanent class struggle* over the distribution of material production and – at least periodically – over the conservation or the overthrow of the existing social order.

On the basis of the dominant relations of production, a broad intricate *superstructure* of ways of thinking and behaving, of juridical and coercive institutions, ideological systems and so forth arises, with

the function of maintaining the existing social order. The most important of these institutions is the state, i.e. a special apparatus separate
from the rest of society and subsidized with the social surplus product,
which maintains a monopoly over the exercise of certain social functions. Since the dominant class controls the social surplus product, it
controls the state. For this same reason the *dominant* (certainly not the
only!) ideology of every society is also the ideology of the dominant
class.

This in itself easily understandable instrumentarium enables Marxism to understand and explain not only economic and social development, but also the history of states, civilizations, of science, religion,
philosophy, literature, art, and ethics in their diversity and transformations, in a profoundly searching way which integrates ever more
empirical data.[3] Therein lies its great superiority. It is the science of
the development of human society, i.e., in the final analysis the science
of mankind *tout court*.

II

The Marxist conception of history and society sets out from the premise
that each mode of production possesses specific laws of development,
which determine their origin, rise, heyday, decay and disappearance.
The greatest theoretical achievement of Karl Marx was his discovery of
the specific laws of motion of the capitalist mode of production. This is
the real content of his chief work, *Das Kapital*.

Capital is older than the capitalist mode of production. It originates
in the context of simple commodity production, when trading becomes
an independent activity based on the circulation of money. Its initial
forms are usury capital and merchant capital. The modern capitalist
mode of production is born only when capital penetrates into the
sphere of production; only when capital begins to dominate the sphere
of production can one speak of a definitively established capitalist
mode of production.

Capital is value generating surplus value, money in search of more
money, the drive for enrichment as the predominant motive for
economic activity. One of Karl Marx's greatest discoveries was that
'capital' in and by itself is not a 'thing'. Neither cattle which reproduce
their kind, nor the mass of accumulated means of production, nor
indeed a treasure of silver and gold is capital. These 'things' become
capital only under definite social conditions, which allow their owners
to *appropriate* the social surplus product, either in part or totally,

depending on the weight of this capital in society. Behind the appearance of relations between people and things Marx discovered the substance of the capital relation to be a relation of social production, a relationship between social classes.

The essence of the capitalist mode of production lies in the relationship of wage labour and capital – in the separation of the direct producers from their means of production and subsistence on the one hand, and on the other, the fragmentation of the power of control over the means of production within the capitalist class, because of private property.[4] Out of this double division of society there emerge straightaway economic arrangements of a structural kind. The direct producers are subject to the economic *compulsion* to sell their labour power as the only way to survive. All the commodities created by these producers are appropriated as private property by alien owners of the means of production. Thus a society of generalized commodity production comes into being, since not only finished goods but also means of production (including land) and labour power itself are offered on the market.

For Marxists, these structural features are the ones which determine the capitalist character of the economy and society, and not, for example, very low wages, impoverished producers, politically powerless wage earners or the absence of state intervention in the economy. Far from having only 'described economic development in the 19th century' and being 'outdated by economic developments in the 20th century', Marx's *Capital* is in reality a genius's anticipation of developmental tendencies which only unfolded fully long after the death of its author. In Marx's own time, the majority of the working population in all capitalist countries – except Britain – consisted of independent small producers and small traders assisted by their immediate families. Only much later was the working population actually reduced to a vast mass of wage and salary earners (which amounts already to 90 per cent in Britain and the USA, and over 80 per cent in most other industrialized capitalist countries), a constantly diminishing class of big, medium-sized and small capitalists, and a vanishing minority of independent small producers who do not employ external wage labour.

To prove that we no longer live within a capitalist mode of production in the Marxist sense of the word, in order to justify the myth of the 'mixed economy', one would have to supply evidence showing that wage earners are no longer compelled to sell their labour power continuously (perhaps because the state will guarantee all citizens a minimum livelihood irrespective of whether they can work or not, or because the means of production have become so cheap that workers can all save enough from their average wages to go into business for themselves), and that economic development is no longer governed by the compulsion for individual firms to maximize profits or growth under the pressure of competition.

It suffices to investigate economic development over the last hundred, fifty or twenty-five years to establish that none of these structural changes have in fact occurred. Capitalism, as Marx defined it, today remains more than ever characteristic of the economic order in the Western world.

At stake here is not purely a question of definition, i.e., a semantic dispute. The scientifically correct definition of the capitalist mode of production makes it possible to discover the *long-range laws of motion and internal contradictions* of this mode of production. Here we encounter once again the remarkable superiority of Marxist economic analysis over the 'neo-classical' schools of economics, which offer nothing to match it in this respect.[5]

Since capitalism is based on private ownership of the means of production – i.e., on a power of control over means of production, the work force and investment decisions exercised by many independent firms, by different capitalists – capitalist production takes place under conditions of inexorable competition and its resulting anarchy of production. Each individual capitalist, each individual firm, attempts to maximize its profits and growth, without regard for the effects of these pursuits on the economy as a whole.

Competition compels the reduction of production costs, in order to retain a share of the market or to expand it. This reduction requires a significant expansion of the scale of production, i.e., ever greater production runs, and these in turn demand ever more perfect machines. Capitalism hence implies a tremendous increase in technological advancement, the constant application of the findings of natural science to material production, and the tendency towards limitless expansion of the mountain of commodities and machines up to semi-automation, which Marx anticipated.

But more and more machines require more and more capital. To survive the battle of competition, the capitalist (the capitalist firm) must constantly try to increase his (its) capital. The accumulation of capital is the main goal and principal motor of economic life and economic growth under capitalism. If the accumulation of capital slows down, economic activity declines and misery and want grow, in spite of the availability of gigantic reserves of goods and productive forces. The compulsion to accumulate capital moreover tendentially forces the capitalist class to raise the rate of exploitation of labour power. For capital is only capitalized surplus value, and surplus value is only unpaid labour – the total new value produced by the labour force minus the reproduction costs of the labour force, i.e., the monetary form of the social surplus product. A rising productivity of labour means, however, that a given basket of consumer goods (or even a growing quantity of consumer goods) can be produced in an ever shorter span of labour time (in a smaller fraction of the working day). It is therefore always possible – especially given a reduced and declining industrial reserve army (unemployment) in the long term – that the real wage of the workers rises, while at the same time the rate of exploitation increases and workers receive a smaller fraction of the new value they themselves produced.

Since only living labour power creates new value and surplus value, and the proportion of capital invested in 'dead' means of production (buildings, machines, raw materials, energy) tendentially grows, there exists a medium- and long-term tendency towards a fall in the average rate of profit, i.e., the relationship between total social surplus value and social capital.

The fluctuations of the rate of profit regulate economic development under capitalism. A falling rate of profit causes a slower accumulation of capital, slackening investment activity, growing unemployment, a drop in production, declining real wages, and a slump. A rising rate of profit causes an upward trend of capital accumulation, increased productive investment, expanding production, and in the long run also more employment and rising real incomes, i.e., a boom, although both in 'good' and in 'bad' times all these developmental tendencies by no means operate simultaneously or in a linear fashion. In the longer term, capitalism exhibits waves of more rapid economic growth (1848–1873, 1893–1913, 1948–1966) and waves of slower growth (1823–1847, 1874–1893, 1914–1939, 1967–. . .), which are in the last instance determined by fluctuations in the average rate of profit and the attendant possibility (or difficulty) of realizing fundamental techno-logical revolutions.

This wave-like movement in the rate of profit conditions the *cyclical pattern of capitalist production* inherent in the system, the regular suc-cession of phases of periodic overproduction (recession) and economic upturn (up to periodic booms). This cyclical motion of capitalist production will continue so long as the capitalist mode of production exists, and no 'refined package of government anti-cyclical policies' can prevent the return of periodic overproduction crises in the long run.[6] Over-production crises are explained by competition, i.e., on the one hand by the anarchy of capitalist production, which necessarily leads to a cyclical movement of over-investment and under-investment, and on the other hand by the trend, equally inherent in the system, to develop production (and productive capacity) beyond the limits of the solvent demand of the vast majority, which remains bounded by capitalist relations of distribution.

To be sure, each of the twenty generalized economic crises[7] which have occurred in the history of the capitalist world market up till now also featured special characteristics, which are tied to special aspects of the development of the world market (witness the partial 'triggering' role of the raw materials boom and the oil shocks for the 1974–75 recession). But it would be unconscientious and unscientific to 'explain' a phenomenon recurring twenty times within a span of 150 years mainly or exclusively by reference to 'special' factors, which could at best explain only this or that specific crisis each time, and to refuse to explain the *general causes of capitalist economic crises* inherent in the system.

It is equally inapposite to regard the regular recurrence of an economic upturn after the crisis as proof of the 'failure' of Marx's analysis. Marx never envisaged an automatic collapse in 'the' great economic crisis. In his analysis, the crisis had precisely the objective function of boosting the valorization and accumulation of capital once again, by means of the massive devalorization of capital and a massive rise in the rate of exploitation of labour power (made possible by unemployment). His conclusion was just that a system which can only achieve economic growth at the price of a periodic, violent destruction of productive forces and a periodic production of mass poverty is an irrational and inhuman system, which ought to be replaced by a better one.

Under structurally-determined competition, the constantly growing accumulation of capital leads to the *increasing concentration and centralization of capital.* The big fish eat up the little fish. In more and more branches of industry, two-thirds or more of production is concentrated in a handful of big corporations. Concentration and centralization of capital pave the way for market monopolies in many areas. Monopoly capitalism takes the place of the liberal capitalism of free competition. Neither the monopolies nor growing state intervention can, in the long run, abolish the operation of the law of value, or control and guarantee prices, markets, production and economic growth. Competition and anarchy suspended at one level reassert themselves just as powerfully at a higher level.

From these general laws of motion of the capitalist mode of production arise a series of *fundamental and growing contradictions in the system.*

Capitalist economic growth is always uneven growth, called forth by the search for surplus profits. Development and underdevelopment mutually condition each other and lead both nationally and internationally to an extreme polarization of economic power. In the leading industrialized capitalist countries, the richest 1 to 2 per cent of the population owns more than 50 per cent of private wealth, and in many cases more than 75 per cent of the shares of all joint-stock companies.[8] Worldwide, fewer than 800 multinational corporations already control between a quarter and a third of capitalist industrial production. One thousand wheat, corn and soya wholesale firms together with a few hundred agro-business corporations control the best part of the trade in foodstuffs. Seventy per cent of the world population (by which is meant the underdeveloped countries plus China) subsists on barely 15 per cent of the world income and account for less than 10 per cent of world energy consumption.

The capitalist mode of production entails a growing alienation of labour and self-alienation of all human beings. When labour is treated merely as a means to earn money, it loses its creative and personality-building dimension to a far-reaching degree. Physical exertion, monotony and the permanent stress caused by the pressure to perform and the fear of failure become a burden and a plague. The human being is no longer an end but only a means of the economic system – degraded to a cog in the machine, so to speak.

Extreme rationality and refined planning in cost and investment calculations within the firm, the minute organization of research and production within the enterprise, are combined with a growing irrationality of the system as a whole. This irrationality manifests itself not merely in the regular recurrence of overproduction crises; it also finds expression in growing waste due to the permanent under-utilization of productive capacity and in the squandering of productive forces on senseless production harmful to health, nature and life.

All these contradictions can be traced to one central contradiction: the contradiction between the growing objective socialization of production and private property. Labour as a private activity aimed at meeting direct consumption needs of individual producers or small communities became insignificant long ago. An ever closer mutual dependence today links hundreds of millions of producers in objectively cooperative labour. Yet the organization, the control and the purpose of this expanding social organism are not determined by those millions themselves. They are in the hands of big capital. Private profit (the profit of each individual firm) remains the alpha and omega of economic organization as a whole. The unlimited drive for private enrichment makes it impossible to put the expanding productive forces at the service of satisfying human needs and emancipating the producers. On the contrary, exchange-value, which has become a law unto itself, transforms these productive forces increasingly into destructive forces, which augur terrible catastrophes. The growing internal contradictions of the system discharge themselves in a series of periodic economic, social and political (military) crises with explosive destructiveness. The annihilation of material culture and elementary human civilization, the regression to barbarism, has become a real and tangible possibility.

Whoever considers the history of our century objectively can only marvel at how well Marx's analytical genius recognized and predicted the main tendencies of economic and social development.

III

The *active and conscious* dimension of Marxism is an integral element of its conception of history. This creates a daily challenge for each individual who regards him or herself as a Marxist.

While bourgeois society appears on the surface as a universal struggle between individuals, Marxism views these clashes as structured by class struggles. The class struggle between wage labour and capital dominates social development in this mode of production. It is in the last instance only the social conflict that gives expression to the economic laws of motion and the inner contradictions of this mode of production.

Every wage earner and every property owner is objectively compelled to enter into this class struggle, whether they like it or not. The capitalist employers are compelled by competition to maximize their profits, i.e., to the maximal exploitation of their employees. The wage workers on their part have no other option than to fight for higher wages and shorter working hours, if they are to maintain or improve their position in bourgeois society.

Practical experience teaches that the first cause of the financial and economic powerlessness of wage workers lies in their individual transactions with capitalist employers. The former must sell their labour power continuously, while the capitalists have sufficient reserves at their disposal to delay this sale until the price suits them. In this way material pressure forces wage earners into coalitions, to collective organization, to the creation of strike funds, trade unions, cooperatives and, when it becomes necessary, workers' political parties.

But this objective compulsion is not mechanically experienced in the same way by all wage earners. Nor do they all react instantly, in like fashion and continuously to this compulsion. Some become aware of the necessity of their coalition and the conditions under which it will be effective better and more quickly than others. Some will draw the practical conclusion from this awareness and act accordingly on a permanent basis, others much less so or not at all. Individuals from other social classes can also join the proletarian class struggle, either out of scientific conviction or because of moral identification with the exploited, or for both reasons at the same time (in some cases this phenomenon can even be explained by the aspiration to an individual career in the mass organizations).

The fact that the proletarian class struggle can only be understood as the outcome of *a dialectic of objective and subjective historical factors* implies in no way that Marxism reintroduces pure coincidence and indeterminacy into historical analysis so to speak 'by the back door', after having thrown it out in the name of the lawfulness of historical processes discovered by historical materialism.[9] It means only that the process of history does not move in a linear and one-sided way, that each historical crisis does not tend towards only one possible outcome, but that it can culminate either in a historical step forwards (a successful social revolution) or in a historical regression (a disintegration of the level of material civilization and culture that has been reached).

The bounding limits of the possible variants, however, remain materially and socially predetermined. At a definite stage in the sharpening of its internal contradictions, the downfall of a given social order is inevitable. Nothing could in the long run save decadent slave society from 300 BC onwards, or decadent late feudalism from the seventeenth century onwards. Only the concrete forms of their supersession were to a certain degree undetermined, i.e., dependent on the evolution of the relationship of forces between the warring social classes (a relationship of forces which incorporates elements of ideological class warfare and political initiative).

Likewise the possibility of finding a way out of the social crisis is materially predetermined. Given the level of development of the productive forces prevailing at the time, the crisis of antiquity could not lead to a communist society, any more than the crisis of feudalism could have, notwithstanding all the conviction and all the efforts of the Essenes and the early Christians, the Hussites and the Anabaptists. And given the development of the productive forces in our own time, a return to petty commodity production and small-scale private production is simply utopian.

Because the class struggle retains a decisive weight in the determin-ation of the concrete course of events within the Marxist conception of history, Marxism tends towards the restoration of the *unity of theory and practice*, destroyed for a long time by the social division of labour and the division of society into classes. It attempts to achieve this at three levels: firstly at the general-epistemological level, since it recognizes practical verification as the ultimate form of proof for every scientific hypothesis – including its own;[10]secondly, in showing the possibility of a socialist transformation of society, of a positive outcome of the proletarian class struggle, i.e., the solution to the dilemma of how people whose individual motivation is deeply conditioned by an alien-ating class society could build a classless society. To this vulgar-materi-alist objection Marxism replies that, while people are the product of their conditions, these conditions themselves are the product of the activity of people.[11] The revolutionary transformation of relations, and the revolutionary self-education of people for the purpose of con-sciously changing their social being, are therefore two inextricably linked processes, whose material basis is created by the internal contra-dictions of the capitalist mode of production, by the high level of development of the productive forces and the intrinsic logic of the proletarian class struggle which unfolds on an ever broader scale. In the proletariat schooled by Marxism, scientific theory and the practical transformation of society are also more and more practically reunited.

Finally, Marxism tends towards the restoration of the unity of scien-tific theory and revolutionary-political practice for every individual convinced by it. A purely contemplative 'lecture-hall Marxism' would be a castrated, self-alienated and reified pseudo-Marxism, not only practi-cally, but also theoretically because it must tend towards a fatalistic-economic determinism.

Does this inescapable connection between Marxist theory and revolutionary-socialist practice imply a tendential loss in scientific detachment and objectivity on the part of Marxist researchers, or a restriction on their ability to explain the totality of social phenomena (which is precisely the intellectual promise and attraction of Marxism)? Not at all! The antithesis of scientific objectivity is subjectivism (preju-dice and arbitrariness in the treatment of empirical data) and not partisanship. Subjectivism leads either to blindness to problems or to the denial of facts which do not fit into some dogmatic category. Nothing is more foreign to Marxism – whose founder's favourite motto was *de omnibus dubitandum est* – than such an unscientific approach to the analysis of social phenomena. Rigorous mastery of the sources and the facts; readiness to test each and every working hypothesis anew, in the event that new trends emerge which seemingly or actually contradict it; unfettered development of the broadest freedom of criticism, and directly following from that a need for scientific-ideological pluralism: these are not only integral to the Marxist method, they are so to speak necessary preconditions for the full flowering of Marxism itself. Without them it degenerates into an anaemic Talmudism or – even worse – a sterile state religion.

Precisely because Marxism is no 'science for the sake of science', precisely because it is 'partisan' in the highest sense, i.e., because it sets itself the goal not only of interpreting the world but also of changing it in the interests of working class emancipation, *precisely for these reasons* it can in no way tolerate a departure from the strictest scientific objectivity in social analysis. Only a scientifically grounded theory accounting for reality can be an effective weapon in the fight for a socialist transformation of society. To violate scientific objectivity for reasons of 'partisanship' means wetting the gunpowder before the shooting starts. And with damp gunpowder no battle is won.

An 'impartial', 'value-free' social science, i.e., one which is 'neutral' in relation to the class struggle, is impossible in a class-divided society, regardless of the subjective aspirations of researchers, who may often tend towards it. A striking example is provided by academic and 'official' economics over the last five years. When institutions like the International Monetary Fund, in *every* single case, demand of nations who request a loan, but whose credit-worthiness is in doubt, that they cut government spending on *social issues*; when they demand without scruple that poor countries like Egypt radically reduce or even abolish government subsidies on staple foods, which literally condemns a section of the population to hunger, then we are obviously confronted with a worldwide attempt to raise the rate of profit by lowering the price of the commodity labour power. That this attempt can also be justified in purely 'technical' terms (with reference to inflation, balance of payments deficits, budget deficits and so forth) only proves one thing. Because it tacitly operates exclusively within the framework of the existing social order, 'official' economics is just as tacitly forced to subordinate itself to the laws of capital accumulation, i.e., to the needs of the class struggle waged by capital.

IV

The proletarian class struggle in its elementary form is not yet a socialist class struggle. It will certainly grow over from a purely economic struggle into an objectively political one as it broadens in scope, inasmuch as it opposes not only individual workers and individual capitalists but also the broad masses of wage and salary earners against the whole of the propertied class.[12] But such an objective and politically elementary class struggle can only, through its subjective impact on the class consciousness of the proletariat, supplement the clashes between capital and labour with periodic opportunities for the conquest of political power, for the purpose of a radical transformation of bourgeois society – i.e., with a conscious anti-capitalist dimension.

These clashes are just as inevitable and inherent in the capitalist system as the decline and decomposition of this system. But neither the victory of socialism nor the formation of proletarian class consciousness at its highest level are inevitable. Here we encounter once more the subjective factor in history, i.e., conscious, purposeful intervention in the objective historical process, as a decisive component of Marxism. A series of important conclusions can be drawn from this.

The socio-economic stratification of the proletariat, the uneven appropriation of scientific knowledge (or, what is simply the negative side of the same phenomenon, the differential receptivity for bourgeois and petty-bourgeois ideology), and variations in the readiness to put continuous personal effort into trade union and political organization lead to an inevitable differentiation of proletarian class consciousness. Only the organization of the class conscious vanguard in a *revolutionary vanguard party* can secure the continuance of this consciousness and, by means of the experiences gained in each new phase of the class struggle, constantly develop it further.

But such a party only becomes the vanguard of the *class* in a genuine objective sense, when it succeeds in transmitting to the majority of wage earners the level of class consciousness essential in the battle for a socialist revolution. This transmission can only be realized through effective intervention in the real class struggle. The necessary dialectical unity of vanguard and class, of organization and spontaneity, flows from the nature of the proletariat as well as the nature of the proletarian revolution and socialist council order.[13]

The means-ends dialectic thus gets an objectively definable framework. Precisely because the socialist goal *cannot* be reached without raising the self-confidence, the feeling of communality and the class solidarity of the workers, only those means, tactics and compromises are useful and permissible – assuming they lead to the *socialist* goal – which raise proletarian class consciousness as a whole and do not lower or divide it.[14] Every tactic which has the opposite effect on the class consciousness of the workers – whatever its apparent immediate effectiveness from a 'purely practical' standpoint may be – will in the long run detract from the socialist goal, instead of bringing it a step closer.

This places special weight on the critical and self-critical components of Marxism. Marxism is not only in essence 'open' and undogmatic because it refers to a historical process, which is constantly in motion and continuously adds to and changes the raw material of the social sciences (not only with regard to the present, but to the past as well). Neither is it only 'open' because its concern with practice continually directs it to the future, which *can never* be completely known in advance, given that conscious and purposive intervention in the historical process can change a given outcome in the meantime. It is also 'open' in addition because the decisive factor in the transition from capitalism to socialism remains the raising of the class consciousness of the proletariat, as well as the level of self-activity, the self-organization, and the initiatives for struggle of the wage earners. In class struggle, every organized intervention, be it in a strike, in elections or in the construction of socialism, every speech made at a workers' meeting and every leaflet read by the workers, must always be looked at from the following standpoint: what effect will this intervention have on class consciousness? Any judgement about this effect, however, remains necessarily hypothetical during the course of action. Only subsequent, practical experience can show whether it was right or wrong. Herein lies the great significance which the history of proletarian class struggles contains for Marxism. It is the only laboratory which makes possible valid pronouncements about tactics and methods of struggle on the basis of previous experience.

Without objective-critical thought, including about oneself, a consciously socialist class struggle, a really revolutionary party and a genuine Marxism are therefore impossible. A pseudo-Marxism which sacrifices relentless self-criticism, the open expression of the truth – however bitter it may be – for no matter what 'practical exigencies' is not only unscientific, but also unworthy of the liberating dimension of Marxism. It is also, in the long run, completely inefficient.

But a *political* class struggle must deal with all social phenomena, phenomena which involve more than single individuals. Its scope, therefore, extends beyond the elementary class struggle over the division of the national income between wages and profits (surplus value). Setting out directly from this elementary class struggle, it cannot pose the question of the abolition of private ownership of the means of production, the question of the 'expropriation of the expropriators'.

The question of the state, the question of the political freedom and self-activity of the workers, the transition from representative to direct democracy, play a very decisive role here. The clear comprehension of all these questions requires the progressive education (self-education) of the proletariat, through involvement with *all* political and social problems affecting *all* social classes of bourgeois society.[15]

That this imperative should be inscribed in the Marxist conception of history and action is by no means accidental, or the product of 'purely tactical' considerations. It arises out of the essence of proletarian class struggle, which conceives itself only as a means to the end of a classless society, a society in which every form of oppression and violence perpetrated by human beings against human beings *must* disappear with the exploitation of human beings by human beings. Indifference, toleration or even the renewed extension of such oppression *cannot* lead to the socialist goal.

Consequently there is also an ethical component of Marxism, which has an objective-materialist basis. When consistent Marxists say that they approach everything from the standpoint of the proletarian class struggle, they imply that this standpoint is based on the theorem that only that which raises proletarian class consciousness and, amongst other things, promotes a deeper understanding by the workers of the fundamental difference between bourgeois and classless society, can advance the class struggle in the long run. This, in turn, entails a recognition of the necessity of practical struggles against every form of exploitation and oppression, of women as well as of all specific races, nationalities, peoples, age-groups and so forth, as necessary components of the worldwide struggle for a socialist social order. Marxism begins 'with the doctrine that *for the human being, the supreme being is the human being,* and thus with the *categorical imperative to overthrow all conditions* in which the human being is a debased, enslaved, neglected and contemptible being'.[16]

This recognition originates without doubt from an individual psychological need for protest and rebellion against every form of unfairness, injustice and inequality. But it also originates from an objective historical necessity.

Only the conscious, worldwide control of humanity over the material productive forces can prevent the latter from transforming themselves more and more into nature- and culture-destroying forces. Conscious control, however, assigns prime importance to both individual and collective capacity for judgement. The self-education of the proletariat in effective emancipation and genuine internationalism, which Marxism promotes, is in the last instance self-education of individual proletarians in a collective framework, in the capacity for judgement and decision-making. Without these, socialist self-management and socialist planned economy would only be a hollow, if not indeed a cynical phrase.

The socialization of the economy can only successfully make the leap from a purely objective process to one brought under subjective control when the collectivization of property relations and management of the productive forces is dialectically accompanied and combined with a progressive individualization of the *capacity* for decision-making.[17] To extend the self-realization of the human personality to *all* producers and *all* human beings is not only the greatest socialist goal; it is also increasingly the indispensable means for the realization of that goal.

V

Marxist theory distinguishes the most favourable conditions for the overthrow of capitalism from those which are essential for the construction of a fully developed socialist social order. The former set of conditions depend above all on the socio-political relationship of forces. This relationship is not just a function of the relative strength of the proletariat and its revolutionary vanguard party, but also of the relative weakness of the bourgeoisie and, for example, the possibility of winning the majority of a still numerous non-proletarian working population – the peasantry – as allies for the proletarian revolution, precisely because of the inability of the bourgeoisie of the underdeveloped capitalist countries in the imperialist epoch to radically overcome the pre-capitalist relations of the rural village. The latter set of conditions are a function of a high level of development of the productive forces and a political-cultural ripeness of the proletariat, which enable a maximal degree of direct council democracy, of self-management, of harmonious economic growth, of systematic elimination of commodity and money relations through the rapid achievement of saturation in the consumption of basic material goods and services (i.e., a gradual transition towards distribution according to need).

It is obvious that the relative underdevelopment of capitalism in certain countries in the imperialist epoch facilitates the conquest of political power by the proletariat for the very same reasons which make the construction of a classless society exceedingly difficult, or even – so long as the revolution in these countries remains isolated – impossible. Trotsky's theory of permanent revolution – together with Lenin's theory of organization the most important progressive development of Marxism since Marx and Engels – allowed him to anticipate *both* contradictory aspects of twentieth-century revolutions correctly as early as 1905–06.[18]

The conclusion which he drew from his recognition of the dialectical character of the socialist revolution in relatively underdeveloped countries was not one of damning these revolutions as 'premature', on the ground that they condemned the revolutionary party and class to defeat.[19] It was, on the contrary, one of understanding the inevitability of such 'premature' revolutions in the epoch of imperialism – the only alternative is to remain stuck in barbaric underdevelopment! – and the necessity of viewing them as springboards for the socialist *world revolution*, which *can* spread by degrees and stages to the most important industrial countries of the world. The tragedy of socialism since 1917 does not lie in the fact that Marxists tried to assist its victory in underdeveloped countries. That should rather be viewed as their world-historical achievement. Its tragedy lies in the fact that the revolution remained isolated in these countries, i.e., that it has still not triumphed in the industrialized West despite numerous favourable historical situations (Germany 1918–19, 1920, 1923; France 1936, 1944–47, 1968; Italy 1919–20, 1945–48, 1969–70; Great Britain 1926, 1945–48; Spain 1936–37, and so forth).[20]

As a result, a new historical phenomenon emerged, first in the Soviet Union, then in Eastern Europe, China, Cuba and Vietnam. There one finds societies which are no longer capitalist, in which none of the laws of motion of capitalism mentioned earlier still operate, but which at the same time are still far removed from the construction of a socialist society in the sense of Marx and Engels' definition of the first stage of classless society.[21] They are societies arrested and frozen in the transitional period between capitalism and socialism, as a result of the delay of the proletarian world revolution.

The concrete, historically specific conditions under which this freezing-up occurred led to the bureaucratic degeneration of these transitional societies. A social layer – the state, economic, party and military bureaucracy – appropriated significant privileges for itself in the sphere of consumption. Because its privileges remain limited to this sphere, and because it performs no vital function in the production process, we are not dealing here with a new ruling *class*. Without parasitism the socially necessary productive accumulation would not sink but rise. Instead of registering a decline, economic growth would increase. But precisely because it is a parasitic layer, the bureaucracy can base its privileges only on unlimited control of the social surplus product, i.e., on an absolute monopoly of management of the state, the economy and defence, and on a lack of political rights, atomization and passivity of the broad working masses.[22] As events in Hungary and Poland in 1956, in Czechoslovakia in 1968 (and partially in China in 1966–67) have shown, every new upswing of political mass activity in these societies entails an almost automatic stimulus towards a real council system, the almost automatic overthrow of the dictatorship of the bureaucracy.

By sticking the label of 'real' or 'actually existing' socialism on this dictatorship, its Eastern and Western apologists did the international bourgeoisie the greatest possible ideological and political service, without which – at least in Western Europe – capitalism would probably have disappeared by now. Today, the identification of socialism with the conditions of political oppression and lack of personal freedom in the East is, for workers in several key countries in the West, the most important reason for a relative acquiescence in bourgeois society, despite its growing susceptibility for crises.

This identification will only be permanently broken when the proletarian revolution triumphs in one or more highly developed countries in the West and presents the world proletariat with a practically realized 'socialist model' (more correctly: a model of a still developing and incomplete socialism) radically different from the USSR. We cannot describe what such a model will actually look like. But its broad outlines can be approximately deduced both from those elements of the new society which have already emerged in the womb of the old, and from the critical assimilation of the totality of (positive as well as negative) experiences of previous proletarian revolutions in the twentieth century.

The chief characteristic of this socialist model at the political level will be that of council democracy, i.e., the direct exercise of political power by the working *class* and its *freely chosen representatives*. The revolutionary party will exercise its leading role within the framework of the councils' regime through political-ideological persuasion of the majority, and not by force and repression of its political opponents. This implies a *multi-party system*, full freedom of organization, assembly, demonstration and of the press, independent trade unions, the right to strike and full respect for ideological, scientific, artistic and philosophical pluralism. These basic democratic rights will, in contrast to bourgeois parliamentary democracy, be all the more *expanded* that they will no longer be purely formal but become achievable in content, i.e., the time and material preconditions will be secured for the masses of citizens to exercise them effectively. It means likewise a growing shift to direct democracy, to the immediate exercise of state power by the workers themselves, to self-management of people and communities in a significant number of social areas, i.e., the onset of a dynamic towards the gradual withering away of the state.

At the economic level this 'model' will be characterized by planned, democratically centralized self-management of the economy, in which the associated producers themselves decide all the priorities determining the development of the economy, and indeed always at the level where these decisions *can* in practice be made most efficiently: for important investment decisions – at national congresses of all councils and congresses of industrial branches; for the organization of work – at the level of industrial branches and individual enterprises (or at the level of enterprises federated in cooperatives); for social investments – at local and regional levels; for decisions regarding the range of goods to be produced – producer-consumer conferences aided by television, referenda and written opinion polls; for a growing number of major investment decisions as well as policies to combat environmental pollution – in international council congresses, and so forth.

Workers' self-management put into practice (and not merely demagogically proclaimed) demands a radical shortening of the working week, a permanent elevation of the level of technical-cultural capacities of the direct producers, a radical reduction of inequalities in remuneration as well as the continual replacement of bourgeois norms of distribution (commodity-money relations). Maximum public control and the broadest political council democracy are the only guarantees against parasitism, corruption and waste, i.e., the retroactive effects of the survival of commodity-money relations in the distribution of consumer goods on the relations of production.

Both in its political and economic aspects, this 'model' is closely bound up with an enduring change in work motivation and the work ethic which, in turn, is inconceivable without a progressive transformation of technology, the organization of labour and the content of the labour process (the elimination of all mechanical and monotonous labour processes experienced only as a passive 'service to society'), the supersession of the division between manual and intellectual labour, between production and management, and the changing of morals and customs. All these changes will interact and condition each other in the self-education of the associated producers and the self-development of the 'socialist human being'. They imply a sudden, qualitative surge of international solidarity, i.e., a significant redistribution of use-values produced worldwide. A 'socialist world' in which abundance and ample free time in the North went hand in hand with hunger and underdevelopment in the South would be a monstrosity, and have nothing in common with true socialism.

Bourgeois ideologues hold Marxism responsible for Stalin and every-thing that went wrong and is still going wrong in the USSR, Eastern Europe and China. This is a bit like condemning modern medicine and calling for a return to institutionalized quackery – on the ground that so many patients could not be cured over the last sixty years due to inadequate medical treatment. We can even turn the tables on these critics. A new demonstration of the superiority of Marxism as social science is offered by its discovery of the causes, secrets and laws of motion of the unforeseen 'bureaucratized transitional society between capitalism and socialism', and its thorough and complete unmasking of the mystification of 'applied pseudo-Marxism' in this society. Com-pared to such achievements, the theoretical analyses attempted by academic 'Sovietology' are bungling, while the relevant 'laws' allegedly discovered by it either boil down to commonplaces or else are over-taken quickly by the objective developments.

VI

If Marxism elevates the fight against every form of exploitation and oppression to a categorical imperative and subjects its alleged 'realiz-ation' in the Soviet Union or elsewhere to thorough-going criticism,[23] it by no means lapses into a kind of historical idealism, which counter-poses a utopian ideal model to the 'real overcoming of the existing conditions'. It only raises the materialist understanding of history to a higher plane, where the unity of theory and practice once more gains a new dimension.

Throughout human history, one can actually find two parallel yet contradictory constants. On the one hand, wars, successive forms of class society and class struggles attest to the inability of people up till now to extend the principles of voluntary collaboration, cooperation in solidarity and association to humanity as a whole. The practical, endur-ing application of these principles remains restricted to greater or smaller *fragments* of the human race: to tribal or village communities, specific forms of extended families, to social classes whose members fight for a common goal. We already know what material causes give rise to this constant tendency towards social self-destruction – and how, given the contemporary level of science and technique, it more and more threatens the continued existence of civilization, and indeed the sheer physical survival of humanity. On the other hand, the yearning for a society of free, equal and associated producers is just as deeply rooted in human history as class divisions and the resulting inequality, injustice and violence perpetrated by people against people. Despite all the ideological influence wielded by the ruling classes, who try to persuade us time and again that 'there have always been rich and poor, powerful and powerless, dominant and dominated people, and there will always be', and that it is therefore senseless to fight for a society of equals, we nevertheless witness throughout history an uninterrupted stream of upsurges, rebellions, revolts and revolutions against the exploitation of the poor and the oppression of the powerless. Time after time these attempts at the self-emancipation of humanity fail. But new attempts are constantly being made – and, viewed historically, in each materially more developed society they are made with a clearer vision of the future, with bolder goals and growing chances to realize them.

We Marxists in the epoch of class struggle between capital and labour are only the most recent representatives of this many centuries-old tendency, which began with the first strike in Egypt under the pharaohs[24] and found its way, through countless slave rebellions in Antiquity and the peasant wars of ancient China and Japan, to the great continuity of revolutionary tradition in modern times and the present.

This continuity is created by the inextinguishable spark of revolt against inequality, exploitation, injustice and oppression, which lights up again and again in the human race. In it lies the certainty of our victory. No Caesar and no Pontius Pilate, no emperor by the grace of God and no Inquisition, no Hitler and no Stalin, no terror and no consumer society has proved successful in extinguishing this spark in the long run. So much does it correspond to our anthropological nature – the fact that humans cannot survive without progressive socialization and walking upright – that it shows itself time and again[25] – if not in one country or continent, then in another, in one social class at one time, in another the next, sometimes only among poets, philosophers and scholars, at other times among great masses of people, according to the tides of history and the material interests and political-ideological class struggle which govern them.

Neurophysiologists, psychologists and behavioural scientists have attempted to reduce this duality in human history to the two sides of our central nervous system, which are said to reflect the combination of instinctive and conscious activity in the individual. Such a thesis can prove at most the possibility of human aggressiveness and destructiveness, the fact that the *potential* for destructiveness – which stems from our pre-human or proto-human past – is deeply embedded in human beings. But it does not explain by any means why this potential is actualized more strongly or weakly in a given epoch; why there have been peaceful and aggressive epochs, cultures and societies; or why there could be no social order which drastically restricts this potential destructiveness on a permanent (or at least very long-term) basis, or channels it into harmless areas. This is the main theme and main goal of Marxism as a science of humanity as a whole.

We believe, though, that it is more to the point to keep the following in view: the weak human race, which for hundreds of thousands of years was ruled by *fear* of the overpowering forces of nature, and developed elementary forms of social cooperation in the struggle against them, could buy the progressive mastery of these natural forces only at the price of a continual erosion of social solidarity. This mastery demanded indeed the accumulation of an ever greater fraction of the social product in place of its immediate consumption, a growing specialization of one section of society in management and intellectual work instead of the exercise of management functions on a rotational basis by all members of society. So long as the social product remained too small, this compulsion led to a permanent conflict; accumulation could grow only by means of forced labour by the direct producers, and the masses of these producers had to remain separated from intellectual work.

The more humans began to master nature, the more they lost social solidarity and control over their social existence. From now on these were regulated by objective, blind laws operating behind people's backs. In capitalism this contradiction has found its highest and sharpest expression.

With the gigantic development of the productive forces by the capitalist mode of production, however, this price for our mastery of nature has not merely become too high and an immediate danger to human survival, but has also become increasingly senseless. For the first time in history a realistic material basis has emerged for a worldwide classless society of associated producers. In creating wage labour, a class more capable of collective organization and mass action than any other in history, capitalism simultaneously generates a social force which – at least periodically – exhibits an instinctive urge to fight for such a society in practice. From the Paris Commune to the Russian Revolution, from Catalonia in 1936–37 to May '68 in France, the history of revolutionary class struggle of the proletariat is a combination of ever bolder and more extensive attempts in this direction, in spite of all dramatic defeats and tragic partial victories.

We do not doubt for one moment that this history is still in its early phase and that its high point still lies ahead and not behind us. This is not a mystical belief but rather a certainty grounded in a scientific analysis of the laws of development of bourgeois society and class struggle in the twentieth century. The great historical achievement of Marxism lies precisely in its ability to provide a rational-scientific basis and direction for the achievement of an ancient dream of humanity, in making possible a superior synthesis of critical thought, moral-human striving and militant emancipatory action.

In the last instance I am a Marxist because only Marxism makes it possible to keep believing in humanity and its future without self-deception – despite all the terrible experiences of the twentieth century, despite Auschwitz and Hiroshima, despite famine in the 'Third World' and the threat of nuclear annihilation. Marxism teaches us to take a positive attitude toward life and human beings and to love them, without a false gloss, without illusions, in full awareness of the never-ending difficulties and unavoidable setbacks in the millions of years which it has taken our species to progress from ape-like creatures to global investigators and conquerors of space. To conquer conscious control over its social existence has today become a matter of life and death for this species. In the end it will succeed in realizing the noblest of all aspirations: the construction of a humane, classless, non-violent world socialism.

Notes

1. See the classical works by Adolf Portmann (*Zoologie und das neue Bild des Menschen. Biologische Fragmente zu einer Lehre vom Menschen*, Rowohlt Verlag, Reinbek 1956) and Arnold Gehlen (*Der Mensch. Seine Natur und seine Stellung in der Welt*, 7th ed., Athenäum Verlag, Frankfurt and Bonn 1962) as well as Gerhard Heberer (*Der Ursprung des Menschen. Unser gegenwärtiger Wissensstand*, Gustav Fischer Verlag, Stuttgart 1969), Trân Duc Thao (*Investigations into the Origin of Language and Consciousness*, D. Reidel Publishing Company, Boston 1984) and the volume edited by V. P. Iakimov (*U istokov tshelowetshestva. Osnoviye problemi antropogenesa* [The Origins of Humankind: Fundamental Problems of Anthropogenesis], Isdatelstvo Moskovskogo Universiteta, Moscow 1964).

2.
   A spider conducts operations which resemble those of the weaver, and a bee would put many a human architect to shame by the construction of its honeycomb cells. But what distinguishes the worst architect from the best of bees is that the architect builds the cell in his mind before he constructs it in wax. At the end of every labour process, a result emerges which had already been conceived by the worker at the beginning, hence already existed ideally.
   Karl Marx, *Capital* Volume 1, Penguin, Harmondsworth 1976, p. 284.

3. Convincing examples of such an application of the Marxist method can be found, e.g., in outstanding works on the history of literature and literary criticism like Franz Mehring's *The Lessing Legend* (*Die Lessing-Legende*, Dietz-Verlag, Berlin 1963), Georg Lukács's *The Theory of the Novel* (Merlin Press, London 1971) and *The Historical Novel* (Penguin, Harmondsworth 1969), and Lucien Goldmann's *Le Dieu caché* (*The Hidden God: A Study of Tragic Vision in the Pensées of Pascal and the Tragedies of Racine*, Routledge & Kegan Paul, London 1964).

4. Private property and capital ownership should not be understood in a purely legal sense here, but in terms of their economic meaning as private (as opposed to collective) power of control over means of production. This economic institution of course cannot consolidate, reproduce and generalize itself in the long run without the requisite juridical recognition. Typical for capitalism is the fact that private *ownership* of large amounts of capital permits private control over even greater amounts of capital than those legally 'owned'.

5. 'However important these technical contributions to the progress of economic theory in the present-day appraisal of Marxian achievements, they are overshadowed by his brilliant analysis of the long-term tendencies of the capitalist system. The record is indeed impressive . . .' (Wassily Leontief, 'The Significance of Marxian Economics for Present-Day Economic Theory' in David Horowitz, ed., *Marx and Modern Economics*, MacGibbon & Kee, London 1968, p. 94.)

6. Understanding this enabled us to predict already in the late 1960s and early 1970s the generalized recession of the international capitalist economy in 1974–75 with sufficient accuracy, including with regard to the time of its outbreak.

7. The economic crises suffered by leading nations on the world market broke out roughly speaking in 1825, 1836, 1847, 1857, 1866, 1873, 1882, 1891, 1900, 1907, 1913, 1921, 1929, 1937, 1949, 1953, 1957, 1960, 1970, 1974.

8. This without taking into account the savings of small savers or pension funds, since in these cases we are obviously dealing not with wealth, but only with differentiated income which is later completely consumed. If moreover owner-occupied dwellings are subtracted from the national wealth (on the ground that they likewise do not represent assets but only durable consumer goods), these percentages become even higher.

9.

> In the history of society . . . the agents are all endowed with consciousness, are men acting with deliberation or passion, working towards definite goals; nothing happens without a conscious purpose, without an intended aim. But this distinction, important as it is for historical investigation, particularly of single epochs and events, cannot alter the fact that the course of history is governed by inner general laws. For here, also, on the whole, in spite of the consciously desired aims of all individuals, accident apparently reigns on the surface. That which is willed happens but rarely; in the majority of instances the numerous desired ends cross and conflict with one another, or these ends themselves are from the outset incapable of realisation or the means

of attaining them are insufficient . . . Historical events thus appear on the whole to be likewise governed by chance. But where on the surface accident holds sway, there actually it is always governed by inner, hidden laws and the important thing is only to discover these laws.

Frederick Engels, *Ludwig Feuerbach and the End of Classical German Philosophy*, in Marx and Engels, *Selected Works in 3 Volumes*, Moscow 1970, vol. 3, pp. 365–6.

10. See V. I. Lenin, *Philosophical Notebooks*, in *Collected Works*, Moscow, vol. 38, p. 191.

11. See the third of the 'Thesis on Feuerbach' by Karl Marx. These 'Theses' are in a certain sense the birth certificate of Marxism.

12. Karl Marx and Frederick Engels, *Manifesto of the Communist Party*, in Marx and Engels, *Selected Works*, vol. 1, pp. 115–16.

13. See on this issue my essays 'The Leninist Theory of Organisation', in Robin Blackburn, ed., *Revolution and Class Struggle*, and 'What Is the Bureaucracy?' in Tariq Ali, ed., *The Stalinist Legacy*.

14. See V. I. Lenin, *Left-Wing Communism: An Infantile Disorder*, in *Collected Works*, vol. 31, p. 74.

15. V. I. Lenin, *What Is to Be Done?* in *Collected Works*, vol. 5, pp. 422ff.

16. Karl Marx, 'Critique of Hegel's Philosophy of Right. Introduction', in *Karl Marx Early Writings*, Penguin, Harmondsworth 1975, p. 251 (modified translation).

17. 'Beyond these three sides – individual subjectivity, inter-subjectivity and objective relation – the primary constitutive interest in the Marxian thinking about praxis is the practical primacy of their synthesis, as determined by the interest in objective *wealth*, in multi-dimensional and autonomous personal *self-activity* and in universal social mutuality, in egalitarian *cooperation* . . .' (Helmut Dahmer and Helmut Fleischer, 'Karl Marx', in Dirk Käsler, ed., *Klassiker des soziologischen Denkens*, vol. 1, Verlag C. H. Beck, Munich 1976, p. 151).

18. Leon Trotsky's *Results and Prospects* was first published in 1906. (English translation by Brian Pearce in Leon Trotsky, *The Permanent Revolution* and *Results and Prospects*, Pathfinder Press, New York 1970.)

19. 'The worst thing that can befall the leader of an extreme party is to be compelled to take over a government in an epoch when the movement is not yet ripe for the domination of the class which he represents and for the realization of the measures which that domination would imply' (Frederick Engels, *The Peasant War in Germany*, International Publishers, New York 1966, p. 135).

20. The explanation of this tragedy must incorporate a concrete analysis of the strategy and tactics of the labour movement in the twentieth century. Some of the most important contributions in this field are Rosa Luxemburg's *Social Reform or Revolution*, her writings on the debates over the mass strike, Lenin's *Left-Wing Communism: An Infantile Disorder* and Trotsky's writings on Germany (*The Struggle Against Fascism in Germany*, Pathfinder Press, New York 1971), France and Spain (*The Spanish Revolution 1931–39*, Pathfinder Press, New York 1973).

21.

> Within the cooperative society based on common ownership of the means of production the producers do not exchange their products; similarly, the labour spent on the products no longer appears *as the value* of these products, possessed by them as a material characteristic, for now, in contrast to capitalist society, individual pieces of labour are no longer merely indirectly, but directly, a component part of the total labour. The phrase "proceeds of labour", which even today is too ambiguous to be of any value, thus loses any meaning whatsoever.

> We are dealing with a communist society, not as it has *developed* on its own foundations, but on the contrary, just as it *emerges* from capitalist society. In every respect, economically, morally, intellectually, it is thus still stamped with the birthmarks of the old society from whose womb it has emerged.
>
> Karl Marx, *Critique of the Gotha Programme*, in *The First International and After*, Penguin, Harmondsworth 1974, pp. 345–6.

Also:

> Direct social production and direct distribution preclude all exchange of commodities, therefore also the transformation of the products into commodities (at any rate within the community) and consequently also their transformation into *values*. From the moment when society enters into possession of the means of production and uses them in direct association for production, the labour of each individual, however varied its specifically useful character may be, becomes at the start and directly social labour . . . It could therefore never occur to it (i.e., society) still to express the quantities of labour put into the products, quantities which it will then know directly and in their absolute amounts, in a third product, in a measure which, besides, is only relative, fluctuating, inadequate, though formerly unavoidable for lack of a better one, rather than express them in their natural, adequate and absolute measure, *time* . . . society will not assign values to products.
>
> Frederick Engels, *Anti-Dühring*, Moscow 1947, pp. 374–5.

22. Thorough analyses of the bureaucratized transitional society between capitalism and socialism can be found in Leon Trotsky, *The Revolution Betrayed: What is the Soviet Union and Where is it Going?*, Pathfinder Press, New York 1977; Isaac Deutscher, *The Unfinished Revolution*, Oxford University Press, Oxford 1967; Jürgen Arz and Otmar Sauer, *Zur Entwicklung der sowjetischen Übergangsgesellschaft 1917–29*, ISP-Verlag, Frankfurt 1976; Jakob Moneta, *Aufstieg und Niedergang des Stalinismus*, ISP-Verlag, Frankfurt 1976.

23. This tendency towards merciless self-criticism of proletarian revolutions was anticipated by Karl Marx already in 1852, in his foreword to *The 18th Brumaire of Louis Bonaparte* (in *Surveys from Exile*, Penguin, Harmondsworth 1973, p. 150).

24. Towards the end of the twentieth dynasty, under Pharaoh Ramses III, i.e.,

some 3500 years ago, the workers of the royal necropolis organized the first known strike or workers' uprising in history. This event was reported in detail on a papyrus at the time, which has been preserved and is currently located in Turin (see François Daumas, *Ägyptische Kultur im Zeitalter der Pharaonen*, Knaur Verlag, Munich 1969, p. 309; translated from the French original: *La Civilisation de l'Égypte pharaonique*, Arthaud, Paris 1965).

25.

And yet ethics as experiment must neither remain boundless nor merely be a formal requirement for individual behaviour. It must draw its light from the class struggle of those who suffer and are heavy laden, from the humiliated and the insulted. In this way only, will enduring ethical postulates become indestructible and imperishable, in spite of their betrayal in reality. This means that the true face of humanity, however vague its features, and despite the weariness and purely loquacious character of its too general determinations . . . is at least present in its self-consciousness.

Ernst Bloch, *Experimentum mundi. Frage, Kategorien des Herausbringens, Praxis*, Suhrkamp Verlag, Frankfurt 1975, p. 184.

Ernest Mandel's Book-Format Works in English

This bibliography of Ernest Mandel is restricted to writings published in book-format in the English language, including contributions to collective works. The huge number of articles Mandel has published in various periodical publications, many of whom have been reprinted as pamphlets in different countries, as well as his contributions of various sorts and various lengths to the numerous party bulletins, organs and pamphlets of the Fourth International and its organizations are not included. To do otherwise would have considerably increased the length of this bibliography and the size of this book.

The bibliography is arranged in chronological order usually according to the date of publication of the first edition of each book, notwithstanding the original date of publication of Mandel's writings when they are included in a collection. There are three sections:

1. Books authored by Mandel alone.
2. Books edited or co-edited by Mandel.
3. Contributions by Mandel to works authored or edited by others.

1. Mandel as single author

1995 – *Long Waves of Capitalist Development: A Marxist Interpretation*, second revised edn, Verso, London, viii+174 pp.

1995 – *Trotsky as Alternative*, transl. by Gus Fagan, Verso, London, vi+186 pp.

1994 – *Revolutionary Marxism and Social Reality in the 20th Century: Collected Essays*, ed. and with an introd. by Steve Bloom, Humanities Press, Atlantic Highlands, NJ, xii+214 pp. [Includes the follow-

ing articles by Ernest Mandel: 'Trotsky: The Man and His Work',
pp. 2–18; 'Solzhenitsyn's Assault on Stalinism . . . and on the
October Revolution', pp. 19–31; 'Rosa Luxemburg and German
Social Democracy', pp. 32–49; 'Trotsky's Economic Ideas and
the Soviet Union Today', pp. 50–57; 'Vanguard Parties',
pp. 60–76; 'The Leninist Theory of Organization: Its Relevance
for Today', pp. 77–127; 'What Is the Theory of Permanent
Revolution', pp. 130–42; 'Reasons for Founding the Fourth
International and Why They Remain Valid Today', pp. 143–78;
'The Marxist Case for Revolution Today', pp. 179–206].

1992 – *Power and Money: A Marxist Theory of Bureaucracy*, Verso, London,
vii+252 pp.

1989 – *Beyond Perestroika: The Future of Gorbachev's USSR*, transl. by Gus
Fagan, Verso, London, xvi+214 pp. (and later rev. edn).

1986 – *The Meaning of the Second World War*, Verso, London, 208 pp.

1984 – *Delightful Murder: A Social History of the Crime Story*, Pluto, London,
viii+152 pp. (and American edn, publ. by University of Minne-
sota Press, Minneapolis, MN).

1980 – *Long Waves of Capitalist Development: The Marxist Interpretation*,
Cambridge University Press, Cambridge, viii+151 pp.

1979 – *Introduction to Marxism*, transl. by Louisa Sadler, second edn,
improved and with new material, Ink Links, London, 192 pp.
(and other ed.; first edn publ. with title: *From Class Society to
Communism*).

1979 – *Trotsky: A Study in the Dynamic of his Thought*, NLB, London,
156 pp.

1979 – *Revolutionary Marxism Today*, ed. by Jon Rothschild, NLB, London, xii+236 pp.

1978 – *The Second Slump: A Marxist Analysis of Recession in the Seventies*,
transl. by Jon Rothschild, NLB, London, 212 pp. (and later edn,
publ. by Verso, London).

1978 – *From Stalinism to Eurocommunism: The Bitter Fruits of 'Socialism in
One Country'*, transl. by Jon Rothschild, NLB, London, 223 pp.
(and later edn).

1977 – *From Class Society to Communism: An Introduction to Marxism*, transl.
by Louisa Sadler, Ink Links, London, 186 pp. (later edn publ.
with title: *Introduction to Marxism*).

1975 – *Late Capitalism*, transl. by Joris De Bres, NLB, London, 599 pp.
(and later edn, publ. by Verso, London).

1972 – *The Decline of the Dollar: A Marxist View of the Monetary Crisis*,
Pathfinder Press, New York, NY, 128 pp.

1971 – *The Formation of the Economic Thought of Karl Marx: 1843 to Capital*, transl. by Brian Pearce, Monthly Review Press, New York, NY, 223 pp. (and other and later edn publ. by NLB, London).

1970 – *Europe versus America?: Contradictions of Imperialism*, transl. from the German by Martin Rossdale, NLB, London, 139 pp. (American edn publ. by Monthly Review Press, New York, NY).

1968 – *Marxist Economic Theory*, transl. by Brian Pearce, Merlin Press, London, 2 vol., 797 pp. (and later edn, publ. by Merlin Press and by Monthly Review Press, New York, NY, respectively).

1967 – *An Introduction to Marxist Economic Theory*, Young Socialist Alliance, New York, NY, 78 pp. (and later edn publ. by Pathfinder Press, New York, NY).

2. Mandel as editor or co-editor

1992 – *New Findings in Long-Wave Research*, ed. by Alfred Kleinknecht, Ernest Mandel and Immanuel Wallerstein, St Martin's Press, New York, NY, xii+348 pp. [Ernest Mandel, 'The International Debate on Long Waves of Capitalist Development: An Intermediary Balance Sheet', pp. 316–38].

1984 – *Ricardo, Marx, Sraffa: the Langston Memorial Volume*, ed. by Ernest Mandel and Alan Freeman, Verso, London, xvi+286 pp. [Ernest Mandel, 'Introduction', pp. ix–xvi, and 'Gold, Money, and the Transformation Problem', pp. 141–63].

1968 – *50 Years of World Revolution 1917–1967: An International Symposium*, ed. by Ernest Mandel, transl. by Gerald Paul, Merit, New York, NY, 366 pp. (and later print.) [Ernest Mandel, 'Introduction', pp. 11–34; 'Economics of the Transition Period', pp. 275–303].

3. Mandel as contributor

1995 – *Marxism in the Postmodern Age: Confronting the New World Order*, ed. by Antonio Callari, Stephen Cullenberg and Carole Biewener, The Guilford Press, New York, xxiii+450 pp. [Ernest Mandel, 'The Relevance of Marxist Theory for Understanding the Present World Crisis', pp. 438–47].

1994 – *Bukharin in Retrospect*, ed. by Theodor Bergman, Gert Schaefer, and Mark Selden, M.E. Sharpe, Armonk, NY, xxiv+251 pp. [Ernest Mandel, 'Bukharin and the Problem of Bureaucracy in the Transition Period', pp. 176–87].

1993 – *The USSR 1987–1991: Marxist Perspectives*, ed. by Marilyn Vogt-Downey, Humanities Press, Atlantic Highlands, NJ, xvi+544 pp. [Ernest Mandel, 'The Causes and Consequences of Bukharin's Rehabilitation', pp. 267–70; 'Soviet Press Does a Turnaround on Trotskyism', pp. 277–9].

1992 – *A Biographical Dictionary of Dissenting Economists*, ed. by Philip Arestis and Malcolm Sawyer, Edward Elgar, Aldershot, xiv+628 pp. [Ernest Mandel, 'Ernest Mandel (born 1923)', pp. 336–41].

1992 – *Interfaces in Economic and Social Analysis*, ed. by Ulf Himmelstrand et al., Routledge, London, xviii+318 pp. [Ernest Mandel, 'Partially Independent Variables and Internal Logic in Classical Marxist Economic Analysis', pp. 33–50].

1991 – *The Socialist Register*, ed. by Ralph Miliband and Leo Panitch, Merlin Press, London, iii+398 pp. [Ernest Mandel, 'The Roots of the Present Crisis in the Soviet Economy', pp. 194–210].

1991 – *Fallacies of State Capitalism*, introd. by Phil Hearse, Socialist Outlook, London, 125 pp. [Ernest Mandel, 'A Theory which Has not Withstood the Test of Facts', pp. 35–60; 'The Impasse of Schematic Dogmatism', pp. 85–125].

1990 – Paul LeBlanc. *Lenin and the Revolutionary Party*, Humanities Press, Atlantic Highlands, NJ, xxxiv+399 pp. (and later edn) [Ernest Mandel, 'Introduction', pp. xvii–xxxiv].

1990 – *The New Palgrave: Marxian Economics*, ed. by John Eatwell et al., Macmillan, London, xii+383 pp. (a selection from *The New Palgrave: A Dictionary of Economics*) [Ernest Mandel, 'Karl Marx', pp. 1–38; 'Communism', pp. 87–90].

1989 – *Capitalist Development and Crisis Theory: Accumulation, Regulation, and Spatial Restructuring*, ed. by Mark Gottdiener and Nicos Kominos, Macmillan, Basingstoke, xv+408 pp. (American edn publ. by St Martin's Press, New York, NY) [Ernest Mandel, 'Theories of Crisis: An Explanation of the 1974–1982 Cycle', pp. 30–58; 'The Infernal Logic of the Debt Crisis', pp. 217–33].

1989 – *The Socialist Register*, ed. by Ralph Miliband et al., Merlin Press, London, viii+306 pp. [Ernest Mandel, 'The Marxist Case for Revolution Today', pp. 159–84].

1987 – *The New Palgrave: A Dictionary of Economics*, ed. by John Eatwell et al., Macmillan, London, 4 vol., vol. 3, xix+949 pp. (and later print.) [Ernest Mandel, 'Marx, Karl Heinrich]', pp. 367–83].

1987 – *The New Palgrave: A Dictionary of Economics*, ed. by John Eatwell et al., Macmillan, London, 4 vol., vol. 1, xxxi+1085 pp. (and later print.) [Ernest Mandel, 'Communism', pp. 512–13].

1987 – *Ending the Nightmare: Socialists Against Racism and Fascism*, ed. by John Lister, Socialist Outlook, London, 128 pp. [Ernest Mandel, 'Learn the Lessons of Germany', pp. 28–42].

1987 – *The World Order: Socialist Perspectives*, ed. by Ray Bush, Gordon Johnston, and David Coates, Polity Press, New York, NY, ix+301 pp. [Ernest Mandel, 'The Soviet Bloc', pp. 26–42].

1986 – *The Socialist Register*, ed. by Ralph Miliband, John Saville, Marcel Liebman and Leo Panitch, Merlin Press, London, iii+489 pp. [Ernest Mandel, 'Marx, the Present Crisis and the Future of Labour', pp. 436–54].

1985 – *Rethinking Marxism: Struggles in Marxist Theory; Essays for Harry Magdoff and Paul Sweezy*, ed. by Stephen Resnick, Autonomedia, Brooklyn, NY, xxxiv+428 pp. [Ernest Mandel, 'Marx and Engels on Commodity Production and Bureaucracy', pp. 223–58].

1985 – *Socialism on the Threshold of the Twenty-First Century*, ed. by Milos Nicolic, Verso, London, ix+311 pp. [Ernest Mandel, 'The Actuality of Socialism', pp. 146–62].

1984 – *The Stalinist Legacy: Its Impact on 20th-Century World Politics*, ed. by Tariq Ali, Penguin, Harmondsworth, 551 pp. [Ernest Mandel, 'What Is the Bureaucracy?', pp. 60–94].

1983 – *A Dictionary of Marxist Thought*, ed. by Tom Bottomore et al., Blackwell, Oxford, xi+587 pp. (and later edn; American edn publ. by Harvard University Press, Cambridge, MA) [Ernest Mandel, 'Joint-Stock Company', pp. 241–4; 'Keynes and Marx', pp. 249–51; 'Uneven Development', pp. 502–03].

1983 – *Monetarism, Economic Crisis and the Third World*, ed. by Karel Jansen, F. Cass, London, xiii+194 pp. [Ernest Mandel, 'World Crisis and the Monetarist Answer', pp. 79–95].

1982 – *The Socialist Register*, ed. by Martin Eve and David Musson, Merlin Press, London, x+314 pp. [Ernest Mandel, 'China: The Economic Crisis', pp. 185–204].

1981 – Karl Marx. *Capital: A Critique of Political Economy*, Volume 3, transl. by David Fernbach, Penguin, Harmondsworth, 1086 pp.(and later edn; American edn publ. by Vintage Books, New York, NY) [Ernest Mandel, 'Introduction', pp. 9–90].

1981 – J.W. Freiberg. *The French Press: Class, State, and Ideology*, Praeger, New York, NY, xxvii+320 pp. [Ernest Mandel, 'Foreword', pp. vii–xvi].

1980 – *Capital and Labour: Studies in the Capitalist Labour Process*, ed. by Theo Nichols, Athlone Press, London, 476 pp. [Ernest Mandel, 'Labour and the State in Nazi Germany', pp. 103–6; 'Planning, Strategy and Capitalist Crisis', pp. 448–64].

1979 – Pierre Frank. *The Fourth International: The Long March of the Trotskyists*, transl. by Ruth Schein, introd. by Brian Grogan, Ink Links, London, 189 pp. [Ernest Mandel, Appendix on 'Trotskyists and the Resistance in World War Two', pp. 173–81].

1978 – Karl Marx. *Capital: A Critique of Political Economy*, Volume 2, transl. by David Fernbach, Penguin, Harmondsworth, 624 pp. (& later ed.; American ed. publ. by Vintage Books, New York, NY) [Ernest Mandel, 'Introduction', pp. 11–79].

1977 – *Revolution and Class Struggle: A Reader in Marxist Politics*, ed. by Robin Blackburn, Fontana/Collins, London, 444 pp. [Ernest Mandel, 'The Leninist Theory of Organization', pp. 78–135; 'Peaceful Coexistence and World Revolution', pp. 266–98].

1976 – Karl Marx. *Capital: A Critique of Political Economy*, volume 1, transl. by Ben Fowkes, Penguin, Harmondsworth, 1141 pp.(and later edn; American edn publ. by Vintage Books, New York, NY) [Ernest Mandel, 'Introduction', pp. 11–86].

1975 – Roy Medvedev et al. *Détente and Socialist Democracy: A Discussion with Roy Medvedev; Essays from East and West*, ed. for the Bertrand Russell Peace Foundation by Ken Coates, Spokesman Books, Nottingham, 163 pp. (and other edn, publ. by Monad Pr., New York, NY) [Ernest Mandel, 'The Social Forces Behind "Détente"', pp. 41–8].

1975 – *The Socialist Register*, ed. by Ralph Miliband and John Saville, Merlin Press, London, vi+318 pp. [Ernest Mandel, 'Liebman and Leninism', pp. 95–114].

1973 – *American Labor Radicalism: Testimonies and Interpretations*, ed. by Staughton Lynd, John Wiley & Sons, New York, NY, vi+217 pp. [Ernest Mandel, 'Where Is America Going?', pp. 187–202].

1972 – *Trotsky: The Great Debate Renewed*, ed. by Nicolas Krassó, introd. by David Horowitz, New Critics Press, St Louis, Mo., xiii+191 pp. [Ernest Mandel, ' "Trotsky's Marxism": An Anti-Critique' pp. 43–70;' "Trotsky's Marxism": A Rejoinder', pp. 91–124].

1971 – *Man and Socialism in Cuba: The Great Debate*, ed. by Bertram Silverman, Atheneum, New York, NY, xvi+382 pp. [Ernest Mandel,'Mercantile Categories in the Period of Transition', pp. 60–97].

1971 – *The Revival of American Socialism: Selected Papers of the Socialist Scholars Conference*, ed. by George Fischer with Alan Block et al., Oxford University Press, New York, NY, xvi+330 pp. [Ernest Mandel, 'Workers and Permanent Revolution', pp. 167–87].

1971 – Leon Trotsky / *The Struggle Against Fascism in Germany*, ed. by George Breitman and Merry Maisel, Pathfinder Press, New York,

NY, 479 pp. (and later edn; Brit. edn, publ. by Penguin Books, Harmondsworth) [Ernest Mandel, 'Introduction', pp. 9–46].

1970 – *'All We Are Saying . . .': The Philosophy of the New Left*, ed. by Arthur Lothstein, Capricorn Books, New York, NY, 381 pp. [Ernest Mandel, 'A Socialist Strategy for Western Europe', pp. 303–19].

1970 – *The Marxist Theory of Alienation: Three Essays by Ernest Mandel and George Novack*, introd. by George Novack, Pathfinder Press, New York, NY, 94 pp. (and later edn) [Ernest Mandel, 'The Causes of Alienation', pp. 13–30; 'Progressive Disalienation through the Building of Socialist Society . . .', pp. 31–51].

1970 – Abram Leon. *The Jewish Question: A Marxist Interpretation*, transl. n.a., Pathfinder Press, New York, NY, 270 pp. (and later edn) [Ernest Germain *alias* Mandel, 'A Biographical Sketch of Abram Leon', pp. 9–26].

1969 – *The New Revolutionaries: A Handbook of the International Radical Left*, ed. by Tariq Ali, Morrow, New York, NY, 319 pp. (and Brit. edn, publ. by Owen, London & Canad. edn, publ. by McClelland and Stewart, Toronto) [Ernest Mandel, 'The New Vanguard', pp. 47–53].

1969 – *Rural Sociology in India*, ed. by A. R. Desai, Fourth Revised Edition, Popular Prakashan, Bombay, xx+968 pp. (First three editions published by The Indian Society of Agricultural Economists in 1938, 1959 and 1961; later edn and print.) [Ernest Germain *alias* Mandel, 'The Industrialization of Backward Countries', pp. 925–38].

1967 – *The Socialist Register*, ed. by Ralph Miliband and John Saville, Merlin Press, London, 256 pp. [Ernest Mandel, 'International Capitalism and "Supra-Nationality"', pp. 27–41].

1964 – *The Socialist Register*, ed. by Ralph Miliband and John Saville, Merlin Press, London, 308 pp. [Ernest Mandel, 'The Economics of Neo-Capitalism', pp. 56–67].

Notes on the Contributors

Gilbert Achcar teaches political science at the University of Paris VIII and the American University of Paris. He is the author of *Communism and Liberalism: Marxist Paradigms of Revolution* (forthcoming).

Jesús Albarracín works as an economic researcher at the Bank of Spain. He is a member of the Federal Executive Commission of the Workers' Commissions. He has published several books on economics, including *La economía de mercado* (Madrid 1994).

Robin Blackburn is the editor of *New Left Review* and the author of many books on politics and history, including *The Making of New World Slavery* (London 1997).

Norman Geras teaches political theory at the University of Manchester. He is the author of several books on politics and philosophy, including *The Contract of Mutual Indifference* (London 1998).

Michel Husson works as an economic researcher at the Institute for Social and Economic Research (IRES) in Paris. He is the author of several works, including *Misère du capital. Une critique du néolibéralisme* (Paris 1996).

Francisco Louçã teaches economics at the University of Lisbon. He is the author of *Turbulence in Economics* (Aldershot 1997).

Michael Löwy is research director of sociology at the National Centre for Scientific Research (CNRS) in Paris. He is the author of many books on philosophy, politics and social sciences, including *Redemption and Utopia* (London 1992).

Pedro Montes works as an economist at the Bank of Spain. He is the author of several books on economics and politics, including *El desorden neoliberal* (Madrid 1996).

Charles Post teaches sociology at the Borough of Manhattan Community College of the City University of New York.

Catherine Samary teaches economics at the University of Paris IX. She is the author of several works on economics and Eastern European affairs, including *Yugoslavia Dismembered* (New York 1995).